# NO PLACE
# HOME
### THE ART OF COOKING FOR FAMILY & FRIENDS

FROM THE JACKSON SERVICE LEAGUE

Copyright © 2002

by

The Jackson Service League, Inc.

441 East Chester Street

Jackson, TN 38301

(731) 427-2080

First Printing, October 2002    5,000 copies

ISBN:
0-9720010-0-X

Printing underwritten by

Kirkland's

# TABLE OF CONTENTS

Entertaining . . . . . . . . . . . . . . . . . . . . . . . 9

Appetizers . . . . . . . . . . . . . . . . . . . . . . . 23

Soups, Salads, and Sandwiches . . . . . . . 57

Brunch, Breads and Beverages . . . . . . . . 91

Side Dishes . . . . . . . . . . . . . . . . . . . . . 125

Entrées . . . . . . . . . . . . . . . . . . . . . . . 161

Desserts . . . . . . . . . . . . . . . . . . . . . . 219

Index . . . . . . . . . . . . . . . . . . . . . . . . 267

## COOKBOOK COMMITTEE

*Chairmen 2000-2001*
Kay Culbreath
Yolanda Harris

*Chairmen 2001-2002*
Pamela Perchik
Katie Kibbe
Teresa Cobb

*Recipe Chairman 2000-2002*
Ceil Cowles

*Section Chairs*
Carol Adkins
Cecilia Alagappan
Laura Camp
Stephanie Freeman
Jenny Lytle
Peggy McGuire
Heather Miller
Ginka Poole
Laura Tomlin

# INTRODUCTION

The mystique of the South is woven inextricably into the American tapestry. As much as the South is part of our national geography, its symbolism and traditions have become part of our very language.

We define warmth and neighborliness as "Southern hospitality." An especially comely and genteel woman is a "Southern belle." We lovingly cherish our church dinners on the grounds and small-town festival parades as "Southern traditions."

And then there is "Southern cooking". It's an old term, but its definition is in transition.

The change of the Southern economic base from agriculture to business and industry has changed the South itself. This socio-economic evolution has brought a diverse influx into the Southern population, which in turn has made some changes in what we once defined as Southern.

Our tastes have changed, and as a result, Southern cooking has changed. Most of us remember grandmother's (some of us called her "mammaw") vegetable garden as rows of tomatoes and bell peppers, sweet corn and purple-hull peas. The noon meal in progress meant the aroma of some vegetable simmering on the stove with a generous application of pork fat for seasoning. Cornbread and biscuits were daily staples. One could scarcely imagine Mammaw growing broccoli or habanero peppers or (gasp!) making croissants.

Today, the Information Age is likely to find Mammaw logging onto the Internet to look up a recipe for Thai cooking, or eschewing the fat in pork seasoning in favor of healthier olive oil, herbs and spices. Indeed, the pace of today's society often finds the cookstove idle while dining out or bringing home takeout becomes the norm.

But that doesn't mean Southern cooking is gone. It's just found some room to grow and flexed its elbows a little.

We have made room for a bit of the new without sacrificing the old and beloved. And while we may have yielded to the temptation of convenience, it has not been allowed to usurp tradition. Staying home to eat, or inviting friends over for a meal, may be the exception more often than the rule, but when we make the time for it, it is a special occasion.

What truly defines Southern cooking is the emotional connection that makes human relationships, longtime traditions, and the pleasure of good eating an entity whose parts cannot be separated. Breaking bread together is an intimacy that renews and strengthens our bonds. We celebrate our holidays and family reunions, birthdays, and high school graduations with that heady mix of a welcoming open front door, a warm hug and a plateful of the best from somebody's kitchen - and heart.

With this collection of recipes, we bring you Southern cooking in the 21st Century. It is a cuisine that reflects how our population has changed, bringing new influences to the local culture that augment and complement those already established. It's a little of then, a little of now — and Southern tradition, as it was, is and always will be.

*Delores Ballard*

## Committee Members

Missy Amrol
Debbie Atkins
Elizabeth Atkins
Becky Baxter
Sybil Benson
Suzanne Boyd
Lynn Cobb
Donna Coffman
Jamie Davis
Connie Garey
Anne Garrard
Lynda Gilbert
Cherie Graham
Mary Claire Hancock
Tracy Hickey
Karen Harris
Anne Sanford Hawks
Denise Homberg
Tiffany Howard
Valerie Johnstone
Michelle King
Stacy Klein
Amy Koerner
Cindy Magee
Clare Markos
Judy Mascolo
Carol Ann Mitchell
Jenny Mitchell
Becky Ozment
Melinda Pierce
Emily Richards
Leslie Rickman
Tammy Roberts
Amy Staggs
Denise Stuart
Jamie Sullivan
Jan Teer
Leslie Underwood
Kim Villarreal
Michele Williamson
Patti Yellen

# FRIENDS OF THE LEAGUE

### *Patron*

Kirkland's

### *Platinum*

Methodist Le Bonheur Hospital, Jackson
Union Planter's Bank, Jackson
BancorpSouth

### *Gold*

Mrs. George (Sara) Dodson, sustainer

Hobert Banks and the Scott Kirk family in memory of Ann Banks

The Spiller and Kibbe families in memory of Gibbs Spiller

Mrs. Don (Catherine) McKnight in honor of Mrs. Roberta Price

Mr. and Mrs. John Chandler in honor of Mrs. J. Hughes Chandler, founding president

Mrs. Oliver (Bettie Gray) Graves, sustainer

Mr. and Mrs. Les Kenney

Mrs. Robert (Janelle) Henderson, sustainer

Mr. and Mrs. W. Eric Underwood

First South Bank by Ed and Lynn Woodside

UBSPaineWebber

The Bank of Jackson

Jackson-Madison County General Hospital

First Tennessee Bank

Mr. and Mrs. Royal Hickey, sustainer

## Silver

- Mrs. F.W. (Merilyn) Hamilton, sustainer
- Mrs. William S. (Patty) Lawrence, sustainer
- Mrs. Ed (Brenda) Whalley, sustainer
- Mrs. Don (Patty) Lewis, sustainer
- Mrs. Sam (Leila) Lawrence, sustainer
- Mrs. Clarence (Gertrude) Driver, sustainer
- Mrs. Jackie (Piper) Taylor, sustainer
- Mrs. Mike (Judy) Cobb, sustainer
- Mrs. Hoyt (Kathy) Hayes, Jr., sustainer
- Mrs. Bruce (Jane) Edenton, sustainer
- Mrs. Jimmy (Lynn) East, sustainer
- Mrs. Tyler (Kathryn) Swindle, sustainer
- Mrs. Augustus (Ann) Middleton, sustainer
- Mrs. Chip (Diane) Edwards, sustainer
- Mrs. Walton (Katherine) Harrison, sustainer
- Mr. and Mrs. Mike McWherter, sustainer
- Mrs. Marda Wallace
- Mr. and Mrs. Jim Jenkins
- Mr. and Mrs. David Hickey
- Mrs. Cornelia Tiller in memory of Martha Douglass
- Mrs. Christy Haynes in honor of Caroline Haynes
- Mrs. Leigh Ann Drew in honor of Ruth Ann Morrison, Sally Rainey and Debbie Allen
- The 2002 Provisional Class
- Katie Smylie in memory of Mildred Warner Smylie
- Kelly and Company Interior Design
- Kitchen Extras
- Madison Lighting
- Signature's Boutique

Contributions have been made to honor the following people who have helped us to make our houses *No Place Like Home*.

- Charleyn Reveire in honor of Peggy Sipes and Sammie Reviere and her family
- Pam Perchik in honor of Rev. and Mrs. William H. Ruff
- Pam Perchik in honor of Mr. and Mrs. Hank Perchik
- Pam Perchik in honor of Joel, Jordan and Madison Perchik
- Janet and Mike Tankersley in honor of Serena Jill McCartney
- Tiffany Howard in honor of Carolyn Grizzard
- Tiffany Howard in honor of Kay Howard
- Janelle Henderson in honor of her precious grandchildren
- Leslie Rickman in honor of her grandparents Mr. and Mrs. Maurice Thrasher
- Stephanie and John Masterson in honor of their children
- Dr. and Mrs. Frank Pierce in honor of Linda Mount
- Dr. and Mrs. Frank Pierce in honor of Mary Pierce
- Stacey Coley in honor of Beth McPipkin
- Stacey Coley in honor of Deanne Camryn Coley
- Celia Jordan in honor of Janie Hickman
- Kay Culbreath in memory of Joseph and Katherine Mitchell

# ABOUT THE ARTIST

Lendon Hamilton Noe is a truly innovative and talented artist who created all artwork that appears in No Place Like Home. An associate art professor at Lambuth University in Jackson, Tennessee, her work is displayed in various galleries and collections across the United States and France.

Lendon donated an enormous amount of her time and talents to make this book a reality. An honorary member of the Jackson Service League, she was raised in Jackson. Her mother, Merilyn Hamilton, is a sustainer.

We cannot express in words the gratitude that we feel for Lendon. She is a pleasure to work with, generous and talented. She translated our love of food into art. Jackson is blessed to have such a wonderful treasure right here in its own backyard. Her work is available for purchase and commission. You may contact Lendon by e-mailing her at noe@lamubuth.edu or by calling (731) 425-3355. You may also view selections of her work on her website www.lendonnoe.com.

# ABOUT OUR PATRON SPONSOR
## Kirkland's

Kirkland's, Inc. is a leading specialty retailer of home décor in the United States, operating over 230 stores in 28 states. Kirkland's has been helping families decorate and accessorize their homes for over 30 years. The company's stores offer a broad selection of distinctive merchandise, including framed art, mirrors, candles, lamps, picture frames, accent rugs, garden accessories and holiday-themed merchandise. The stores also carry many items that are perfect for gift giving throughout the year. Kirkland's offers its customers a unique combination of style and value that has made it a leader in home décor.

The company was co-founded in 1966 by Carl Kirkland, a native of West Tennessee who today is the company's chairman. Kirkland's corporate headquarters are located in Jackson, Tennessee, and the company and its people are strong supporters of the Jackson community. A generous contribution from the company was an important part of making *No Place Like Home* a reality.

We are fortunate to have Kirkland's as a friend, and we appreciate the company's partnership with the Jackson Service League in producing this fine cookbook and entertaining guide. You can shop online or learn more about Kirkland's, including the location of the store nearest you, by visiting www.kirklands.com.

Entertaining at home can be one of life's greatest pleasures. The most memorable evenings tend to be the ones spent at home because there is NO PLACE LIKE HOME. This Entertaining Guide is organized to give a step-by-step approach to entertaining. We hope that you will find inspiration to entertain at home.

One of the nicest gifts one can give friends is to open one's home. When entertaining at home, remember that you want guests to feel welcome and have fun! Focus on this goal during each phase of planning as well as on the day of the event.

Following this guide we have included several party themes with suggestions for invitations, decorations, menus, and ideas for getting guests involved. Use our party ideas as a whole, or take from them those things that compliment your style and get going! Remember, there is no one way to entertain that is right or wrong, as long as you feel comfortable, your guests will too!

**Four to six weeks before the party:**
1. Set the date.
    a. Allow enough time to prepare for the event, so you will be able to relax and enjoy the party.
    b. Consult a calendar (and friends) for major events competing for guests' time.
    c. Consider which night of the week works best for your schedule.
2. Decide if you want a theme.
    a. A theme can flow from the design of the invitations until the very last guest leaves.
    b. Develop the theme with invitations, decorations and the menu.
    c. Think about how to make the theme come to life. The more creative you are, the more memorable the event will be!
3. Creating the invitations.
    a. Create unusual invitations to catch guests' attention.
    b. Use invitations not just to inform guests about the party, but to create excitement!
    c. An innovative invitation will have guests eagerly anticipating the event.
4. Remain organized with all of the details.
    a. Keep a list of all guests invited, and the date and time of the event.
    b. Update the list with responses from guests.
    c. Keep all lists in an entertaining journal for future reference.

**Two to three weeks before the party:**

1. Mail the invitations. If you are having a small dinner party, ask if your guests have any special dietary needs when they respond to the invitation. (It is important to know any health conditions or food allergies of guests.)

2. Plan the menu.
   a. Choose the entrée first and then develop the menu.
   b. Keep the menu simple with only the number of courses that you feel comfortable preparing. Develop a back up menu of appetizers and a dessert that are quick to assemble if you run out of time and are unable to complete the entire menu. Gourmet crackers and cheese and bakery pastries are wonderful any time!
   c. When serving alcohol, it is more economical to offer a specialty drink, beer, wine, and soft drinks than to offer a full bar. A specialty drink should compliment the theme. Beverages such as sangría, margaritas, and Bellinis, etc. are a fun addition to a party and show guests that you have developed the theme down to the last detail. Remember to have water, bottled or in a pretty pitcher, available for the guests, also.

---

Things to consider when developing the menu:

- Use fruits and vegetables that are in season.
- Bear in mind the presentation and service of the food.
- Consider the foods that will be served from start to finish; vary the richness, texture, color and flavors of all courses.
- A colorful plate of food is appealing to the eye as well as the palate. Imagine the presentation of the food on the plate.
- Avoid duplicating prominent ingredients. For example, do not serve a tomato appetizer, tomato salad and tomato side dish.
- If serving one dish that is highly seasoned, complement it with one of a simple flavor.
- Pair a heavy meal with a light dessert or vice versa.
- Consider courses that can be prepared in advance. This will allow for assembling and reheating food during the party instead of starting from scratch once guests have arrived.
- Think about the number of ovens you can access immediately before the party to heat and cook the food.
- Note the cooking times and temperatures of each dish so that you are not cooking during the entire party.

3. Plan the decorations!

   Decorations can add so much to any special event. They can be as simple as extra candles on the table and fresh flowers or as elaborate as a transformation of your home for the evening. When thinking of decorations, imagine being a guest at the party. Let your imagination run wild! Consult magazines, books, and the Internet to get ideas. We have suggestions throughout this book for decorating ideas. Attention to detail can be time consuming, but the extra effort will make guests feel special which is the main goal of entertaining at home.

   These details create the atmosphere for the party. Make a great first impression starting with the front door. Entice your guests by using flowers, interesting potted plants, outdoor lighting, or a festive wreath for the front door. Decorating your front door before the party will increase your excitement about the event as well as any guests who stop by before the big day. Each table and serving area may further develop the theme as well. Have a great time with decorating! Do as much or as little as you wish.

   Think of the "big picture" when decorating.
   - Use two or three colors that can be repeated in every aspect of the decorations (wreath, tablecloth, napkins, flowers, candles, party favors etc.).
   - Repeat a symbol throughout the decorations. It could be something that you collect (rabbits, bees, books, or garden tools) or something associated with your theme (Santa and Christmas; sand pails and summer).
   - Do not purchase a lot of new things; use what you already own in a new way!
   - When you find good quality linens, dishes, glassware or accessories on sale, stock up on items that can be used in a variety of ways!

4. Plan the music!

   Enhance the mood of the party with theme music (i.e. Mexican Fiesta and Mariachi music). Consider the music when developing the theme. Borrow or buy CD's several weeks in advance. Remember, if the "theme" music for the party is fun, play it while preparing for the party to keep yourself motivated. Also, make tapes or CD's for guests to get them excited, too!

### Ten days before the party:

1. Inventory party supplies, make a list of what you have and what is needed. Deciding in advance the supplies needed will give you time to purchase or borrow what you do not have.
2. Determine the expected attendance for the big event
3. Make sure you have enough of the following: tables, chairs, dishes, serving dishes, utensils, glasses, and flatware.
4. Determine where and how everything will be served and where guests will be seated.
5. Prepare any food that can be frozen to allow more free time immediately before the party to concentrate on last minute details.
6. Consider hiring someone to help clean your house or help serve the meal. A little extra help on the day of the party will help you relax and enjoy the party as a guest.

### Four to seven days before the party:

1. Make sure everything to be used for the party is clean, pressed and polished.
2. Set the table if it is in an area that remains undisturbed.
3. Label each of the serving dishes with the name of the food that it will hold for the party. It is extremely helpful to have a visual presentation to see if anything is missing.
4. Collect all of the recipes and create a Master Shopping List. Include all ingredients (and amounts) needed for each dish you are preparing.
5. Check off all ingredients you have at home. This will reduce the number of trips to the store.
6. Make a separate list for things that you are not preparing but need to pick up before the party (ice, rolls, dessert, drinks, etc.).
7. Shop for all items that are not perishable.
8. Remember to buy paper goods and trash bags for the party. You can never have too many of these items and you will sorely miss them if there are too few.

### Two days before the party:

1. Begin preparing those courses that can be cooked ahead of time.
2. Clean out the refrigerator to accommodate all of the platters and trays.
3. Make sure that the ice maker is on or that there are enough containers to accommodate the bagged ice.

**The day before the party:**
1. Arrange the flowers and continue food preparation. Having the flowers arranged in advance will allow time for them to settle and look natural. You can add last minute flowers before the party, if necessary, but the majority of the work will be done, and you will not have a big mess to clean up just before your guests arrive.
2. Locate your camera to avoid a lost photo opportunity. Also, make sure that all of the music is ready to go in the stereo. Turn on the music and keep yourself energized while you are preparing for the next day.
3. Clean all of the areas of the house that guests will see during the party. Take care of spot cleaning the day of the party, but the big jobs should be done in advance, if possible. Make sure that area where coats and purses will be stored is clean.
4. Create a Last Minute List for yourself of the things that need to be done immediately before and during the party (see page 15). Include baking times for each dish that needs to be cooked before or during the party. Determine the time that it needs to be put in the oven and place this time on your list! This list is an invaluable memory aid when trying to do many things at once. It also allows you to enlist the aid of friends if they volunteer to help in the kitchen.
5. Remember to thaw all items prepared in advance. With less than twenty-four hours until the party, the last thing on your mind is what to prepare for dinner. Take a break and eat out or order a pizza!
6. If you have time, pick out your special outfit for the party. With this decided in advance, you will not have to spend time in your closet wondering what to wear.

**The morning of the big day:**
1. Prepare all of the ingredients needed for any dishes left to be cooked.
2. Chop, measure, and place ingredients in individual zip top bags.
3. Pick up any last minute items.

**Four hours before the party:**
1. Clean the kitchen, run and empty the dishwasher.
2. Vacuum the areas of the house where guests will be mingling and clean the bathrooms guests will use. Straighten the rest of the house in case someone wanders.
3. Make sure there is enough toilet paper and hand towels for the guests and that they are accessible during the party if you run low.

4. Take pictures of the tables that are set and the decorations for future reference.
5. Continue last minute food preparations.
6. Consult and update the Last Minute List for anything that needs to be done immediately before or during the party.

**Two hours before the party:**

1. Fill your coolers or containers with ice.
2. Prepare one container with ice only to use for drinks.
3. Use the other coolers to ice down canned drinks, beer, or bottles of wine.
4. Prepare (and sample!) the specialty drink for the party.
5. Make sure all of the appetizers are prepared and serving trays are ready if the appetizer must be baked immediately before serving.
6. Have your Last Minute List handy so that you will not have to rely on your memory to get everything done.

**One hour before the party:**

1. Get ready and take a few minutes to relax. Light the candles and turn on the music!
2. Remember, the party will be a success because you are there! Your friends are coming to spend time with you and each other.

**After the party:**

1. Keep an entertaining journal to remember what you served and who attended. After your party is over, make notes about what worked, what did not, and what you wanted to do differently.
2. Use your guest list, party supply inventory, Master Shopping List, and Last Minute List from each party, small or large, to create a file or a journal.
3. Remember to include notes about the menu and drinks served (amount of liquor, beer or wine needed).
4. Make a list of supplies that you need to purchase for your next party.
5. Include photographs of your decorations and table setting in your journal. This is especially helpful when you want to duplicate your party in the future for different guests or create an annual event.

We hope this Entertaining Guide provides suggestions for entertaining with ease and grace. Use the ideas that fit your home and lifestyle. Whether a formal dinner or backyard cookout, any time that you share your home with family and friends you are sharing yourself. Remember, when you are with your friends and family, there is NO PLACE LIKE HOME to entertain!

# LAST MINUTE LIST

| Menu Item: | Start Cooking At: | Temperature: | Baking Time: |
|---|---|---|---|
|  |  |  |  |
|  |  |  |  |
|  |  |  |  |
|  |  |  |  |
|  |  |  |  |
|  |  |  |  |
|  |  |  |  |

| Items to be thawed: | Items to be chopped: |
|---|---|
|  |  |
|  |  |
|  |  |
|  |  |
|  |  |
|  |  |
|  |  |

# HOUSEKEEPING CHECKLIST

- ☐ Clean Kitchen
- ☐ Run and Empty Dishwasher
- ☐ Stock up on cleaning supplies
- ☐ Vacuum party area
- ☐ Clean and Supply Bathrooms
- ☐ Fill coolers with ice
- ☐ Put ice in container for drinks
- ☐ Prepare and sample specialty drink
- ☐ Serving trays prepared
- ☐ Appetizers ready
- ☐ Check lighting at front door
- ☐ Music loaded in Stereo or CD player
- ☐ Light Candles
- ☐ Cameras ready
- ☐ Designated area for coats and purses
- ☐ Extra plastic storage containers, bags and wrap for leftovers

## MENU:

Mimosas,
fresh juice, coffee

Gingerbread Muffins,
p. 110 and Orange
Curd, p. 242

Winter Fruit Salad, p. 65

Mushroom, Tomato,
and Bacon Puff, p. 99

Grits Gruyère, p. 94

Black-Eyed Peas with
Caramelized Onion and
Country Ham, p. 135

Mandarin Orange
Brunch Cake, p. 109

## MENU:

Watermelon Margaritas,
p. 121 or Sangría
Blanca, p. 124

Shrimp Quesadillas, p. 45

Green Chili
Pick-Me-Ups, p. 39

Spiced Pork Tenderloin
with Jalapeño Honey
Sauce, p. 164

Jícama Slaw, p. 68

Guacamole with
Roasted Corn, p. 52

Almond Cream
Cheese Cookies, p. 256

Espresso Ice Cream
Sundaes, p. 260

# NEW YEAR'S DAY BRUNCH

Is there a better way to spend the first day of the New Year than with good friends or close family? The food served should bring good luck to your guests! In the South, many serve black-eyed peas and turnip greens on New Year's Day to bring financial good luck. Some cultures believe you should eat ring-shaped foods on the first day of the New Year, symbolizing the completion of one year and the beginning of the next.

For this brunch, use a ring as the continuing symbol. A low ring of flowers can serve as a centerpiece, a round wreath for the front door, and a ring of flowers around the Winter Fruit Salad. Decorate napkin rings by gluing black-eyed peas to an inexpensive napkin ring.

Have guests write their New Year's resolutions down when they arrive. Hold a contest to see who can match the guests with their resolutions. Prepare prizes for those who have the most and least matches.

# MEXICAN FIESTA

South of the Border parties are always fun! At the party, hold a Sombrero Contest. For invitations, attach a note to a large straw hat informing the guests of the time and place of the party. Also, let guests know that they need to decorate their sombreros and bring them to the party for a contest! This will help encourage guests' participation.

Once guests arrive they can wear their sombreros or you can use them as table centerpieces. Have Mexican mariachi music playing in the background and wear brightly colored clothes during the party, to carry the theme further.

Tables can be decorated with bright cotton tablecloths made from fabric with finished edges or Mexican blankets. Place piñatas on the main buffet table and enlist the help of school age children to make tissue paper flowers, a fun accent to the tables also.

After dinner, hold a contest to judge the creativity of sombrero decorations and award prizes.

# MILESTONE PARTY

Upon reaching a "milestone" in life, everyone deserves a celebration. This party can be adapted for any "milestone" reached. A "milestone" may be graduation, promotion, birthday or anniversary. The events that you can celebrate are limited only by your imagination.

For the invitation, scan a childhood picture of the guest of honor into a computer. The picture can be the cover of the invitation and the information can be on the inside. Many copier stores have the capability to do this for you.

Enlisting the help of friends is always important. For this party, ask friends from different stages of the guest of honor's life to help decorate a table for the party. For instance, if the guest of honor has lived in several cities, some tables can be named after each place. (Friends from Houston will decorate the Houston table, friends from San Francisco decorate the San Francisco table and friends from New Orleans decorate the New Orleans table.) Or you can focus on different aspects of his or her life such as high school, college, first job, military service, or hobbies. You can make the table assignment for the guests based upon the time of life when the guest met your guest of honor. This will make for several "mini-reunions".

When creating your menu, highlight the guest of honor's favorite dishes. Here are some of ours.

### MENU:

*Spinach, Artichoke, and Gruyère Pinwheels, p. 28*

*Mixed greens with marinated Vegetable Salad Dressing, p. 74*

*Chicken Jambalaya, p. 178*

*Creole Bread Pudding, p. 243*

## MENU:

*Smoked Salmon Spread,
p. 48, with Toast Points*

*Brie Tartlets
with Grape Salsa, p. 23*

*Tropical Romaine Salad,
p. 79*

*"Ready When You
Need Them" Dinner Rolls,
p. 113*

*Mushroom Stuffed Beef
Tenderloin, p. 194*

*Tomatoes Rockefeller,
p. 147*

*Caramelized Onion and
Porcini Risotto with Sage,
p. 153*

*Warm Chocolate Soufflé,
p. 247 or Chocolate
Truffle Cake with
Raspberry Sauce, p. 228*

---

## MENU:
### LUNCH

*Citrus Black Bean
Salsa, p. 50*

*Turkey and Caramelized
Onion Wraps, p. 89*

*Mocha Fudge Brownies,
p. 251*

### DINNER

*Spicy Spiked Slush, p. 123*

*Monterey Salsa with
Corn and Olives, p. 51*

*Sun-Dried Tomato
Spread, p. 48*

*Spicy Baked
Barbeque Shrimp, p. 202*

*Orange Walnut Salad with
Sweet and Sour Dressing,
p. 67*

*Corn on the Cob*

*French Bread*

*Tennessee Peach Pie, p. 236*

---

# FORMAL DINNER FOR EIGHT

Rarely do we take the time to dress up and enjoy a really nice meal at home. If you do not have an occasion, create one!

The invitation can be a simple phone call or an invitation written with calligraphy. Decorations should be simple candles and a low flower arrangement on the table. Play classical or jazz music during appetizers and dinner.

With a small dinner party, use place cards to seat guests. There are many ways to seat people. One idea is to separate married couples and place guests male-female-male. This will keep the conversation flowing across the table and will encourage guests to visit with each other. Use silver frames with the guests names written in calligraphy on the inside of the frame as a place card. Allow the guests to take the frame home as a token of friendship. At some point during the night, try to take a picture of everyone together. Deliver the picture after the party for them to enclose in the frame.

While enjoying dinner, remember to brew a pot of coffee so that everyone can linger around the table during dessert.

# SUMMER SOLSTICE

On the longest day of the year, find a way to celebrate with friends. What better way than to spend the day on the lake or at the beach? Extend the invitation by filling a beach bucket with sunscreen, beach toys and information about the party.

Have your guests arrive about 11:00 a.m. They can get acquainted and settled in before lunch. Serve lunch in picnic baskets. If you have time, wrap the food attractively. Your attention to detail will go a long way to making your friends feel special. Spread blankets on the ground for your guests to relax upon.

After lunch, you and your guests can enjoy the water and each other's company. Badmitton or volleyball could be fun for those who tire of being in the water. Have some frisbees or soft footballs to throw also! Vacation days bring out the child in all of us.

Have your friends gather at the house about 4:30 to start freshening up and get ready for cocktails and appetizers.

After dinner, roast marshmallows for some romancing around a bonfire!

# BABY SHOWER

When celebrating life's great events, it is time to bring out the finest china and silver. What better way to welcome a new baby than to have a tea party!

The buffet table can be covered with a simple white linen or damask tablecloth. Use silver baby cups (tied with pink or blue ribbons) and baby shoes (lined with plastic) as vases for the baby shower. Cluster them together on the buffet table between the trays of food. Baby roses (with a little baby's breath, of course) will be a simple yet elegant touch.

Before the shower, have the guests mail you a copy of their baby picture. Frame each and place on a table together. Ask your guests to guess who is the baby in each picture. This is a great way to get the conversation going.

### MENU:

Banana Punch, p. 120

Artichoke Cheese Puffs, p. 29

Pepper Pecan Cheese Wafers, p. 34

Ginger and Water Chestnut Dip with Crudités, p. 55

Old Hickory's Chicken Salad, p. 63, on croissants

Raspberry Pecan Bread, p. 103 with assorted Cream Cheese Spreads, p. 101

Almond Apricot Tartlets, p. 234

# PATRIOTIC PARTY

During the summer, there are three holidays that celebrate America: Memorial Day, Fourth of July and Labor Day. Many celebrate these holidays with family and friends with a cookout in the back yard. The invitation is a simple phone call saying "Come on over!" When your friend responds, "What can I bring?" make sure that you delegate a side dish or dessert!

Use the colors red, white, and blue in every aspect of the party from invitations to decorations. The symbol repeated throughout the party can be a star. Tie bunches of red, white, and blue balloons around the buffet table and on the chairs. Paint stars on a galvanized tub to hold the cold drinks. If serving fruit salad, try to find star fruit to include in it. Make star shaped cookies with red, white, and blue icing.

Have the children bring their bathing suits and let them run in the sprinkler and play water games. Have several water guns, water balloons and a big tub of bubbles set up to entertain the young ones. Remember to have a lot of jars with lids available once it gets dark to catch fireflies!

### MENU:

Fresh Tomato Tart, p. 32

Summer Strawberry Salad, p. 76 with blueberries and bananas

Summertime Orzo Salad, p. 78

Flank Steak with Summer Salsa, p. 190

Angel Food Cake with raspberries, blueberries, star fruit and fresh vanilla whipped cream

Watermelon

## MENU:

*Cowboy Caviar, p. 54*

*Tailgate Cheese Spread, p. 37, with crusty bread and crudités*

*Picnic Chicken with Cumin and a Pine Nut Crust, p. 169*

*Basil Marinated Corn, p. 134*

*Sesame Marinated Asparagus, p. 126*

*Mediterranean Cous Cous, p. 160*

*Tunnel of Love Cupcakes, p. 230 with Grand Marnier Buttercream Frosting, p. 230*

# STARLIGHT SYMPHONY

Our community is very fortunate to have a wonderful Symphony. The Starlight Symphony is a fabulous annual event in Jackson. The Jackson Symphony holds its first concert of the season in August under huge trees on the grounds of First Presbyterian Church. With as many as 6,000 in attendance, some arrive at dawn to "stake out their ground" for the event. Everyone brings a picnic dinner and catches up on all that has happened during the summer. As dinner concludes, the birds begin to wind down their chorus, the sun begins to set behind the church, and the Symphony plays under the trees. It is a most magical evening that everyone enjoys. The concert is concluded when the Symphony plays Tchaikovsky's 1812 Overture and real cannons are fired!

A successful dinner at the Starlight Symphony requires planning. Some necessities to have at a outdoor concert include: blankets, lawn chairs, wagon (for pulling all of the food, supplies and later to entertain the children), a cooler, lanterns or candles, insect repellent, paper plates, plastic cups and plastic utensils, paper towels and baby wipes. It is helpful to bring a folding table for food service. While planning the menu, take into consideration the amount of time that the food can remain at room temperature before spoiling. Finger foods are most convenient for this casual affair.

The children will love having individual box dinners. Each little box could contain a peanut butter and jelly sandwich, fruit and a cookie. Wrapping the box like a "happy meal" will make the children feel even more special. Include a special toy in the box to entertain the children. If you are sitting in the back include some bubbles and glow-in-the-dark necklaces. (This also makes it easy to find each other in the dark.)

# HARVEST MOON

When the weather begins to cool down and everyone has gotten into the routine of school, a Harvest Moon party is a great way to get together with friends. Harvest Moon is the name given to the full moon nearest the autumnal equinox and marks the first day of fall. The harvest moon occurs when the full moon of mid-September rises to the same level in the east as the position of the sun as it is setting in the west.

To celebrate the Harvest Moon, invitations can be simple or elaborate. Write the invitation on a dried cornhusk with a permanent marker. Roll the husk into a tube and tie at each end with raffia. Or decorate mini-pumpkins with dried flowers and silk leaves. (Wash the pumpkins in bleach first to kill bacteria and prevent rotting.) Attach the flowers and leaves with hot glue. Write the invitation on a card, attach the card with raffia, and hand deliver.

For the table, begin with a layer of large colorful leaves. Add Autumn harvest foods such as Indian corn, pumpkins, apples and gourds on top of the leaves. The insides of mini-gourds can be hollowed out and candles can be placed inside for instant candleholders.

For a flower arrangement, add something unexpected to the vase to hold the flowers in place such as small pumpkins or gourds. Any fresh flower added to this arrangement will really stand out, especially Gerber daisies.

To add to the theme, buy bales of hay to decorate your front porch.

## MENU:

*Savory Goat Cheese and Walnut Cheesecakes, p. 26*

*Grilled Portobello Mushrooms with Hazelnut Topping, p. 44*

*Pumpkin Harvest Soup, p. 85*

*Spinach Salad with Cranberries, p. 74*

*Ginger Orange Roasted Carrots, p. 131*

*Apricot Glazed Cornish Hens with Wild Rice, p. 186*

*Sweet Potato Biscuits, p. 114*

*Apple Cream Pie, p. 135 or Baked Apples in Puff Pastry, p. 245*

# CHRISTMAS CAROLING\ PROGRESSIVE DINNER

## MENU:

**House 1**
Sun-Dried Tomato Pesto Torte, p. 38, with assorted crackers

Marinated Cheese Tortellini, p. 37

**House 2**
Hot Christmas Cider, p. 124

Pepperoni Praise, p. 35

**House 3**
Burgundy Lasagna, p. 212

The Overnight Salad, p. 71

Artichoke Garlic Bread, p. 115

**House 4**
Miss Bess' Famous New York Cheesecake, p. 219 with Raspberry Sauce, p. 229

Brownie Trifle, p. 239

Coffee

---

It is easy to entertain when your home is decorated for the holidays. If you are lucky enough to live in a neighborhood in which you are friends with your neighbors, this party will be fun to throw and attend. If you do not know your neighbors, this may be a good way to meet them. First, recruit at least two other neighbors to host the party with you. Each house should be located close by so that the guests can sing their way from house to house as they progress along the meal. The first family can host the appetizers, the second family can host dinner and the final house can host the dessert, coffee and hot chocolate. The only thing that is mandatory is a song sheet with the lyrics for the songs to be sung as you go caroling along.

Your invitation can be sent in a poem that can be sung to the tune of Jingle Bells. Wrap the invitation festively in a box and top it with a kazoo. With this invitation, your guests will become aware that this will not be an ordinary Christmas event.

If you can find Santa hats, have one for each guest to wear during the caroling. During the appetizers, play familiar holiday tunes to get everyone in the spirit. After everyone has arrived and had a chance to unwind and visit, you may want to practice a few songs so that everyone will be ready for the caroling!

Everyone will get into the holiday spirit if you ask them to bring a gift to be donated to the needy in your community.

# APPETIZERS

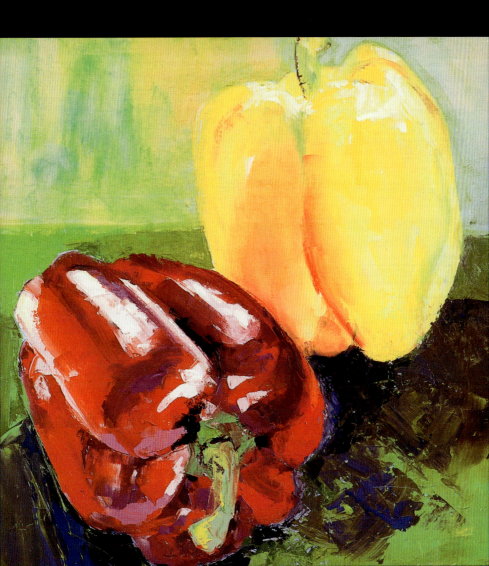

# APPETIZERS

Brie Tartlets with Grape Salsa ........................... 23
Asparagus with Wasabi Dip ........................... 24
Bombay Blues ........................... 25
Savory Goat Cheese and
  Walnut Cheesecakes ........................... 26
Chinese Chicken Bites ........................... 27
Spinach, Artichoke and
  Gruyère Pinwheels ........................... 28
Artichoke Cheese Puffs ........................... 29
Petite Crab Cakes with Fresh
  Tomato Tartar Sauce ........................... 30
Cheesy Bacon Delights ........................... 31
Fresh Tomato Tart ........................... 32
Garden Party Canapés ........................... 33
Pepper Pecan Cheese Wafers ........................... 34
Festive Bite-Size Cheese Balls ........................... 34
Pepperoni Praise ........................... 35
Gorgonzola and Walnut Terrine ........................... 36
Tailgate Cheese Spread ........................... 37
Marinated Cheese Tortellini ........................... 37
Sun-Dried Tomato Pesto Torte ........................... 38
Green Chili Pick-Me-Ups ........................... 39
Five Pepper Quesadilla ........................... 40
Rosemary's Walnuts ........................... 41

Tomato Bruschetta ........................... 41
Devils and Angels on Horseback
  with Balsamic Syrup ........................... 42
Cece's Samosas ........................... 43
Grilled Portobellos with Hazelnut Topping ........ 44
Shrimp Quesadillas ........................... 45
Cilantro Lime Grilled Shrimp ........................... 46
Skewered Shrimp with Warm Plum Sauce ........ 47
Smoked Salmon Spread ........................... 48
Sun-Dried Tomato Spread ........................... 48
Mediterranean Salsa ........................... 49
Easy Everyday Salsa ........................... 49
Citrus Black Bean Salsa ........................... 50
Jackie's Salsa ........................... 50
Monterey Salsa with Corn and Olives ............. 51
Chive Talking Fondue ........................... 51
Guacamole with Roasted Corn ........................... 52
In A Crunch Corn Dip ........................... 52
Three-Way Queso ........................... 53
Cowboy Caviar ........................... 54
Nutty Fruit Dip ........................... 55
Ginger and Water Chestnut
  Dip for Crudités ........................... 55
Cranberry Citrus Salsa ........................... 56

# BRIE TARTLETS WITH GRAPE SALSA

*A unique appetizer, great for showers or brunches!*

| | | | |
|---|---|---|---|
| 1 | cup seedless red grapes, cut in halves | ¼ | teaspoon chopped fresh rosemary |
| ¼ | teaspoon kosher salt | ¼ | teaspoon minced garlic |
| 2 | tablespoons finely chopped green onion, green part only | ⅛ | teaspoon freshly ground pepper |
| | | 30 | mini phyllo shells |
| 1 | tablespoon balsamic vinegar | ½ | cup chopped walnuts, toasted |
| 2 | teaspoons walnut oil (or olive oil) | 8 | ounces Brie, rind removed |

- Preheat oven to 300 degrees.
- Combine grapes and salt in a food processor and pulse until the grapes are coarsely chopped. Place in strainer and let sit for at least 10 minutes.
- Mix green onions, vinegar, walnut oil, rosemary, garlic, and pepper together in a small bowl. Add grapes and mix well.
- Arrange shells on a baking sheet.
- Fill each shell with ½ teaspoon walnuts, ½ teaspoon Brie, and ½ teaspoon salsa (use fork to transfer salsa to avoid getting any liquid).
- Bake until cheese begins to melt, about 5 minutes. Do not overbake.
- Serve immediately.

*Yield: 30 tartlets*

*Note: Grape salsa can be made one day in advance and refrigerated (do not add the walnut oil until ready to assemble). Tarts can be assembled with walnuts and Brie up to 6 hours in advance and salsa can be added up to 30 minutes in advance.*

---

*The Jackson Service League, Incorporated was chartered in 1952 for the purpose of fostering interest among its members in the social, economic, educational, cultural, and civic conditions of the community and to make efficient their volunteer service, specifically the support of benevolent and charitable undertakings for the underprivileged. For fifty years, the League has worked to help the Jackson community.*

# ASPARAGUS WITH WASABI DIP

*Try this spicy dip for asparagus. You will not be disappointed!*

| | | |
|---|---|---|
| 3 | pounds fresh asparagus, cut approximately 4-inches long, tough ends discarded | Wasabi Dip |

- Blanche asparagus in salted water until bright green and crisp-tender.
- Remove from water and pat dry.
- Cover and chill.
- Arrange asparagus on a platter and serve with Wasabi Sauce in a bowl for dipping.

### Wasabi Dip

| | | | | |
|---|---|---|---|---|
| 1 | cup real mayonnaise | 1½ | teaspoons sugar |
| 3 | teaspoons fresh lemon juice | 1 | tablespoon wasabi paste |
| 3 | teaspoons soy sauce | | |

- Combine all ingredients in a small bowl.
- Cover and chill several hours or overnight.

*Yield: 12 to 15 servings*

*Note: May be made the day before serving. Using the wasabi paste is essential to this recipe! If you are unable to find wasabi paste, ask your local Japanese restaurant if you can purchase some from them.*

*Try this dip with snowpeas or sugar snap peas if asparagus is not in season.*

---

*When choosing asparagus look for firm, bright green stalks with tight tips. It tastes best cooked the day it is purchased. Store asparagus tightly wrapped in a plastic bag in the refrigerator. When you are preparing the asparagus, remove the outer layer of the stalk with a vegetable peeler.*

# BOMBAY BLUES

*Blue cheese lovers will think they are in heaven with this pick up appetizer.*

- ½ cup sharp blue cheese, at room temperature
- 3 tablespoons unsalted butter, softened at room temperature
- ½ cup all-purpose flour
- ¼ cup cornstarch
- ¼ teaspoon pepper
- ¼ teaspoon kosher salt
- ⅓ cup chopped walnuts
- 3 tablespoons soft cream cheese (in the tub)
- 3 tablespoons mango chutney
- ½ cup walnut pieces, toasted, for garnishing
- Parsley leaves for garnishing

- Combine the blue cheese and butter in a food processor; process until creamy.
- Mix the flour, cornstarch, pepper, and kosher salt together in a small bowl; add to blue cheese mixture. Pulse to combine.
- Add the chopped walnuts and process just until incorporated. Do not over process.
- Remove from the food processor and shape into a ball.
- Cover with plastic wrap and refrigerate until firm, at least 1 hour.
- Preheat oven to 325 degrees.
- Place chilled dough on a piece of plastic wrap and cover with another piece of plastic wrap.
- Roll the dough out about ⅛-inch thick. Remove the plastic wrap and cut into 1-inch circles using a fluted cookie cutter.
- Place on a parchment paper-lined baking sheet. Repeat until all the dough is used.
- Bake until light brown, about 25 minutes. Do not overbake.
- Let cool.
- To assemble, spread ¼ teaspoon cream cheese on each shortbread. Top with a toasted walnut piece, ¼ teaspoon chutney, and a leaf of parsley.

*Yield: 36 shortbreads*

*Note: The shortbread can be prepared up to 3 days in advance and stored in an airtight container, or frozen for up to 2 weeks. Assemble up to 1 hour before serving.*

# SAVORY GOAT CHEESE AND WALNUT CHEESECAKES

*Easy and elegant!*

| | | | |
|---|---|---|---|
| ½ | cup fresh breadcrumbs | 4 | ounces cream cheese, softened |
| ½ | cup finely ground walnuts plus 15 to 18 halves for garnish | 5 | ounces soft goat cheese |
| 2 | tablespoons melted butter | 1 | tablespoon fresh thyme leaves or 1 teaspoon dried |
| ½ | teaspoon salt, divided | 1 | egg, beaten |
| ½ | teaspoon black pepper | | |

- Preheat oven to 350 degrees.
- Butter generously an 18-count mini muffin pan.
- In a bowl, combine breadcrumbs, walnuts, melted butter, ¼ teaspoon salt, and pepper, mixing well until combined. Spoon into muffin tins to cover bottoms well.
- With mixer or food processor, beat cream cheese until soft and fluffy. Add goat cheese mixing until well blended. Add egg, thyme and remaining ¼ teaspoon salt, mixing until well blended. Spoon mixture into muffin tins, dividing equally.
- Smooth tops and garnish with walnut half.
- Bake 12 to 18 minutes until puffed, watching crust carefully so as not to burn.
- Let sit 5 minutes before unmolding.
- Serve warm or at room temperature.
- Garnish with fresh thyme, if desired.

*Yield: 15 to 18 cheesecakes*

---

*If you are in a hurry and need a simple flower arrangement for your table, float a day lily or magnolia blossom in a silver bowl of water for a centerpiece. The arrangement will not last long, but it makes a strikingly elegant statement. Additionally, it is free if you can grab one of the flowers from your yard!*

# CHINESE CHICKEN BITES

*Serve these warm for your next football party!*

| | | | |
|---|---|---|---|
| ½ | cup lemon juice | ¼ | teaspoon cayenne pepper |
| ¼ | cup soy sauce | 1 | pound boneless, skinless chicken breasts, cut into 1-inch cubes |
| ¼ | cup Dijon mustard | | |
| 2 | teaspoons vegetable oil | | |

- Mix lemon juice and next 4 ingredients to make a marinade.
- Put marinade and chicken cubes into a 1-gallon zip top plastic bag. Marinate 8 hours in the refrigerator (or freeze).
- To prepare, remove chicken from marinade (thaw, if frozen).
- Preheat broiler.
- Heat marinade in a small saucepan over medium high heat.
- Place chicken cubes on broiler pan prepared with nonstick spray. Broil 4 to 5-inches from heat for 7 minutes, brushing with marinade once. Turn cubes and broil another 4 minutes.
- Place on serving platter with toothpicks.

*Yield: 8 servings*

*Note: Serve with Warm Plum Sauce on page 47.*

# SPINACH, ARTICHOKE AND GRUYÈRE PINWHEELS

*Serve these elegant pinwheels with a light white wine.*

| | | | |
|---|---|---|---|
| 1 | (10-ounce) package frozen chopped spinach, thawed | ½ | cup grated Gruyère cheese |
| 1 | (14-ounce) can artichoke hearts, drained and chopped | 1 | teaspoon onion powder |
| | | 1 | teaspoon garlic powder |
| ½ | cup mayonnaise | ½ | teaspoon pepper |
| | | 1 | (17.3-ounce) package frozen puff pastry |

- Drain spinach well, pressing between layers of paper towels.
- Stir together spinach, artichoke hearts and next 5 ingredients.
- Thaw puff pastry at room temperature for 30 minutes. Unfold pastry and place on a lightly floured surface.
- Spread ¼ spinach mixture evenly over pastry sheet, leaving a ½-inch border.
- Roll up pastry, jelly roll fashion, pressing to seal seam. Wrap in plastic wrap.
- Repeat procedure with remaining pastry and spinach mixture.
- Freeze for 30 minutes.
- Preheat oven to 400 degrees.
- Remove rolls from freezer, remove plastic wrap and cut into ½-inch thick slices.
- Bake for 20 minutes, or until golden brown.

*Yield: 48 hors d'oeuvres*

*Note: Rolls may be frozen for up to 3 months.*

---

*Gruyère cheese has a rich, sweet, nutty flavor that can be enjoyed alone or prepared in a recipe. It is usually aged for 10 to 12 months and has a golden brown rind and firm, pale yellow interior with well-spaced, medium-sized holes.*

# ARTICHOKE CHEESE PUFFS

*These have a light and airy texture you are sure to enjoy.*

| | |
|---|---|
| 1 tablespoon olive oil | 1 teaspoon Worcestershire sauce |
| 1 tablespoon butter | 3 drops hot sauce |
| 1/3 cup chopped onion | Salt and pepper, to taste |
| 1 clove garlic, minced | 1 1/4 cups milk |
| 1/2 cup sliced fresh mushrooms | 2/3 cup biscuit mix |
| 2 tablespoons chopped fresh parsley | 4 eggs |
| | 1/4 teaspoon garlic powder |
| 1 (14-ounce) can artichoke hearts, drained and chopped | 1/4 teaspoon pepper |
| | 2/3 cup grated Parmesan cheese |
| | 2/3 cup grated Swiss cheese |

- Preheat oven to 350 degrees.
- In a sauté pan, heat olive oil and butter.
- Sauté onion, garlic, mushrooms, and parsley until onions are clear. Add artichokes, Worcestershire sauce, hot sauce, and salt and pepper to taste; mix well.
- Spray miniature muffin tins with cooking spray. Fill each tin 1/2 full with onion mixture.
- Blend milk, biscuit mix, eggs, garlic powder, and pepper until well blended. Pour over onion mixture.
- Mix together Parmesan and Swiss cheeses and divide evenly over each tin.
- Bake for 20 minutes until light brown.
- Cool in tin for 10 to 15 minutes, remove from tins carefully and serve.

*Yield: 24 cheese puffs*

---

*In 1964, the League opened the Thrift Store allowing Jacksonians to purchase second hand clothing and household items. League members staffed and managed the store, the revenue from the store was donated back to the community. The Thrift Store closed in 1979, and the annual Thrift Sale began.*

# PETITE CRAB CAKES WITH FRESH TOMATO TARTAR SAUCE

*You will enjoy the combination of flavors this recipe offers!*

> To peel and seed tomatoes, immerse in boiling water for 20 seconds. Remove with slotted spoon and place in ice water immediately. Cut an X at both ends of the tomato with a paring knife and slip off the skin. Cut off ends of tomato, push seeds out with fingers and remove remaining seeds from ends. Do this over the sink as it is very messy.

### Crab Cakes

| | | | |
|---|---|---|---|
| 3 | tablespoons butter | ¼ | cup green onion, finely sliced |
| ¼ | cup all-purpose flour | 2 | teaspoons fresh lemon juice |
| ¼ | teaspoon salt | 1 | teaspoon dry mustard |
| ⅛ | teaspoon pepper | ¼ | teaspoon ground red pepper |
| 1 | cup milk | 1 | pound lump crabmeat, cleaned |
| ½ | cup red pepper, finely chopped | 2 | cups fine dry breadcrumbs, divided |
| ½ | cup yellow pepper, finely chopped | ½ | cup vegetable oil |
| ½ | cup celery, finely chopped | | Fresh Tomato Tartar Sauce |

- Make a white sauce base by melting butter in saucepan over low heat. Stir in flour, salt, and pepper, mixing well. Slowly add milk, stirring constantly until thickened and bubbly. Cook 2 minutes more and set aside.

- In large mixing bowl, combine peppers, celery, onion, lemon juice, mustard, ground red pepper, and white sauce.

- Gently fold in crabmeat and ½ cup breadcrumbs.

- Shape crab cakes using 1 to 2 tablespoons of mixture. Make cakes about ½-inch thick. Dip each cake in remaining 1½ cups breadcrumbs to coat.

- In a large skillet, heat ¼ cup oil (or enough to cover bottom of pan) over medium heat.

- Cook crab cakes 4 to 5 minutes on each side or until golden brown. Replenish skillet with remaining oil as needed.

- Serve with chilled Fresh Tomato Tartar Sauce.

## Petite Crab Cakes continued

**Fresh Tomato Tartar Sauce**

| | |
|---|---|
| 3 | Roma tomatoes, seeded, peeled, chopped and drained of excess juice |
| 3 | tiny dill pickles, finely chopped |
| 1 | tablespoon canned chopped green chilies, drained |
| 1 | tablespoon lemon juice |
| 1 | tablespoon onion, finely chopped |
| 1 | tablespoon capers, minced |
| ¼ | teaspoon salt |
| ¼ | teaspoon black pepper |
| 1 | cup mayonnaise |

- Combine all ingredients in a small bowl. Cover and chill at least 2 hours before serving.

*Yield: 8 servings*

*Do not protect yourself by a fence, but rather by your friends.*

*Czech proverb*

# CHEESY BACON DELIGHTS

*Serve this easy delicious pick up appetizer at your next outdoor party or picnic!*

| | |
|---|---|
| 2 | cups shredded sharp Cheddar cheese |
| ¼ | cup grated onion |
| 8 | slices bacon, cooked crisp and crumbled |
| 1½ | ounces sliced almonds |
| 1 | cup mayonnaise (not low fat) |
| 1 | loaf of thin sliced white bread, crust removed, and ends discarded |

- Mix first 5 ingredients.
- Spread each slice of bread with about 1 tablespoon of cheese mixture to cover entire slice. Cut each slice into 3 strips. Lay flat on cookie sheet and freeze until firm.
- Once firm, remove from freezer and place in zip-top bags or freezer containers.
- When ready to bake, preheat oven to 400 degrees. Bake frozen slices on cookie sheet for 10 minutes.

*Yield: 30 pieces*

# FRESH TOMATO TART

*A great way to use tomatoes fresh from your garden or the farmer's market! Pretty and easy to make!*

| | | | |
|---|---|---|---|
| 1 | refrigerated 9-inch pie crust | 3 | large, ripe tomatoes, seeded and sliced ½-inch thick |
| 2 | tablespoons Dijon mustard | | Extra-virgin olive oil |
| 2 | cups shredded mozzarella cheese | | Fresh basil leaves, finely sliced |
| 2 | tablespoons minced garlic | | |

- Preheat oven to 400 degrees.
- Press pie crust into tart pan with a removable bottom. Brush bottom of pie crust with Dijon mustard to lightly coat. Sprinkle mozzarella cheese and garlic onto crust.
- Place tomatoes on top in concentric circles, overlapping edges. Brush top of tomatoes with olive oil.
- Place in oven uncovered for 10 minutes or until edges of tart crust are brown and cheese has melted.
- Remove from oven and sprinkle generously with fresh basil.
- Remove sides of tart pan, cut into desired size wedges, and serve warm or at room temperature.

*Yield: 8 first course servings*

*Variation: Roma tomatoes can be substituted for tomatoes in the winter. Mixed shredded cheeses can be substituted for mozzarella cheese. If you substitute a frozen pie shell, reduce the amount of cheese to 1½ cups.*

---

*Be sure to visit the farmer's market in your area. You will be sure to find the freshest fruits and vegetables from local growers. It is a great way to help the farmers in your community and to learn about different varieties of fruits and vegetables!*

# GARDEN PARTY CANAPÉS

| | | | |
|---|---|---|---|
| 2 | medium seedless cucumbers, peeled and quartered | 1 | tablespoon Worcestershire sauce |
| 2 | carrots, peeled and cut in half | 2 | teaspoons dried dill |
| 1 | small onion, quartered | 8 | ounces cream cheese, softened |
| ½ | cup diced celery | ⅛ | teaspoon black pepper |
| 1 | red bell pepper, seeded and quartered | ¼ | teaspoon salt |
| 2 | tablespoons fresh lemon juice | | Thin sliced white and wheat bread |
| 2 | tablespoons mayonnaise | | |

- Combine all vegetables in bowl of food processor and finely mince, being careful not to puree.
- Put vegetable mixture in cheesecloth and squeeze out all the liquid.
- Place vegetables in a bowl and combine with next 7 ingredients and mix until smooth.
- Spread mixture evenly on bread slices that have been cut in decorative shapes with small cookie cutters.

*Yield: 1 pint*

*Note: This vegetable spread may be served on top of cucumber slices, also. The vegetable spread can be prepared ahead of time and refrigerated until you are ready to prepare the canapés or sandwiches.*

# PEPPER PECAN CHEESE WAFERS

*These small wafers are cookie like in texture.
Make them in advance and freeze!*

| | | | |
|---|---|---|---|
| 1 | cup butter at room temperature | 2½ | cups sifted all-purpose flour |
| 2 | (5-ounce) jars sharp, processed cheese spread | 1 | teaspoon salt |
| | | ½ | teaspoon cayenne pepper |
| | | 1 | cup finely chopped pecans |

- In a medium bowl, cream together the butter and cheese until smooth. Beat in flour, salt, and cayenne. Fold in pecans.
- Form the dough into a ball and divide the dough in half. Form each half into a 1-inch log.
- Wrap in plastic wrap and chill until firm.
- Preheat oven to 400 degrees. Slice the dough into ¼-inch thick slices and bake in oven for 12 minutes.

*Yield: 48 wafers*

*Note: Cheese wafers can be stored in sealed plastic containers and frozen.*

# FESTIVE BITE-SIZE CHEESE BALLS

*This is a unique twist on an old favorite. Try it at your next party!*

| | | | |
|---|---|---|---|
| 3 | (8-ounce) packages cream cheese, softened | 1 | (8-ounce) package chopped dates |
| 1 | (4-ounce) package blue cheese, crumbled | 1 | cup golden raisins |
| | | 2 | cups pecans, toasted |
| 1 | cup shredded sharp Cheddar cheese | | |

- Combine the first 5 ingredients. Divide and roll into 1-inch balls. Roll in chopped pecans.
- Chill until ready to serve.
- Serve on platter or in a bowl alone or with table water crackers.

*Yield: 60 balls*

# PEPPERONI PRAISE

*A delicious pick up hors d'oeuvres.*

| | | | |
|---|---|---|---|
| ½ | cup finely grated Gruyère cheese | 1 | puff pastry sheet, thawed |
| ¾ | teaspoon dried sage | 2 | tablespoons country or spicy Dijon mustard |
| ¾ | teaspoon dried oregano | 1 | (2-ounce) package sliced pepperoni |
| ¼ | teaspoon freshly ground pepper | 1 | egg, lightly beaten |

- Mix Gruyère, sage, oregano and pepper together in a small bowl.
- Lay the puff pastry on a lightly floured surface with the short side closest to you. Cut crosswise and lay sheets with longest sides closest to you.
- Spread with mustard leaving a 1-inch border at the top. Lay pepperoni over mustard in single layer and top with Gruyère mixture. Brush egg over border at the top.
- Roll lengthwise very tightly. Lay seam-side down on platter. Cover with plastic wrap and chill for 30 minutes.
- Preheat oven to 400 degrees. Cut prepared puff pastry into ½-inch slices and place flat on parchment lined baking sheet. Bake 1 sheet at a time until browned, about 14 minutes.
- Serve warm.

*Yield: 48 hors d'oeuvres*

*Note: Can be frozen for up to 2 weeks or chilled for 1 day after being covered in plastic.*

---

*The Thrift Sale is the largest yearly project of the League. During our Thrift Sale, League members work for three days setting up, cleaning, and tagging donated merchandise. This one-day sale allows the Jackson community to purchase high quality second hand clothing, toys, and household items for very reasonable prices. All profits are then returned to the community through various projects.*

# GORGONZOLA AND WALNUT TERRINE

*This makes a lovely presentation.*

| | | |
|---|---|---|
| 1 | cup walnuts, toasted | Lettuce leaves |
| ½ | pound Gorgonzola at room temperature | Fuji or Granny Smith apples |
| ¼ | cup sour cream | Sourdough baguette |

- Line a 5½x3x2-inch loaf pan with plastic wrap, leaving 3-inches of wrap overhanging all around.
- In a large bowl, break up cheese with fork until slightly chunky. Add walnuts and sour cream; mix thoroughly.
- Turn mixture into loaf pan and spread evenly.
- Cover with the overhanging plastic wrap; refrigerate overnight until very firm.
- Unfold the plastic and invert the terrine onto a platter lined with lettuce leaves. Discard plastic wrap.
- Core and slice the apples into wedges.
- Cut the baguette into ½-inch slices.
- Arrange apple and baguette slices along with terrine and serve.

*Yield: 12 to 16 servings*

*Note: If you dip the apple slices in lemon juice after slicing, they will not turn brown.*

---

*When making a mold such as a terrine, line the pan with plastic wrap. Press firmly into place and secure on outside of pan. Fill pan with hot water. Discard the hot water then fill the lined pan with whatever you are making. Refrigerate according to the recipe. When finished, invert the pan onto the serving dish. Remove plastic wrap. There should not be many lines on the mold.*

# TAILGATE CHEESE SPREAD

*Don't forget to bring this spread when you are cheering your team on to victory!*

| | | | |
|---|---|---|---|
| 1 | (3-ounce) package cream cheese, softened | 1 | tablespoon Worcestershire sauce |
| 8 | ounces sharp Cheddar cheese, shredded | ½ | teaspoon dry mustard |
| 1 | clove garlic, minced | ¼ | teaspoon ground red pepper |
| | | ¼ | cup beer |

- Beat 2 cheeses on medium with electric mixer until smooth.
- Add garlic and next 3 ingredients.
- With mixer running, gradually add beer and mix until incorporated and cheese has smooth consistency.
- Cover and chill a minimum of 1 hour before serving.
- Serve with crusty bread, crackers or raw vegetables

*Yield: 2½ cups*

Note: Will last up to 1 week in refrigerator.

*A smiling face is half the meal.*

*Latvian proverb*

# MARINATED CHEESE TORTELLINI

*Quick and full of flavor.*

| | | | |
|---|---|---|---|
| 1 | (9-ounce) package refrigerated cheese tortellini | ½ | cup soy sauce |
| 1 | cup lemon juice | 2 | tablespoons dried oregano |
| ¾ | cup olive oil | 1 | tablespoon garlic powder |

- Cook tortellini according to package directions, removing 1 minute prior to time directed. Tortellini should be slightly undercooked. Rinse tortellini in cold water.
- Combine remaining ingredients. Add tortellini and marinate 4 to 24 hours covered in refrigerator.
- Drain, reserving ¼ cup of the marinade. Place on a platter and pour reserved marinade over the tortellini.

*Yield: 6 to 8 servings*

Note: Tortellini tastes better when marinated overnight as the flavors have time to marry. You may serve these with toothpicks to pick them up.

# SUN-DRIED TOMATO PESTO TORTE

*This recipe captures the best flavors of summer.*

| | | | |
|---|---|---|---|
| 10-12 | stone ground wheat crackers, crushed | ⅛ | teaspoon salt |
| 2 | (8-ounce) packages cream cheese, softened | ¼ | cup sun-dried tomatoes packed in oil, drained |
| 1 | egg | ⅛ | cup grated Parmesan cheese |
| | | 1 | cup prepared pesto |

- Preheat oven to 375 degrees.
- Butter a 7 to 9-inch springform pan and sprinkle bottom evenly with cracker crumbs.
- With an electric mixer, beat cream cheese until smooth then mix in egg and salt until well blended. Set aside.
- In a food processor, chop sun-dried tomatoes. Blend in pesto and Parmesan cheese.
- Spread ½ cream cheese mixture into the pan. Use fingers to carefully spread over crumbs, carefully.
- Top with tomato pesto mixture.
- Top with remaining cream cheese mixture.
- Bake 35 minutes.

**Topping**

| | | | |
|---|---|---|---|
| ¾ | cup sour cream | ⅛ | cup grated Parmesan cheese |
| 1 | teaspoon flour | 1½ | tablespoons fresh parsley |

- While torte is baking, make topping. In a small bowl, combine sour cream, flour, Parmesan cheese and parsley.
- After baking, remove torte from oven and spread topping evenly over top of torte.
- Return to oven and bake for 5 to 10 minutes until set.
- Cool. Cover and chill 4 to 24 hours.
- Remove sides of pan and place on a platter.
- Garnish with fresh basil, parsley and sun-dried tomato.
- Serve with cracker, pita, or French bread.

*Yield: 24 servings*

Note: You may make this in a round cake pan by doubling the number of crackers used for the crust. Carefully invert the torte onto a plate lined with plastic wrap. Flip the torte over onto a serving plate and remove plastic wrap.

---

*Cookbook-Guidebook – Use your cookbooks as guidebooks. Make notes about which recipes you tried. It is helpful to note the date that you made a dish and for whom. If friends ask for the recipe you can easily find it. Also, note the changes to the recipe that you thought should be made to suit your pallette!*

# GREEN CHILI PICK-ME-UPS

*We dare you to eat just one! They are addictive!*

| | | | |
|---|---|---|---|
| 2 | cups shredded Monterey Jack cheese | 2 | teaspoons cumin |
| 2 | cups shredded Cheddar cheese | 1 | teaspoon dried oregano, or more to taste |
| 1 | cup sour cream | 60 | wonton wrappers |
| 1 | (4.5 ounce) can chopped green chilies | | Vegetable oil |
| ½ | cup minced green onions (approximately 1 bunch), green part only | | |

- Combine first 7 ingredients (cheeses through oregano) and refrigerate at least 4 hours or overnight.
- Preheat oven to 350 degrees.
- Grease the bottoms of each cup of a muffin pan.
- Place 1 wonton wrapper in the each muffin cup pressing the middle of the wrapper into the bottom and sides of the muffin cup creating a cup. Brush each wrapper with a very small amount of vegetable oil.
- Bake empty wonton wrappers until lightly browned, approximately 8 to 10 minutes. Remove cups from the muffin tin and cool. Repeat this process until you have made all wrappers into cups.
- Place wontons in an air tight container until ready to fill.
- Once the flavors of the filling have had time to blend, place the cups on a baking sheet and preheat the oven to 375 degrees.
- Spoon filling into cups being careful not to overfill. Bake until the filling is hot and bubbly, approximately 10 minutes.
- Serve immediately.

*Yield: 60 pieces*

*Note: You could garnish these Pick-Me-Ups with a dollop of sour cream and a small amount of chopped cilantro.*

---

*With the help of the Jackson Service League, the West Tennessee Hearing and Speech Clinic opened in 1953. For the past 50 years, the League has continued to support the Clinic through volunteer support and financial contributions.*

# FIVE PEPPER QUESADILLA

*This is served in many Mexican restaurants, now you can serve it at home!*

| | | | |
|---|---|---|---|
| ½ | cup unsalted butter, divided | 1 | tomato, diced |
| 1 | green bell pepper, cut in strips | 1 | jalapeño pepper, seeded and diced |
| 1 | yellow bell pepper, cut in strips | ½ | cup vegetable oil, divided |
| 1 | red bell pepper, cut in strips | 1½ | cups shredded Cheddar cheese |
| 1 | sweet onion, ½ cut in strips, ½ diced | 1½ | cups shredded Monterey Jack cheese |
| 1 | (4-ounce) can chopped green chilies | 10 | (6-inch) flour tortillas |
| | | ¼ | cup sour cream |
| 3 | chipolte peppers, seeded and cut in thin strips | ¼ | cup salsa |

- Melt 2 tablespoons butter in a skillet over medium heat. Sauté green, yellow and red peppers, and onion until soft. Remove to a medium sized bowl. Add green chilies and chipolte peppers.
- Combine tomato, jalapeño and diced onion in a small bowl.
- Combine cheese in a small bowl.
- Melt 1 tablespoon butter and 1 tablespoon oil in a skillet. Place 1 tortilla in the skillet. Spoon 3 tablespoons cheese over the tortilla. Top cheese with peppers and 1 tortilla. Cook until golden brown and flip onto other side. Remove to warm serving plate until ready to serve.
- Repeat with remaining tortillas, cheese and pepper mixture.
- Combine sour cream, salsa, and 2 tablespoons tomato mixture.
- Cut into wedges, top with tomato mixture and sour cream salsa mixture.

*Note: You may prepare these by baking them in the oven. Place prepared quesadillas on a greased baking sheet. Brush top tortilla with vegetable oil. Bake in a 425 degree oven for 7 minutes or until cheese is melted.*

---

*In the South mint julep cups are a popular wedding gift. There are several patterns. What to do with them if you do not serve mint juleps on a regular basis? They are wonderful to cluster on your table and fill with flowers for a centerpiece. Or, fill them with greenery and line them on a ledge for a simple decoration at Christmas. You can also use them in the guest room for any guests who need a sip of water at night.*

# ROSEMARY'S WALNUTS

- 2½ tablespoons unsalted butter, melted
- 2 teaspoons dried rosemary, crumbled
- 1 teaspoon salt
- ½ teaspoon cayenne pepper
- 2 cups walnuts

- Preheat oven to 350 degrees.
- Combine butter, rosemary, salt, and cayenne in a bowl.
- Pour mixture over walnuts and toss them to coat, distributing coating evenly.
- Place nuts in a single layer on a cookie sheet. Bake for 5 minutes and stir, return to oven and bake an additional 5 minutes.

*Yield: 2 cups*

# TOMATO BRUSCHETTA

*A simple and popular Italian appetizer, great to serve when tomatoes are in season!*

- 1 (8-ounce) French bread baguette
- 3 tablespoons extra virgin olive oil, divided
- 2 medium Roma tomatoes, chopped
- ⅛ teaspoon pepper
- ⅓ cup thinly sliced green onion
- 2 tablespoons basil, finely sliced or 1 tablespoon dried basil
- ½ cup freshly grated Parmesan cheese

- Preheat oven to 425 degrees.
- Cut bread into ½-inch thick slices. Brush both sides lightly with 1 tablespoon oil. Place bread in single layer on ungreased cookie sheet. Bake for 5 minutes or until golden brown.
- Combine tomatoes, remaining 2 tablespoons of oil, and next 3 ingredients in a bowl to make topping.
- Place tomato mixture on each bread slice, dividing it evenly amongst the slices. Sprinkle with cheese.
- Bake 2 to 3 minutes longer or until cheese is melted.

*Yield: 8 to 10 servings*

*Variation: Oregano can be substituted for basil.*

*Hold a true friend with both hands.*

*Nigerian proverb*

# DEVILS AND ANGELS ON HORSEBACK WITH BALSAMIC SYRUP

| 10 | pitted prunes (devils) |
| 3½ | ounces goat cheese |
| 10 | slices bacon cut in half crosswise |

| 10 | dried apricots (angels) |
| 1 | cup balsamic vinegar |

- Preheat oven to 350 degrees.
- Cut one side of prunes lengthwise ¾ of the way through the fruit, leaving in one piece. Fill cavity of prune with small amount of goat cheese. Wrap with bacon and secure with toothpick. Repeat with each prune.
- Perform same procedure with apricots.
- Place on rack in roasting pan and bake about 10 minutes, until bacon is crisp.
- For syrup, place vinegar in small, heavy saucepan. Heat to low boil and reduce until thick and syrup-like.
- Remove from heat and cool.
- Place cooled syrup in squirt bottle. Swirl syrup decoratively on serving platter. Arrange Devils and Angels over syrup.

*Yield: 20 hors d'oeuvres*

*Note: Devils and Angels can be assembled the same day and cooked immediately before serving. Syrup can be made up to a week ahead and kept in the refrigerator.*

# CECE'S SAMOSAS

*Introduce your friends to this Indian appetizer with curry!*

| | | | |
|---|---|---|---|
| 4 | medium potatoes, cut into ½-inch cubes | 1 | cup frozen peas, thawed |
| 1 | tablespoon vegetable oil plus vegetable oil for deep-frying | 1 | jalapeño pepper, seeded, deveined and diced |
| | | 2 | teaspoons curry powder |
| 1 | medium onion, chopped | 1 | (8-count) package flour tortillas |

- Fill a large saucepan ½ full of water and bring to a boil. Add potatoes and cook about 20 minutes until potatoes are soft (almost to the point of being able to mash). Drain potatoes and set aside.

- Heat 1 tablespoon oil in a medium-sized saucepan over medium heat; add onion and sauté until transparent, 5 to 10 minutes. Add potatoes, peas, jalapeño pepper, and curry powder to onions and cook 10 minutes on low heat.

- Cut tortillas in half and place 2 tablespoons potato mixture onto top corner of tortilla. Fold over about 3 times to make a triangle. Seal edges by slightly wetting your fingers and pressing edges together.

- In medium to large saucepan, pour oil to measure 2-inches deep. Heat oil. Fry samosas in oil until golden brown. Serve warm.

*Yield: 8 first course servings*

*Note: Can keep warm on baking sheet in 250 degree oven until ready to serve.*

---

*These fried, triangular shaped pastries are a traditional Indian dish. They can be filled with vegetables, meat or a combination of the two. In India, street pushcarts sell delicious samosas to passersby who need some "fast food".*

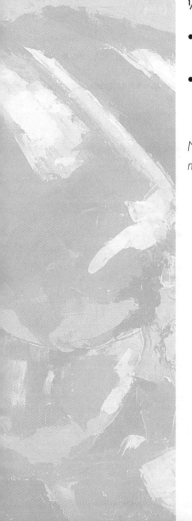

*Store mushrooms in a non-recycled brown paper bag in the refrigerator to keep from turning brown. You may wash mushrooms by rinsing them quickly under running water. This will not damage the flavor of the mushroom.*

# GRILLED PORTOBELLOS WITH HAZELNUT TOPPING

| 4 | portobello mushrooms, stems and veins removed |
|---|---|

**Extra virgin olive oil**

Kosher salt and freshly ground pepper, to taste

- Brush mushrooms on both sides with olive oil and season with salt and pepper to taste.
- Grill over medium heat for 5 to 6 minutes on each side until just cooked through.

**Hazelnut Topping**

- 2 cups hazelnuts, toasted and coarsely chopped
- 2 cloves garlic, finely chopped
- ¼ cup parsley, finely chopped
- 2 tablespoons finely grated lemon zest

Kosher salt and pepper, to taste

- Combine all topping ingredients in a medium bowl and season with salt and pepper to taste.
- Sprinkle topping evenly between mushroom caps and serve immediately.

*Yield: 4 servings*

*Note: Use a small teaspoon to scrape the black veins from the underside of the mushroom tops.*

# SHRIMP QUESADILLAS

*You can serve these as a main course with a salad!*

- 2 tablespoons olive oil
- 1 cup chopped onion
- Salt and freshly ground black pepper, to taste
- 1 large clove garlic, chopped
- 1 pound small shrimp
- 1 medium avocado, peeled and diced
- ½ cup thinly sliced scallions
- ½ cup Monterey Jack cheese, grated
- ½ cup sharp Cheddar cheese, grated
- 12 large flour tortillas
- ½ cup vegetable oil
- 1 cup sour cream
- 1 tablespoon finely chopped fresh cilantro leaves

- Heat olive oil in skillet over medium heat.
- Add onions, season with salt and pepper and sauté until onions are soft. Add the garlic and shrimp and continue to sauté until shrimp are heated through, about 1 minute. Remove from heat and cool completely.
- In a bowl, combine the shrimp mixture, avocado, scallions, and cheeses. Season with salt and pepper and mix well.
- Spoon mixture evenly over half of tortilla. Fold tortilla in half.
- Heat a large griddle over medium heat. Brush each side of tortilla with vegetable oil and cook Quesadillas for 2 to 3 minutes on each side or until crisp and cheese is melted.
- Remove from griddle and cool slightly.
- Slice into thirds and serve with sour cream. Garnish with cilantro.

*Yield: 6 to 8 servings*

*Note: Quesadillas can also be grilled. These are great served with Summer Salsa on page 190.*

---

*Children's Theater, another Jackson Service League project, began in 1978. Prior to that, the League performed puppet shows for area elementary schools. Each year, League members gather together to perform a different well-known children's play at each elementary school in Jackson over a four-day period. This is a wonderful introduction to theater for many children who have never seen a play! Our Children's Theater troupe has touched many lives over the years and sparked a lot of imaginations.*

# CILANTRO LIME GRILLED SHRIMP

*A refreshing start to your next outdoor gathering!*

| | | | |
|---|---|---|---|
| ½ | cup fresh lime juice | 1 | tablespoon soy sauce |
| ¼ | cup orange marmalade | ½ | teaspoon dried red pepper flakes |
| 3 | large garlic cloves, mashed to a paste with 1 teaspoon kosher salt | | Kosher salt and freshly ground pepper, to taste |
| ½ | cup fresh cilantro, washed well, dried and finely chopped | 1 | pound large shrimp, shelled, leaving tail intact and deveined |
| 3 | tablespoons olive oil | | |

- In a measuring cup, whisk together lime juice, marmalade, garlic paste, cilantro, olive oil, soy sauce, red pepper flakes and salt and pepper to taste. Reserve ⅓ cup of the mixture in a small bowl for dipping.

- In a large zip-top bag, combine shrimp with remaining mixture and marinate in refrigerator 45 minutes, tossing occasionally.

- Drain shrimp and lightly pat dry on paper towels.

- Place shrimp on oiled grate or use skewers and grill over medium hot coals about 1½ minutes on each side until cooked through.

- Garnish with cilantro sprigs and serve with reserved dipping sauce.

*Yield: 24 hors d'oeuvres*

*Note: The shrimp can also be sautéed in skillet with oil.*

---

*If you do not have a juicer, you can get the most juice from a lime by cutting it into quarters or eighths and then squeezing the juice out with your fingers. If you cut the lime in half and then squeeze, the pulp may come out of the middle and not release the juice.*

# SKEWERED SHRIMP WITH WARM PLUM SAUCE

*This innovative combination of flavors is sure to delight all who sample!*

| | | | |
|---|---|---|---|
| ⅓ | cup vegetable oil | 24 | large shrimp, peeled and deveined |
| ¼ | cup fresh lemon juice | | Bamboo, wooden, or metal skewers |
| ¼ | cup soy sauce | | |
| 2 | tablespoons dry sherry | 12 | slices thin sliced bacon |
| 2 | cloves garlic, minced | | Warm Plum Sauce |
| ¼ | teaspoon fresh ground pepper | | |

- Mix oil, lemon juice, soy sauce, dry sherry, garlic and pepper in a large bowl. Place shrimp in a zip-top plastic bag. Pour marinade over shrimp and marinate in refrigerator for 3 hours, stirring occasionally.
- If using bamboo or wooden skewers, soak in water for 1 hour.
- Preheat oven to 450 degrees.
- Cut bacon slices in half and cook on paper towels in microwave until limp, but not crisp.
- Wrap each shrimp with bacon and secure on skewer putting 1 or 2 shrimp per skewer.
- Bake on rack in roasting pan 8 to 10 minutes or until shrimp are pink and bacon is crisp.
- Serve immediately with Warm Plum Sauce.

**Warm Plum Sauce**

| | | | |
|---|---|---|---|
| 1 | (12-ounce) jar plum preserves | 1 | tablespoon Dijon mustard |
| 1 | tablespoon ketchup | 2 | tablespoons brown sugar |
| 2 | tablespoons fresh lemon juice | | |

- Combine all ingredients in small saucepan. Bring to boil, reduce heat and simmer 10 minutes stirring occasionally.

*Yield: 6 to 8 servings*

## SMOKED SALMON SPREAD

*An easy classic beginning to a wonderful meal.*

- 1 cup sour cream
- 4 ounces cream cheese, softened
- 2 green onions, thinly sliced
- 1 tablespoon lemon juice
- 4-6 ounce package smoked salmon, chopped
- 2 tablespoons capers, rinsed and drained

- Mix sour cream, cream cheese, onion and lemon juice until smooth. Fold in salmon.
- Cover and chill at least 6 hours or overnight.
- Place spread in serving bowl and garnish top with capers before serving.
- Serve with toasted bagel slices, toast points or Melba rounds.

*Yield: 1½ cups*

---

*Place the rinds of lemons in the disposal after juicing them. Run the disposal and freshen up the smell of the kitchen.*

---

## SUN-DRIED TOMATO SPREAD

- ⅓ cup or 12 whole sun-dried tomatoes packed in oil, drained and chopped
- 8 ounces cream cheese at room temperature
- ½ cup mayonnaise
- ½ cup sour cream
- ½ teaspoon salt
- ¾ teaspoon freshly ground pepper
- 10 drops hot sauce
- ¼ teaspoon dried rosemary
- 1 green onion, thinly sliced, white and green part

- Puree all ingredients, except green onions, in a food processor, until smooth. Add the green onions and pulse only twice.
- Place in a serving bowl. Garnish with chopped green onion, 1 whole sun-dried tomato, and/or sprig of fresh rosemary.
- Serve at room temperature with assorted vegetables and crackers or toasted pita bread.

*Yield: 4 cups*

*Note: You may store up to 1 week covered in refrigerator.*

# MEDITERRANEAN SALSA

*A unique twist on the traditional tomato salsa you are sure to enjoy!*

| | | | |
|---|---|---|---|
| 1 | large avocado, peeled and seeded | ½ | teaspoon dried oregano |
| 2 | plum tomatoes | 1 | tablespoon olive oil |
| ¼ | cup chopped purple onion | ½ | tablespoon red wine vinegar |
| 1 | clove garlic, minced | 2 | ounces feta cheese, crumbled |
| 1 | tablespoon dried parsley | | Salt and fresh ground pepper |

- Chop avocado and tomatoes and place in large bowl.
- Add onion, garlic, oregano, parsley, olive oil, and vinegar tossing to coat.
- Fold in cheese and season with salt and pepper.
- Cover and chill.
- Serve with tortilla chips.

*Yield: 4 to 6 servings*

*The most important work you and I will ever do will be within the walls of our own homes.*

Harold B. Lee

# EASY EVERYDAY SALSA

*Dive into this quick and easy dip.*

| | | | |
|---|---|---|---|
| 1 | (28-ounce) can crushed tomatoes | 1 | tablespoon dried parsley |
| ½ | Vidalia onion, diced (or other variety of sweet onion) | ½ | teaspoon salt |
| | | ½ | teaspoon garlic powder |
| 1 | (4.5-ounce) can chopped green chilies | ½ | teaspoon ground cumin |
| | | ½ | teaspoon freshly ground pepper |
| 1 | tablespoon sugar | ¼ | teaspoon cayenne (optional) |

- Combine all ingredients in a medium-sized bowl, stirring well.
- Cover and chill 30 minutes or longer before serving.

*Yield: 4 cups*

Note: This is a mild salsa that is great to serve for family if you have someone who cannot tolerate spicy food. Do not be afraid to add some heat if you wish.

## CITRUS BLACK BEAN SALSA

*A zesty combination for your next Mexican Fiesta!*

| | | | |
|---|---|---|---|
| 2 | (15-ounce) cans black beans, rinsed and drained | 1 | tablespoon chopped pickled jalapeño pepper |
| 1 | (6.1-ounce) can Mandarin oranges, drained | ¼ | cup fresh chopped cilantro |
| ½ | small purple onion, chopped | ¼ | cup vegetable oil |
| 1 | large green bell pepper, chopped | ¼ | cup red wine vinegar |
| 1 | cup frozen whole kernel corn, thawed | ⅓ | cup orange juice |
| | | ¼ | teaspoon salt |

- Stir together first 7 ingredients. Whisk oil and next 3 ingredients. Drizzle over bean mixture, and toss.
- Cover and chill. Serve with tortilla chips.

*Yield: 8 cups*

## JACKIE'S SALSA

*This fresh salsa is addictive!*

| | | | |
|---|---|---|---|
| 6 | medium tomatoes, diced | 1 | tablespoon minced fresh oregano or 1 teaspoon dried oregano, crushed |
| ⅓ | cup tomato ketchup | | |
| ⅓ | cup chopped purple onion | 3 | tablespoons fresh lime juice (2 limes) |
| 4 | cloves garlic, minced | | |
| 3-4 | fresh jalapeño peppers, seeded, deveined, and chopped | 1 | teaspoon salt |
| | | ¼ | teaspoon cayenne pepper, more or less to taste |
| 2 | tablespoons minced cilantro | | |

- Combine all ingredients stirring well.
- Cover and chill at least 4 hours.
- Serve with tortilla chips.

*Yield: 4 cups*

*Note: Great with grilled meats.*

# MONTEREY SALSA WITH CORN AND OLIVES

| | |
|---|---|
| 1 (15¼-ounce) can white whole kernel corn, drained | 4 green onions, chopped |
| 1 (3¼-ounce) can black olives, chopped | 1 cup Monterey Jack cheese, shredded |
| 1 (4-ounce) can green chilies, chopped | 1 tomato, chopped |
| | ½ cup Italian salad dressing |
| | ¼ cup chopped fresh cilantro |

- Combine all ingredients, stirring well. Serve with tortilla chips.

*Yield: 6 to 8 servings*

*In 1982, League members began volunteering in the Jackson nursing homes. Over the years, our program has evolved and we currently hold several parties during the year in two different nursing homes. During each party our members visit with the residents and participate with them in different activities. We also bring a small gift to the residents during their birthday month.*

# CHIVE TALKING FONDUE

*This is great to serve your guests as they gather in the kitchen to visit while you finish dinner preparation!*

| | |
|---|---|
| 1 cup heavy cream | Fresh ground pepper |
| 11 ounces fresh goat cheese, cut into chunks | Assorted crudités: pear and fennel wedges, endive spears, toasted baguette slices |
| 1 tablespoon finely snipped chives | |

- Warm the cream in a heavy saucepan until hot but not boiling. Gradually add the goat cheese, whisking until smooth.
- Remove from heat, stir in the chives and season with pepper.
- Pour into a fondue pot and serve with crudités.

*Yield: 12 servings*

*To roast corn, remove husks and silks. Lightly coat fresh corn with olive oil. Place directly on hot grill until brown and caramelized, turning frequently. Cut off cob with sharp knife.*

*To ripen an avocado, place in a brown paper bag. When it is soft, it may be refrigerated for up to 10 days.*

# GUACAMOLE WITH ROASTED CORN

*This old favorite has a new twist! Once you try it you will find many ways to include it in your menus!*

| | | | |
|---|---|---|---|
| 3 | avocados, peeled, seeded and coarsely chopped | ¼ | cup coarsely chopped cilantro plus extra to garnish, if desired |
| 2 | ears corn, roasted and kernels removed | ¼ | cup fresh lime juice |
| ⅓ | cup finely chopped red onion | 2 | tablespoons sour cream |
| | | | Kosher salt and freshly ground pepper |

- Combine avocados, corn, onion, cilantro, lime juice and sour cream in a bowl and mix well.
- Season with salt and pepper to taste.
- Serve with tortilla chips and garnish with cilantro, if desired.

*Yield: 4 servings*

# IN A CRUNCH CORN DIP

*During our testing, this received rave reviews!*

| | | | |
|---|---|---|---|
| 2 | (11-ounce) cans mexicorn, drained | 2 | cups shredded Monterey Jack cheese |
| 2 | (4½-ounce) cans chopped green chilies, drained well | ¾ | cup shredded Parmesan cheese |
| | | 1 | cup mayonnaise |

- Preheat oven to 350 degrees.
- Combine all ingredients in a large bowl and mix together. Pour into a baking dish and bake for 30 to 40 minutes until lightly browned.
- Pour into a serving bowl and serve warm with corn chips.

*Yield: 12 servings*

# THREE-WAY QUESO

**Basic Cheese Dip**
1 pound processed cheese loaf, cubed
1 (10-ounce) can diced tomatoes with green chilies, undrained

- Heat cheese and tomatoes in a double boiler, stirring frequently until cheese is melted.
- Serve warm with tortilla chips.

**Spinach Queso**
Basic Cheese Dip
1 (10-ounce) package frozen chopped spinach
1 (4-ounce) can sliced mushrooms, drained
1/3-1/2 purple onion, chopped

- Cook spinach according to package directions. Drain well.
- Place Basic Cheese Dip, spinach, mushrooms, and onion, in a double boiler stirring frequently, heating through.
- Serve warm with tortilla chips

**Jose's Queso**
Basic Cheese Dip
1 pound ground beef
1 envelope taco seasoning mix

- Cook ground beef with taco seasoning mix according to package directions.
- Add to Basic Cheese Dip and heat through.
- Serve warm with tortilla chips.

*Yield: 1 quart more or less*

*Note: Any of these quesos will be even more delicious with 1/4 cup Jackie's Salsa (page 50) added before serving.*

---

*The area north of Jackson is called "three-way". It is the point where Highway 45 forks to go either to Humboldt or Milan. There is also a tiny town at the fork in the road named Three Way.*

# COWBOY CAVIAR

*This is a fabulous dip for a large gathering!*

---

*When cooking dried beans, add salt at the end of the cooking. Adding it at the beginning slows the cooking.*

---

- 1 (15½-ounce) can hominy, drained
- 1 (15½-ounce) can black-eyed peas, drained and rinsed
- 1 (15½-ounce) can kidney beans, drained and rinsed
- 1 (15½-ounce) can black beans, drained and rinsed
- 1 (15¼-ounce) can white corn, drained
- 1 large red bell pepper, seeded and chopped
- 1 large green bell pepper, seeded and chopped
- 1 large yellow bell pepper, seeded and chopped
- 1 large orange bell pepper, seeded and chopped
- 1 red onion, chopped
- 2 large tomatoes, seeded and chopped
- 1 (4.5-ounce) jar minced garlic
- 1 (8-ounce) bottle vinaigrette dressing

- Mix all beans and vegetables.
- Add vinaigrette and garlic; toss to combine.
- Cover and chill 4 hours to overnight.
- Stir well and spoon into a serving bowl with a slotted spoon.
- Serve with corn chips.

*Yield: 24 servings*

*Note: If you have any left over, use it to top a baked potato or pasta! It would also make a great side dish for a picnic!*

## NUTTY FRUIT DIP

*This is a nice dip to serve at a shower.*

| | |
|---|---|
| 8 ounces cream cheese, softened | ¾ cup unsalted peanuts, chopped (optional) |
| ¾ cup light brown sugar, packed | 8 ounces whipped topping |
| 1 cup sour cream | |
| ⅓ cup coffee flavored liqueur | |

- Combine cream cheese, brown sugar, sour cream and liqueur in a bowl and mix until combined, do not over mix. Stir in peanuts and fold in whipped topping.
- Cover and chill for 12 to 24 hours.
- Serve with fruit or gingersnaps.

*Yield: 24 servings*

*Variation: ⅓ cup strong coffee can be substituted for coffee flavored liqueur*

*To remove husks from peanuts or hazelnuts, rub in a clean tea towel.*

## GINGER AND WATER CHESTNUT DIP FOR CRUDITÉS

*Delightfully refreshing and light!*

| | |
|---|---|
| 1½ cups sour cream | ½ cup minced onion |
| ½ cup mayonnaise | ¼ cup chopped parsley |
| ¼ cup finely chopped water chestnuts | 1 tablespoon soy sauce |
| ¼ cup finely chopped crystallized ginger | Assorted fresh vegetables |

- In a medium bowl, stir together sour cream, mayonnaise, water chestnuts, ginger, onion, parsley and soy sauce.
- Cover and chill for up to 5 days before serving.
- Serve with fresh vegetables for dipping.

*Yield: 8 servings*

# CRANBERRY CITRUS SALSA

| | | | |
|---|---|---|---|
| 4-5 | cups fresh cranberries | 4 | tablespoons fresh lime juice |
| 4 | teaspoons fresh grated ginger | 4 | oranges with juice, peeled, sectioned, and diced |
| 2 | large jalapeño peppers, seeded, deveined and finely diced | 3 | inner stalks celery, finely diced |
| | | 1 | cup sugar |
| ½ | cup finely diced red onion | 1 | (8-ounce) package cream cheese, softened |

- Place cranberries in food processor and pulse 5 to 7 times.
- Place cranberries in bowl and add all ingredients, except cream cheese.
- When ready to serve, place cream cheese on serving dish and top with salsa.
- Serve with gingersnaps or crackers.

*Yield: 4 to 6 cups*

Note: Salsa keeps well for up to 2 months in the refrigerator. Cranberry Citrus Salsa can be served as a replacement for traditional cranberry sauce. You can add chopped cilantro or mint and serve with chicken.

---

*Buy cranberries when you see them in the store whole in the bag. Freeze them in the bag and store for up to a year. Fresh berries are hard to find out of season.*

# SOUPS, SALADS, AND SANDWICHES

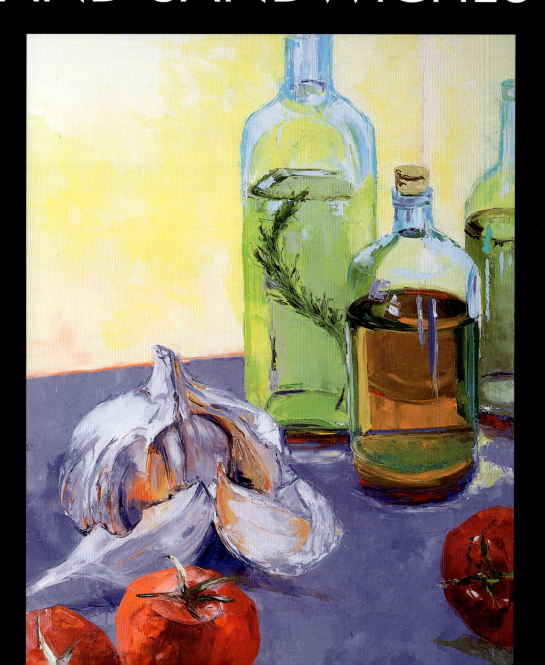

# SOUPS, SALADS, AND SANDWICHES

| | |
|---|---|
| Caesar Ravioli Salad ................................... 57 | Spicy Thai Chicken Salad with Ginger Peanut Dressing .............................. 73 |
| Greek Pasta Salad ........................................ 57 | Spinach Salad with Cranberries ..................... 74 |
| Bow Tie Pasta with Olives and Pine Nuts ........ 58 | Marinated Vegetable Salad Dressing .............. 74 |
| Summertime Cherry Tomato and Green Bean Pasta ............................. 59 | Tossed Salad with Caramelized Almonds and Spicy Vinaigrette Dressing ................. 75 |
| Couscous Chicken Salad with Orange Ginger Vinaigrette ....................... 60 | Summer Strawberry Salad with Sweet Surprise Pecans ............................ 76 |
| Pasta Salad with Sherry Dressing ................... 61 | Summertime Orzo Salad ............................... 78 |
| Crunchy Chicken Salad ................................. 62 | Tropical Romaine Salad ................................ 79 |
| Old Hickory's Chicken Salad ......................... 63 | Fruit Salad with Mint Syrup .......................... 80 |
| Mediterranean Tomato Salad ........................ 64 | Chicken Tortilla Soup ................................... 81 |
| Winter Fruit Salad ........................................ 65 | Curried Corn Soup ....................................... 82 |
| Artichoke and Blue Cheese Salad .................. 66 | Fabulous Chili .............................................. 83 |
| Orange-Walnut Salad with Sweet and Sour Dressing .......................... 67 | Mexican Chowder ........................................ 84 |
| Jícama Slaw ................................................. 68 | Pumpkin Harvest Soup ................................. 85 |
| Oriental Slaw ............................................... 69 | White Chicken Chili with Pine Nuts ................ 86 |
| Pear Salad with Creamy Raspberry Dressing ................................ 70 | Cucumber Sandwiches ................................. 87 |
| The Overnight Salad ..................................... 71 | Green Chile-Pimento Cheese ........................ 88 |
| Shrimp and Black Bean Salad ....................... 72 | Turkey and Caramelized Onion Wraps .......... 89 |
| | Turkey Basil Bites ........................................ 90 |

## CAESAR RAVIOLI SALAD

*The pasta in this salad makes is hearty and filling!*

| | | | |
|---|---|---|---|
| 9 | ounces refrigerated cheese ravioli | ¼ | cup freshly grated Parmesan cheese |
| 2 | cups cherry tomatoes | ½ | teaspoon pepper |
| ½ | cup purple onion, chopped | ¾ | cup Caesar salad dressing |
| ¼ | cup or 1 (2.5-ounce) can sliced ripe black olives | 4 | cups romaine lettuce, torn |

- Cook ravioli according to package directions. Rinse with cold water and drain.
- In a large bowl, combine ravioli with next 6 ingredients.
- Cover and chill.
- Serve over lettuce.

*Yield: 4 servings*

## GREEK PASTA SALAD

| | | | |
|---|---|---|---|
| 8 | ounces vermicelli | ⅓ | cup kalamata olives, chopped |
| ½ | cup extra virgin olive oil | ¼ | cup roasted red peppers, chopped (optional) |
| 2 | tablespoons Greek seasoning | 4-5 | green onions, chopped |
| 3 | tablespoons fresh lemon juice | | |

- Cook vermicelli for 6 minutes; drain.
- Pour olive oil, Greek seasoning, and lemon juice in a bowl. Whisk to combine.
- Add olives, roasted red peppers, and green onions, stir to combine.
- Add pasta and toss to coat.
- Cover and chill at least 1 to 2 hours for flavors to blend.

*Yield: 4 to 6 servings*

*Note: Salad is actually better the next day! You may add more olives if desired.*

---

In 1983, the League began providing volunteer support to Youth Town, a residential facility for youth in our area. Each year our Youth Town project changes based upon the needs of the children living there. We currently hold a yearly field day and participate in activities with both the male and female residents of Youth Town. Some of the activities in the past have been tennis lessons, make-overs, and skating parties. The experience with the young people has touched our members lives and is considered by many to be the highlight of their time in the League.

# BOW TIE PASTA WITH OLIVES AND PINE NUTS

*A terrific pasta salad for your next picnic!*

*There are many uses for a vinaigrette. You can use it as traditional salad dressing or a marinade for meat. Consider pouring over cheese and serve with crackers, toss with cooked vegetables, and rice or pasta to serve as a cold salad. You can also use instead of butter to pour over bread or rolls before baking.*

**Red Wine Vinaigrette**

- ¼ cup red wine vinegar
- ¼ cup extra virgin olive oil
- 2 teaspoons Dijon mustard
- ¼ cup fresh basil leaves, sliced thinly
- 2-3 teaspoons minced garlic

- Prepare vinaigrette by combining all ingredients in a tightly sealed container. Shake well to combine. Chill until ready to assemble salad.

**Salad**

- 1 pound bow tie pasta (or pasta of your choice), prepared according to package directions
- 1 ounce sun-dried tomatoes, reconstituted and sliced (yields about ½ cup)
- ⅓ cup pitted kalamata olives, sliced
- 3 tablespoons pine nuts, lightly toasted
- 1 cup freshly grated Parmesan cheese, divided
- Salt and fresh ground black pepper to taste

- Combine warm pasta with vinaigrette. Add tomatoes, olives and pine nuts.
- Toss with ⅔ cup freshly grated cheese, reserving ⅓ cup for garnish.
- Serve warm or at room temperature with fresh Parmesan cheese and fresh ground pepper sprinkled on top.

*Yield: 8 side-dish or 4 main-dish servings*

# SUMMERTIME CHERRY TOMATO AND GREEN BEAN PASTA

*Fresh and crisp!*

- ½-1 pound thin green beans, washed and strung
- ⅓ cup red wine vinegar
- ⅓ cup extra virgin olive oil
- 1 teaspoon Dijon mustard
- 1 teaspoon minced garlic
- ¼ teaspoon salt
- ½ teaspoon ground black pepper
- 3 tablespoons fresh basil or dill, chopped
- 12 ounces cavatappi or penne pasta, cooked according to package directions
- 1½-2 cups feta cheese, crumbled
- ½-1 pint cherry or grape tomatoes, halved
- ½ red bell pepper, seeded and diced
- ½ green bell pepper, seeded and diced
- ⅓ cup pitted kalamata olives, chopped

- Steam green beans until crisp tender, about 3 to 5 minutes. Drain and rinse in cold water to stop cooking process, then drain again.
- Whisk together vinegar, oil, mustard, garlic, salt, and pepper in a large bowl. Stir in basil or dill. Taste and adjust seasonings. Add the green beans and all other remaining ingredients.
- May be served chilled or at room temperature.

*Yield: 4 main dish servings or 8 side dish servings*

*Variation: May substitute dried basil or dill, but only use half of the suggested measure for fresh.*

---

*You can add edible flowers to salads. Examples of edible flowers are pansies, Johnny jump-ups, violets, roses, forget-me-nots, scented geranium leaves, nasturtiums, daises, day lilies, chamomile, roses, lilacs, orange blossom, sweet peas, snapdragons, lavender, marigolds and honeysuckle.*

*Add one cube sugar to bottle of olive oil to increase life of oil.*

# COUSCOUS CHICKEN SALAD WITH ORANGE GINGER VINAIGRETTE

*A refreshing end to a hot Southern summer day!*

**Orange Ginger Vinaigrette**

- 1/3 cup fresh orange juice
- 1/3 cup extra virgin olive oil
- 1/4 cup chopped fresh parsley
- 2 tablespoons fresh lemon juice
- 2 tablespoons soy sauce
- 1 teaspoon finely chopped ginger
- 1/8 teaspoon pepper
- Dash of salt

- Combine all dressing ingredients in a bowl, whisk to combine.

**Salad**

- 1 cup couscous, cooked according to package directions and cooled
- 2 cups shredded cooked chicken
- 1 cup chopped green pepper
- 1 cup sliced celery
- 1/2 cup shredded carrots
- 2 green onions, sliced
- Orange Ginger Vinaigrette

- In a large bowl, combine couscous and all remaining salad ingredients. Toss gently.
- Pour Orange Ginger Vinaigrette over salad, tossing gently.
- Cover and refrigerate for 1 to 2 hours to blend flavors.
- Serve chilled.

*Yield: 7 to 8 servings*

*Note: May be served on lettuce-lined plates.*

# PASTA SALAD WITH SHERRY DRESSING

*Wonderful to serve for a luncheon.*

**Sherry Dressing**

| | | | |
|---|---|---|---|
| ¾ | cup mayonnaise | ½ | teaspoon Italian seasoning |
| ⅓ | cup dry sherry | | Salt and pepper to taste |

- Combine dressing ingredients in a sealed container; mix well. Add 1 to 2 tablespoons of dressing to cooked pasta.

**Salad**

| | | | |
|---|---|---|---|
| 1 | (12-ounce) package vegetable rotini pasta, cooked according to package directions | 1 | can hearts of palm, drained and cut into bite-size pieces |
| 1 | cup tomatoes, cut into bite-size pieces | 8 | ounces fresh mushrooms, sliced |
| 1 | (8-ounce) can sliced black olives | 4 | fresh green onions, sliced thinly |
| 1 | (6-ounce) jar artichoke hearts, drained and cut into bite-size pieces | 1 | bag frozen green peas, lightly thawed and uncooked |
| | | ½ | cup fresh Parmesan cheese, shredded |

- In a large bowl, combine tomatoes, black olives, artichoke hearts, hearts of palm, mushrooms, and green onions. Top the vegetables mixture with the dressing. Place uncooked peas on top of dressing; add rotini pasta as next layer.
- Cover salad and chill for several hours, preferably overnight.
- Before serving, top with Parmesan cheese, tossing gently.

*Yield: 10 servings*

---

*The Jackson Service League provides many volunteer hours to the community as well as funding a variety of charitable organizations in Jackson, Tennessee. The combined efforts of our membership have had a large impact in Jackson. Since 1997, the Jackson Service League has raised over $100,000.00 to support many different organizations in Jackson.*

# CRUNCHY CHICKEN SALAD

*Wonderful to serve for your next Bunko party!*

**Salad**

- 2 skinless, boneless chicken breasts, cooked and cut into bite-sized pieces
- 1 medium cabbage, chopped
- 1 bunch green onions, sliced
- 1 cup slivered almonds, toasted
- ¼ cup sesame seeds
- 2 (3-ounce) packages chicken flavor Ramen noodles, uncooked and broken into pieces
- 1 flavor packet from 1 Ramen noodle package
- ¼ cup sugar
- 1 cup extra virgin olive oil
- 6 tablespoons oriental rice vinegar
- 1 teaspoon pepper
- ½ teaspoon salt

- Combine chicken and next 6 ingredients in a large bowl. Toss gently.
- To prepare dressing, combine the next 5 ingredients (sugar through salt) in a bowl. Whisk to combine.
- Pour dressing over salad, tossing well.

*Yield: 8 servings*

---

*Home is an invention on which no one has yet improved.*

Ann Douglas

# OLD HICKORY'S CHICKEN SALAD

*This is a true Southern favorite! Serve this for your next luncheon. This chicken salad is so delicious it will convert the pickiest eater into a chicken salad fan!*

| | | | |
|---|---|---|---|
| 4 | cups chicken, cooked and cubed (approximately 4 boneless, skinless, breasts) | 1 | tablespoon onion juice |
| 1½ | cups chopped celery | ½ | cup mango chutney, large pieces chopped |
| 1 | cup mayonnaise | ¾ | cup sliced almonds, toasted, divided |
| 2 | tablespoons freshly squeezed lemon juice | ½ | cup water chestnuts, chopped |
| 2½ | tablespoons soy sauce | 1¼ | cups seedless green grapes, halved |

- Mix chicken, celery, mayonnaise, lemon juice, soy sauce, onion juice, and chutney in large bowl. Cover and chill 8 to 12 hours, or overnight.
- Before serving, add ½ cup almonds, water chestnuts and grapes.
- Scoop salad onto plate, sprinkle remaining almonds evenly over each portion.

*Yield: 6 servings*

---

*Andrew Jackson, for whom Jackson was named, was called Old Hickory.*

# MEDITERRANEAN TOMATO SALAD

*An alternative to your traditional green salad!
Serve for a summertime lunch or with a light dinner!*

| | | | |
|---|---|---|---|
| 6 | medium fresh tomatoes, sliced | 2 | teaspoons parsley, minced |
| 1 | medium cucumber, peeled and sliced | 4 | teaspoons sugar |
| 1 | cup feta cheese, crumbled | 1 | teaspoon chopped fresh basil or ½ teaspoon dried basil |
| ¼ | cup sliced kalamata olives | | Dash salt |
| ½ | cup extra virgin olive oil | | Dash freshly ground black pepper |
| ⅓ | cup red wine vinegar | | |

- Layer first 4 ingredients in order given in a shallow dish.
- Combine remaining ingredients in a blender, food processor. Pulse several times to blend.
- Pour dressing over salad; cover and chill 2 hours before serving. Garnish with fresh basil before serving.

*Yield: 6 servings*

*Variation: May substitute cubed fresh mozzarella cheese for feta cheese.*

---

*Keep parsley, cilantro, and basil fresh in the refrigerator by putting their stems in water and covering the leaves with a plastic bag. Stored this way, herbs will keep fresh for several days.*

# WINTER FRUIT SALAD

*You will cure the winter blues when you serve this salad with fruit in the dressing!*

| | |
|---|---|
| 1 | cup diced panettone (½-inch dice) |
| 2 | tablespoons dried cherries |
| 2 | tablespoons diced dried apricots (¼-inch dice) |
| 2 | tablespoons golden raisins |
| 2 | tablespoons honey |
| 2 | tablespoons champagne vinegar or white balsamic vinegar |
| 5 | tablespoons extra-virgin olive oil |
| 1 | large pear, peeled, cored and cut into slivers about ¼-inch by 1½-inches |
| ¼ | large fennel bulb, cut into slivers equal in size to pear |
| | Salt and freshly ground pepper, to taste |
| 2 | cups mixed baby greens |
| ¼ | cup pistachios, toasted (optional) |

- Preheat oven to 250 degrees.
- Scatter panettone cubes on baking sheet and bake, tossing occasionally, until crisp and brown, approximately 1 hour. Set aside and allow to cool. Once cooled store in a zip-top bag.
- Place cherries, apricots, and raisins in a medium bowl.
- Add honey and vinegar to a small saucepan and heat until just warm. Whisk in olive oil and taste to make sure that the oil and vinegar are balanced.
- Remove from heat and pour over the dried fruit.
- Add pear, fennel and salt and pepper to taste.
- Place dressing in an airtight container and store in the refrigerator until ready to serve.
- To assemble the salad, pour the dressing over the mixed greens in a large salad bowl. Toss well to coat greens with dressing. Top with croutons and pistachios (if desired) and toss again. Serve immediately.

*Yield: 4 servings*

---

*You can find panettone during the holiday season. It is a sweet bread made with raisins, citron, pine nuts, and anise. If you cannot find panettone, you may substitute raisin bread croutons. The baking time for the croutons will decrease as the raisin bread is thinner.*

# ARTICHOKE AND BLUE CHEESE SALAD

*Using store bought grated cheese is a convenience that does not sacrifice flavor. Most cheeses keep for extended periods in the refrigerator. Therefore, it may be economical to stock up on grated cheese when it is on sale. If you choose to grate your own, add oil to grater before grating to make cleanup easier.*

### Dressing

| | | | |
|---|---|---|---|
| ¼ | small onion | ½ | teaspoon salt |
| 3 | tablespoons cider vinegar | ¼ | teaspoon freshly ground pepper |
| 2 | teaspoons spicy brown mustard | 1 | cup extra virgin olive oil |
| ½ | teaspoon sugar | | |

- To prepare dressing, puree onion with vinegar in a food processor. Add mustard, sugar, salt and pepper. With the motor running, add oil into mixture through the feed tube in a thin steady stream until mixed well.

### Salad

| | | | |
|---|---|---|---|
| ½ | pound bacon, cooked and crumbled | 1 | (8½-ounce) jar marinated artichokes, drained and quartered |
| 2 | heads romaine lettuce, torn | 4 | ounces blue cheese, crumbled |

- In a salad bowl, combine salad ingredients.
- Toss salad with dressing immediately before serving.

*Yield: 6 to 8 servings*

*Note: Dressing can be made ahead of time and refrigerated shaking well before serving.*

# ORANGE-WALNUT SALAD WITH SWEET AND SOUR DRESSING

*This is delicious served with chicken or pork.*

**Salad**

| | | | |
|---|---|---|---|
| 1 | head Boston lettuce | ½ | medium onion, sliced and separated into rings |
| 1 | pound fresh spinach, torn and coarse stems discarded | ½ | cup chopped walnuts |
| 2 | oranges, peeled, seeded, and sectioned | | Sweet and Sour Dressing |

- Place first 4 salad ingredients in a large bowl.
- Lightly toast walnuts in a skillet, allow to cool.
- Top salad with walnuts.
- Shake chilled dressing to combine oil and vinegar.
- Pour dressing over salad, tossing gently.
- Serve immediately.

**Sweet and Sour Dressing**

| | | | |
|---|---|---|---|
| 1 | cup vegetable oil | 1 | teaspoon celery seeds |
| ½ | cup vinegar | 1 | teaspoon dry mustard |
| ½ | cup sugar | 1 | teaspoon paprika |
| 1 | teaspoon salt | 1 | teaspoon grated onion |

- Prepare dressing by combining all ingredients in a sealed container. Shake vigorously. Chill dressing for several hours.

*Yield: 6 to 8 servings*

---

*To peel an orange, cover with boiling water and let stand 5 minutes, remove and peel. The white membrane (pith) will be easily removable. This method also works for peaches, the skins will be easily removed if you place them in boiling water for one minute. Immediately immerse in ice water to stop the cooking process.*

# JÍCAMA SLAW

*Serve this slaw at your next outdoor occasion. Wonderful with Spiced Pork Tenderloin (page 164).*

Jícama, also known as a Mexican potato, is a brown skinned root vegetable with a crunchy white flesh. It has a sweet flavor and can be eaten raw or cooked. You can find jícama in most supermarkets in the vegetable section. The skin should be removed before eating.

- 2 large shallots
- 1½ teaspoons salt, divided
- ¼ cup lime juice (about 4 limes)
- ⅓ cup extra virgin olive oil
- 1½ teaspoons sugar
- ¼ teaspoon fresh ground back pepper
- ⅛ teaspoon cayenne pepper (optional)
- 2 pounds jícama, peeled and cut into julienne strips (7 to 8 cups)
- ⅓ cup fresh cilantro, chopped

- Soak shallots in 1 cup cold water with ½ teaspoon salt for 15 to 20 minutes to make flavor milder. Drain and rinse under cold water. Finely chop shallots.
- Whisk together remaining 1 teaspoon salt with lime juice, oil, sugar and peppers in a large bowl.
- Add shallots, jícama, cilantro and toss well.
- Salt to taste and serve chilled.

*Yield: 8 servings*

# ORIENTAL SLAW

*Enjoy this updated version of coleslaw at your next barbeque!*

## Salad

| | | | |
|---|---|---|---|
| 2 | tablespoons butter | 1 | large head Napa cabbage, shredded |
| ½ | cup sesame seeds | | |
| 1 | can rice noodles | 5 | green onions, sliced |
| ½ | cup sliced almonds | 1 | can water chestnuts, chopped |

- Melt butter in a skillet. Sauté sesame seeds. Add rice noodles and almonds. Sauté mixture until golden brown. Remove from heat.
- Toss cabbage, green onions, water chestnuts, and sautéed mixture.

## Dressing

| | | | |
|---|---|---|---|
| ½ | teaspoon salt | 1 | cup sugar |
| ¼ | teaspoon pepper | ½ | cup red wine vinegar |
| 2 | tablespoons soy sauce | 1 | cup extra virgin olive oil |

- Prepare dressing by combining salt, pepper, soy sauce, sugar, and vinegar in a small bowl. Whisk together and slowly add oil.
- Immediately before serving, add dressing to cabbage mixture, tossing lightly.

*Yield: 6 to 8 servings*

---

*The Jackson Service League makes annual financial contributions to various organizations in the Jackson community. Each year, we support the West Tennessee Hearing and Speech Clinic, WRAP, American Cancer Society, and other organizations who assist women and children.*

# PEAR SALAD WITH CREAMY RASPBERRY DRESSING

*An elegant salad to serve with any meat!*

*A house is made of walls and beams; a home is built with love and dreams.*

*Author Unknown*

### Salad

| | | | |
|---|---|---|---|
| 4 | firm, ripe pears | ¼ | cup freshly grated Parmesan cheese |
| 1 | tablespoon lemon juice | 6 | bacon slices, cooked and crumbled (optional) |
| 1 | tablespoon lime juice | ½ | cup fresh raspberries |
| 1 | head Bibb lettuce, torn | | |
| 1 | small head romaine lettuce, torn | | |

- Peel and quarter pears. Combine juices and brush over pears.
- Arrange Bibb and romaine lettuce on 4 plates. Lay pear quarters over lettuce.
- Drizzle salads with Creamy Raspberry Dressing. Sprinkle cheese, bacon, and raspberries over each salad.
- Serve immediately.

### Creamy Raspberry Dressing

| | | | |
|---|---|---|---|
| ¾ | cup sour cream | 3 | tablespoons red wine vinegar |
| ¼ | cup raspberry preserves | ⅛ | teaspoon Dijon mustard |

- Whisk together dressing ingredients. Cover and chill until ready to assemble salad.

*Yield: 4 servings*

# THE OVERNIGHT SALAD

*The full-bodied flavor of the blue cheese compliments the sweet Mandarin oranges.*

**Red Wine Vinaigrette**

- ¾ cup extra virgin olive oil
- ¼ cup red wine vinegar
- ¼ teaspoon sugar
- ½ teaspoon salt
- ¼ teaspoon black pepper
- 1 (14-ounce) can artichoke hearts, drained and quartered
- 1½ cups frozen baby green peas, frozen and thawed
- 1 red onion, thinly sliced

- In a small mixing bowl, combine the first 5 ingredients (olive oil through pepper); whisk to thoroughly blend.
- Add artichokes, peas, and onions to vinaigrette.
- Refrigerate overnight to marinate vegetables.

**Salad**

- 2 bags mixed field greens, torn into small pieces
- ½ cup blue cheese, crumbled
- 1 (15-ounce) can Mandarin oranges, drained

- Place greens in a serving bowl. Add cheese, oranges, and vinaigrette with vegetables. Toss well.
- Serve immediately.

*Yield: 6 servings*

*Note: May substitute canned baby peas for frozen peas. This salad is also delicious with one head romaine lettuce and ½ pound spinach, instead of mixed field greens.*

---

*To remove sand and dirt from fresh greens, soak them in salted warm water for five minutes.*

# SHRIMP AND BLACK BEAN SALAD

*This unique make ahead salad is wonderful to serve for a luncheon or light dinner.*

**Black Bean Salsa**

| | | | |
|---|---|---|---|
| 1 | (15-ounce) can black beans, rinsed and drained | ⅔ | cup picante sauce |
| 1 | small green pepper, seeded and finely chopped | ¼ | cup lime juice |
| ½ | cup diced purple onion | 2 | tablespoons vegetable oil |
| 2 | tablespoons chopped fresh cilantro | 3 | tablespoons honey |
| | | ¼ | teaspoon salt |

- Combine salsa ingredients in a medium-sized bowl, tossing gently. Cover and chill 8 hours.

**Salad**

| | | | |
|---|---|---|---|
| 2 | pounds medium shrimp, boiled, peeled, deveined, and chilled | | Lettuce leaves |
| | | 8 | cherry tomatoes, halved |

- Arrange shrimp around edge of lettuce-lined plates, spoon black bean mixture in center. Garnish with cherry tomatoes.

*Yield: 4 servings*

*Note: The black bean salad could be served without the shrimp or as a dip with tortilla chips!*

---

*When coring a head of lettuce, strike the bottom of the lettuce on the counter, twist the core and remove.*

# SPICY THAI CHICKEN SALAD WITH GINGER PEANUT DRESSING

*A great one dish meal for a hot summer day!*

**Salad**

| | | | |
|---|---|---|---|
| 7 | ounces thin spaghetti, prepared according to package directions | 1 | cucumber, thinly sliced |
| 4 | skinless, boneless chicken breasts, grilled and sliced | 1 | red bell pepper, seeded and cut into strips |
| 4 | cups romaine lettuce, torn | ¼ | cup fresh cilantro, chopped |
| 2 | cups Napa cabbage, thinly sliced | | Chopped peanuts to garnish (optional) |
| 2 | medium carrots, coarsely shredded | | Sliced cucumber to garnish (optional) |
| | | | Ginger Peanut Dressing |

- Combine pasta with 3 tablespoons of dressing; mix well.
- Combine grilled chicken with 3 to 4 tablespoons dressing, reserving remaining dressing.
- Marinate chicken and pasta in separate covered containers in the refrigerator for 8 hours.
- Combine lettuce and next 5 ingredients, tossing well. Arrange on a serving platter or individual plates.
- Top lettuce with pasta, then chicken. Sprinkle with peanuts; garnish with cucumbers, if desired.
- Serve immediately with reserved Ginger Peanut Dressing.

*Yield: 6 servings*

**Ginger Peanut Dressing**

| | | | |
|---|---|---|---|
| 1 | cup rice wine vinegar | ¼ | cup honey |
| 4 | cloves garlic, minced | 2 | tablespoons molasses |
| ⅔ | cup peanut butter | 2 | tablespoons hot sauce |
| ½ | cup fresh lime juice | 1 | tablespoon peeled and grated ginger |
| ½ | cup fresh cilantro | 2 | tablespoons soy sauce |
| ¼ | cup apple cider vinegar | | |

- Prepare dressing by combining all ingredients in a blender. Process until smooth.

*Yield: 4 cups*

*Note: This recipe provides a generous quantity of dressing. It can be easily halved if desired.*

---

*Fresh ginger will last longer if you store it in a plastic bag in the freezer. It is not necessary to thaw it before slicing. Just pull out and cut off the amount that you need.*

*There are many ways to welcome a new neighbor. Include all ingredients for a salad in a basket: dry ingredients for dressing, bottle of olive oil and bag of greens along with a note on how to put it together.*

# SPINACH SALAD WITH CRANBERRIES

*This is wonderful served with any pork dish. Try it with the Spiced Pork Tenderloin (page 164).*

**Dressing**

| | | | |
|---|---|---|---|
| ½ | cup balsamic vinegar | ¼ | cup brown sugar |
| ½ | cup extra virgin olive oil | | |

- Combine dressing ingredients in a sealed container. Shake well.

**Salad**

| | | | |
|---|---|---|---|
| 1 | (12-ounce) bag spinach | ½ | cup feta cheese, crumbled |
| ⅓ | cup dried cranberries | ¼ | cup pistachios or walnuts, toasted and cooled |

- Toss spinach, cranberries, and feta cheese with desired amount of dressing.
- Top with toasted nuts.
- Serve immediately.

*Yield: 4 to 6 servings*

*Variations: Substitute dried cherries for cranberries and goat cheese for feta cheese. Also, may add grilled chicken.*

# MARINATED VEGETABLE SALAD DRESSING

| | | | |
|---|---|---|---|
| ¼ | cup red wine vinegar | 1 | (6-ounce) jar artichoke hearts, quartered |
| 1 | cup extra virgin olive oil | | |
| 6 | tablespoons fresh, grated Parmesan cheese | 1 | teaspoon salt |
| | | 1 | teaspoon garlic powder |
| 1 | (2-ounce) jar pimientos | 1 | teaspoon dry mustard |
| 1 | small purple onion, chopped | 1 | teaspoon black pepper |
| | | 1 | tablespoon sugar |

- Combine all ingredients in a sealed container. Shake to combine.
- Cover and chill at least one day before serving over salad greens.

*Yield: 8 servings*

# TOSSED SALAD WITH CARAMELIZED ALMONDS AND SPICY VINAIGRETTE DRESSING

*This salad will impress your guests with its beauty and wonderful flavor!*

**Tossed Salad**

| | | | |
|---|---|---|---|
| 1 | head lettuce, torn | 1 | (15-ounce) can Mandarin oranges, drained |
| 1 | cup chopped celery | | Caramelized Almonds |
| 2-4 | green onions, sliced | | Spicy Vinaigrette Dressing |

- Combine all salad ingredients in a large bowl. Toss with almonds and dressing. Serve immediately.

*Yield: 4 to 6 servings*

**Spicy Vinaigrette Dressing**

| | | | |
|---|---|---|---|
| ¼ | cup extra virgin olive oil | ½ | teaspoon salt |
| 2 | tablespoons white vinegar | 5 | drops hot sauce |
| 2 | tablespoons sugar | 1 | tablespoon minced parsley (optional) |

- Prepare dressing by combining all ingredients in a small sealed container and shake well; chill until ready to serve.

**Caramelized Almonds**

| | | | |
|---|---|---|---|
| ½ | cup slivered almonds | 3 | tablespoons sugar |

- Combine almonds and sugar in a large nonstick skillet, over medium heat and sauté, stirring constantly until sugar melts and coats almonds, approximately 8 minutes. Almonds will be brown and look like almond brittle.
- Remove almonds to waxed paper to cool; break into small pieces. Store in an airtight container until ready to serve.

---

*Monroe Dunaway Anderson was once a bank teller in Jackson. Today he is best remembered as the man who founded M.D. Anderson Cancer Center in Houston, Texas. The M.D. Anderson Planetarium at Lambuth University bears his name.*

*A person travels the world over in search of what he needs and returns home to find it.*

— George Moore

# SUMMER STRAWBERRY SALAD WITH SWEET SURPRISE PECANS

*This salad is sure to please every palate and satisfy everyone's appetite!*

**Salad**

| | | | |
|---|---|---|---|
| 2 | bags mixed baby greens | 2 | pints fresh strawberries, hulled and sliced |
| 1 | head romaine lettuce, torn into bite-size pieces | 1 | cup Sweet Surprise Pecans |
| 4 | Lemon Thyme Chicken breasts, cubed (page 184) | | Strawberry Poppy Seed Dressing |

- Assemble salad by tossing baby greens and lettuce in a large bowl. Add dressing to salad, coating leaves lightly.
- Divide salad evenly among 8 plates, sprinkling even amounts of Lemon Thyme Chicken over salad greens.
- Layer the sliced strawberries on top of chicken and top with Sweet Surprise Pecans.
- Garnish plates with any extra whole strawberries. Serve immediately.

*Yield: 8 servings*

**Strawberry Poppy Seed Dressing**

| | | | |
|---|---|---|---|
| ⅓ | cup white balsamic vinegar | ¾ | cup sugar |
| 1 | teaspoon salt | 1 | cup vegetable oil |
| 1 | teaspoon dry mustard | 10 | fresh or frozen strawberries |
| 1 | teaspoon finely grated onion | 2 | teaspoons poppy seeds |

- Combine first 4 ingredients of dressing in a blender or a food processor. Add sugar and process until dissolved. Continue processing while slowly adding oil through top or feeder tube. Add strawberries; process until blended.
- Pour into a bowl and stir in poppy seeds; cover and chill at least 30 to 45 minutes. Stir before serving.

*Yield: 2½ cups*

*Variation: You may make raspberry poppy seed dressing by substituting raspberries for the strawberries.*

*Summer Strawberry Salad continued*

**Sweet Surprise Pecans**

| | | | |
|---|---|---|---|
| 2 | tablespoons butter | 2 | teaspoons chili powder |
| 3 | cups pecan halves | 1 | tablespoon ground cumin seed (optional) |
| ½ | cup brown sugar, firmly packed | ¼ | cup apple cider vinegar |

- Preheat oven to 350 degrees. Measure all pecan ingredients and have prepared on counter.
- Melt butter in a large nonstick skillet over medium heat; add pecans and sauté until lightly browned. Add brown sugar and cook until lightly caramelized. Stir in chili powder and cumin, combining well. Add vinegar and cook until all liquid has evaporated.
- Spread pecans evenly on a greased cookie sheet; bake 3 to 5 minutes until crisp. Cool pecans; place in an airtight container.

*Yield: 3 cups*

# SUMMERTIME ORZO SALAD

*Showcase homegrown vegetables with this salad!*

| | | | |
|---|---|---|---|
| 3 | tablespoons extra virgin olive oil, divided | 1 | large red bell pepper, seeded and chopped |
| 1 | medium-sized sweet onion, chopped | 1 | large zucchini, chopped |
| 1 | cup orzo, cooked according to package directions | 4 | tablespoons white balsamic vinegar |
| 4 | large carrots, coarsely shredded or chopped | 2 | tablespoons honey |
| | | ¾ | teaspoon salt |
| | | ½ | teaspoon freshly ground pepper |

- Heat 1 tablespoon of olive oil in a small skillet over medium heat. Add onion and sauté for 10 minutes or until browned; stirring often. Remove from heat.

- In a medium-sized bowl, combine onion, orzo, and remaining 2 tablespoons oil. Stir in remaining ingredients.

- Cover and chill at least 2 hours.

*Yield: 4 servings*

*Variation: You may substitute white wine vinegar for balsamic vinegar*

# TROPICAL ROMAINE SALAD

*A very colorful and easy salad!
The fruit combination adds an exotic flare to your meal!*

**Salad**

| | | | |
|---|---|---|---|
| 1 | head romaine lettuce, torn | ½ | cup toasted pecan halves |
| 3 | kiwis, peeled and sliced | 3 | ounces crumbled blue cheese |
| 1 | pint strawberries, hulled and sliced | | Orange Lime Dressing |

- Place lettuce, kiwi, and strawberries in a salad bowl.
- Immediately before serving, drizzle Orange Lime Dressing over salad; top with pecans and blue cheese.

*Yield: 6 to 8 servings*

**Orange Lime Dressing**

| | | | |
|---|---|---|---|
| ½ | cup extra virgin olive oil | 5 | tablespoons orange marmalade |
| ¼ | cup fresh lime juice | | Salt and pepper to taste |
| 2 | tablespoons white balsamic vinegar | | |

- Combine dressing ingredients in a blender, blending until smooth.
- Cover and chill until ready to serve. Shake well before serving.

*Yield: 1 cup*

*Note: Use this versatile salad as a base recipe and add any fruit you enjoy. Changing this salad by adding seasonal fruits highlights their flavors!*

---

*Highland Park was an amusement center from the 'Gay Nineties' and early 20th century. Located between Crescent and Westwood Avenue it had a baseball park, roller coaster, skating rink, and pavilion for band concerts.*

# FRUIT SALAD WITH MINT SYRUP

*Try this unique presentation for your next luncheon or brunch!*

**Salad**

| | | | |
|---|---|---|---|
| 1 | jar mangoes, drained and sliced lengthwise | 6 | kiwis, sliced thin |
| 2 | pints raspberries | 2 | pints strawberries, halved |
| 1 | jar apricots, drained and sliced | 2 | pints blueberries |
| 2 | star fruit, sliced | 1 | pomegranate (optional) |
| | | | Mint leaves |

- In a glass trifle bowl, layer fruit individually beginning with the mangoes on the bottom followed by the raspberries and apricots.
- After the layer of apricots, place star fruit vertically against the wall of the trifle bowl and continue layering kiwi, strawberries, and blueberries.
- Cut pomegranate in half, remove pulp and scatter across top of salad.
- Pour ½ cup mint syrup over the top of the salad.
- Cover and refrigerate until ready to serve.
- Prior to serving garnish with mint leaves.

**Mint Syrup**

| | | | |
|---|---|---|---|
| 2 | cups water | 1 | bunch fresh mint leaves |
| 2 | cups sugar | | |

- Bring water and sugar to a boil in a saucepan over medium heat.
- Add mint leaves and simmer 5 minutes. Let stand 2 hours, strain, and store in an airtight container in the refrigerator.

*Yield: 8 servings*

---

*When purchasing fruit smell it when you are at the store. It is fresh if, at room temperature, it smells like it should taste.*

# CHICKEN TORTILLA SOUP

*You will love this hearty soup!*

| | | | |
|---|---|---|---|
| 2 | tablespoons vegetable oil and oil to fry tortilla strips | 1 | teaspoon chili powder |
| 1 | small onion, chopped | 1 | teaspoon salt |
| 1 | (4.5-ounce) can chopped green chiles | 1/8 | teaspoon pepper |
| 1 | teaspoon minced garlic | 2 | teaspoons Worcestershire sauce |
| 1 | cup canned chopped tomatoes | 1 | tablespoon Heinz 57 steak sauce |
| 1 | (14-ounce) can beef broth | 1 | pound uncooked chicken breast, cubed |
| 1 | (14-ounce) can chicken broth | 8 | corn tortillas, cut in strips |
| 1½ | cups water | | Salt to taste |
| 1½ | cups spicy tomato-vegetable juice cocktail | 4 | ounces Monterey Jack cheese, shredded |
| 1 | teaspoon cumin | | |

- In a large skillet, heat 2 tablespoons oil. Add onion, chiles, and garlic; sauté until soft.
- Transfer to a large stockpot and add tomatoes, broths, water, spicy tomato juice, spices, and sauces. Bring to a boil, then reduce heat and simmer for 1 hour.
- Add chicken pieces and simmer 45 minutes longer.
- In a skillet, pour enough oil to measure 1-inch. Heat over high heat and add tortilla strips to fry. When crispy, put on paper towel and salt lightly. To serve, divide cheese evenly and place in bowls, add soup, then drop crispy tortillas into the soup.

*Yield: 6 to 8 servings*

*Variation: May substitute store bought tortilla chips as a shortcut.*

---

*If you put too much salt in the soup, you can fix your soup by adding a pinch of brown sugar. Continue to add by pinches until the soup reaches the desired flavor.*

# CURRIED CORN SOUP

*This is a great winter soup with a unique flavor.*

| | | | |
|---|---|---|---|
| 1 | tablespoon olive oil | 2 | large ripe tomatoes, seeded and chopped |
| 1 | large onion, chopped | | |
| 1 | tablespoon garlic, finely chopped | 4 | cups chicken broth or stock |
| | | ¼ | teaspoon hot pepper sauce |
| 1 | tablespoon curry powder | 2 | cups cooked corn |
| 3 | tablespoons all-purpose flour | ½ | cup plain low-fat yogurt |

- Heat olive oil in saucepan over moderate heat. Add onion and sauté for 2 minutes. Add garlic and cook for 1 minute more. Stir in the curry powder and flour. Mix in the tomatoes, chicken broth and hot pepper sauce. Simmer soup for 20 minutes.

- Puree the soup in a blender. Return to the pot and bring to a simmer. Add the corn and cook for 1 minute.

- Remove pot from heat, stir in yogurt and serve.

*Yield: 6 servings*

*Note: This soup may be prepared ahead of time up to point of adding yogurt. Refrigerate and reheat; add yogurt before serving. It also freezes well if you freeze before adding yogurt.*

---

*Home is where the heart is and hence a movable feast.*

Angela Carter (1940-1992)

# FABULOUS CHILI

*The men will love this full bodied chili!*

| | | | |
|---|---|---|---|
| 2 | pounds ground beef, venison, or turkey | ½ | fresh jalapeño pepper, seeded, deveined, and chopped |
| 2 | medium onions, chopped | 2 | tablespoons chili powder |
| 1 | large green pepper, seeded and chopped | 2 | teaspoons dried oregano, crushed |
| 2 | cloves garlic, chopped | 1 | teaspoon ground cumin |
| 3 | (16-ounce) cans tomatoes, coarsely diced and undrained | 1 | teaspoon dried basil, crushed |
| | | 2 | teaspoons salt |
| 3 | (16-ounce) cans kidney beans rinsed and drained | ½ | teaspoon pepper |
| | | ½ | cup ketchup |
| 2 | (10-ounce) cans diced tomatoes with green chilies, undrained | | Monterey Jack cheese, shredded (optional) |
| | | | Sour cream (optional) |
| 3 | (8-ounce) cans tomato sauce | | Green onion, chopped (optional) |
| 1 | (4.5-ounce) can chopped green chilies | | |

- Cook meat, onion, pepper, and garlic until meat is browned. Drain well. Add tomatoes, beans, and tomatoes with green chilies. Stir. Add tomato sauce, chopped green chilies, and next 8 ingredients.
- Cook over medium heat for 20 minutes. Reduce heat and simmer on low for 1 to 2 hours.
- When serving, top each bowl of chili with cheese, sour cream and chopped green onion, if desired.

*Yield: 8 to 12 servings*

*Note: This chili is best if made 1 to 2 days ahead of time, refrigerated and reheated. You may also serve chili over cooked white rice.*

# MEXICAN CHOWDER

*Try this spicy chicken corn chowder.*

| | | | |
|---|---|---|---|
| 3 | tablespoons butter | 28 | ounces frozen cream style corn, defrosted |
| 4 | skinless, boneless chicken breasts, cubed | 1 | (4.5-ounce) can chopped green chiles, undrained |
| 1 | small onion, chopped | ½ | teaspoon hot sauce |
| 1 | garlic clove, minced | ¼ | teaspoon salt |
| 2 | cups half-and-half | ½ | teaspoon ground cumin |
| 2 | cups shredded Monterey Jack cheese | 2 | tablespoons chopped fresh cilantro |

- Melt butter in a Dutch oven over medium to high heat. Add chicken, onion, and garlic; and sauté 10 minutes.
- Stir in the next 7 ingredients. Cook over low heat for 15 minutes, stirring often. Stir in 2 tablespoons cilantro.

*Yield: 6 to 8 servings*

*Variation: May use fat-free half-and-half.*

---

*Worries go down better with soup than without.*

*Jewish proverb*

# PUMPKIN HARVEST SOUP

*This is the perfect fall soup. Beautiful and delicious!*

| | | | |
|---|---|---|---|
| 4 | tablespoons butter | ¼ | teaspoon ground nutmeg |
| 1 | large onion, diced | ¼ | teaspoon ground ginger |
| 1 | medium leek, white part only | 1 | bay leaf |
| 1 | (16-ounce) can pumpkin | 1 | cup half-and-half |
| 4 | cups chicken broth | | Nutmeg |
| ⅓ | teaspoon curry powder | | Mint leaves |

- In a medium soup pot, melt butter over medium-high heat. Add onion and leek, sauté, stirring until soft.
- Stir in pumpkin, broth, spices, and bay leaf. Bring to a boil; lower heat and simmer for 15 minutes, stirring occasionally.
- Remove bay leaf.
- Puree the mixture in batches in a blender until texture is smooth.
- Return mixture to soup pot. Add half-and-half; cook over medium heat, stirring occasionally until heated through. Adjust seasonings if needed.
- Garnish with nutmeg and sprig of mint, as desired.

*Yield: 6 to 8 servings*

*Note: You may refrigerate soup for up to 2 days or freeze after pureeing in blender. Add half-and-half when reheating. Consider serving this soup in carved out miniature pumpkins.*

---

*Use pumpkin as a container for flowers (hollow and insert glass container in center) or candles. Pumpkins can also be used as a name card holder. Spray paint it gold or silver and tie the name card on the stem with raffia.*

*You can also use hollowed out pumpkins to serve soups in the fall. Use a large pumpkin as a tureen and minature pumpkins as bowls.*

# WHITE CHICKEN CHILI WITH PINE NUTS

*In December of 1862, Confederate General Nathan Bedford Forest swept through West Tennessee. While skirmishing near Jackson, he fought a brief engagement at Old Salem Cemetery on Cotton Grove Road.*

| | |
|---|---|
| 4-6 | boneless skinless chicken breasts |
| 1 | large onion, chopped |
| 1 | teaspoon white pepper |
| ¼ | teaspoon salt |
| 2 | cans cream of chicken soup |
| 3 | cans great Northern beans, drained |
| 2 | (4-ounce) cans chopped green chilies |
| ½ | teaspoon garlic powder |
| 1 | teaspoon cumin |
| 2 | teaspoon chili powder |
| ½ | teaspoon dried oregano |
| 1 | can chopped tomatoes and green chilies, drained |
| | Toasted pine nuts (optional) |
| | Sour cream (optional) |
| | Monterey Jack or Cheddar cheese, shredded (optional) |
| | Salsa (optional) |

- Place chicken and onion in large pot with water to cover. Add salt and pepper. Boil until chicken is cooked and tender.
- Remove chicken, leaving onions in pot. Allow chicken to cool and cut into ½-inch pieces.
- Drain broth, reserving onions, into a separate container and reserve.
- Return chicken to pot with onions; add soup, beans, and next 6 ingredients, stir to blend.
- Cook over medium heat until heated through.
- Add reserved chicken broth until you reach the desired consistency.
- Reduce heat to low at least 30 minutes or in a crock pot for several hours.
- Top with toasted pine nuts, sour cream, cheese, and salsa, as desired.

*Yield: 6 to 8 servings*

# CUCUMBER SANDWICHES

*Perfectly refreshing for your next meeting or luncheon.*

- 1 large cucumber, peeled, seeded and grated
- 1 (8-ounce) package cream cheese, softened
- 1 tablespoon mayonnaise
- 1 small shallot, minced
- ¼ teaspoon seasoned salt
- 1 (16-ounce) loaf thin sandwich bread, ends discarded
- Cucumber slices, optional

- Drain cucumber well, pressing between layers of paper towels.
- Stir together cucumber and next 4 ingredients.
- Spread mixture evenly over half of bread slices. Top with remaining bread slices.
- Trim crusts from sandwiches and cut in half diagonally.
- Garnish with cucumber slices if desired.
- Store sandwiches in an airtight container.

*Yield: 16 sandwiches*

---

*Use an electric knife to make quick work of removing bread crusts for luncheon sandwiches.*

# GREEN CHILE-PIMENTO CHEESE

*Serve this at your next Autumn occasion.*

- 2 (8-ounce) blocks extra sharp Cheddar cheese, shredded
- 1 (8-ounce) block Monterey Jack cheese with peppers, shredded
- 1 cup mayonnaise
- 1 (4.5-ounce) can chopped green chilies
- 1 (4-ounce) jar diced pimento, drained
- 1 medium poblano chile pepper, seeded and minced
- 1 teaspoon Worcestershire sauce (or to taste)

- Combine all ingredients in large bowl.
- Cover and chill. Once chilled, serve on sandwiches or crackers.

*Yield: 6 cups*

# TURKEY AND CARAMELIZED ONION WRAPS

*This light and easy lunch is delicious with a cool fruit salad. Perfect for picnics!*

**Turkey Wrap**

- 8 (10-inch) whole grain flour tortillas
- 2 (6.5-ounce) packages lite garlic and herb-flavored cheese, softened
- 1½ pounds deli-style smoked turkey, sliced thin
- 16 turkey bacon slices, cooked crisp and crumbled
- 4 cups loosely packed arugula or mixed baby salad greens

- Spread a thin layer of the softened cheese evenly over each tortilla.
- Top cheese evenly with caramelized onions, turkey, bacon and greens.
- Roll wraps by folding sides of tortilla towards the middle. Starting from unfolded side, roll up.
- Serve immediately or wrap in waxed paper and chill.
- Cut in half to serve.

**Caramelized Onions**

- 2 tablespoons olive oil
- 2 large sweet onions, diced
- 1 tablespoon sugar
- 1 teaspoon balsamic vinegar

- Heat olive oil in a large skillet over medium-high heat. Add onions and sugar, stirring often.
- When onion is caramel in color, remove from heat, and stir in vinegar. Let cool.

*Yield: 8 servings*

*Variation: Also delicious with pita bread instead of tortillas.*

> *My home is not a place, it is people.*
>
> Lois McMaster Bujold

# TURKEY BASIL BITES

*These little sandwiches are delicious and beautiful. Serve them for a light lunch.*

**Scallion Cream Cheese**

| | | | |
|---|---|---|---|
| 8 | ounces cream cheese, softened to room temperature | ½ | cup minced green onions, both the white and green parts |
| 6 | ounces sour cream | | |

- Combine cream cheese, sour cream, and onions with an electric mixer on low speed. Cover and chill until ready to assemble sandwiches.

**Sandwiches**

| | | | |
|---|---|---|---|
| 1 | loaf raisin nut or cinnamon raisin bread, cut into ¼-inch thick slices | 10 | thin slices fresh or smoked turkey breast |
| | | 1 | package fresh basil leaves |

- Spread a thin layer of Scallion Cream Cheese on each slice of raisin bread.
- Place 1 slice of turkey on half of the bread slices, cutting turkey to fit each sandwich.
- Layer basil leaves on top of turkey.
- Place other slices of bread on top, cream cheese side down.
- Put sandwiches on cookie sheet; wrap in plastic; refrigerate until very cold.
- Cut into triangles for a seated luncheon or 3 rectangles for a buffet luncheon.
- Serve chilled.

*Yield: 10 servings*

*Note: Fresh basil is an essential part of these sandwiches. Dried basil cannot achieve the same flavor. Also, these Turkey Basil Bites may be made a day ahead and refrigerated if covered with damp paper towels and wrapped in plastic to keep moist.*

# BRUNCH, BREADS, AND BEVERAGES

# BRUNCH, BREADS AND BEVERAGES

French Toast Soufflé ........................................ 91
Panettone French Toast ................................... 92
Blueberry and Lemon Soufflé Pancakes ............ 93
Grits Gruyère .................................................... 94
Artichoke Frittata ............................................. 95
Santa's Breakfast Surprise ................................ 96
Sausage Mushroom Quiche
    with Parmesan ............................................ 97
Breakfast Strata ................................................ 98
Mushroom, Tomato, and Bacon Puff ................ 99
Tom's Favorite Fruit and Nut Granola ............ 100
Cream Cheese Spreads ................................... 101
Spiced Orange Banana Bread ......................... 102
Raspberry Pecan Bread ................................... 103
Cinnamon Strawberry Bread .......................... 104
Zesty Zucchini Bread ..................................... 105
Cherry-Lemon Scones .................................... 106
Almond Cream Cheese Danish ....................... 107
Cinnamon Roll Ups ........................................ 108
Mandarin Orange Brunch Cake ...................... 109
Gingerbread Muffins ...................................... 110
Good Morning Glory Muffins ........................ 111

"Good for You" Orange
    Cranberry Bran Muffins ........................... 112
"Ready When You Need Them"
    Dinner Rolls ............................................. 113
Sweet Potato Biscuits ..................................... 114
Artichoke Garlic Bread ................................... 115
Miss Jeanne's Corn Light Bread ..................... 116
Guilt Free Popovers ........................................ 117
Refreshing Almond Tea .................................. 118
Famous Iced Tea ............................................. 118
Coffee Punch .................................................. 119
Aunt Lizzie's Punch ....................................... 119
Queen's Punch ............................................... 120
Banana Punch ................................................ 120
Frozen Watermelon Margarita ........................ 121
Sea Breeze in a Pitcher .................................. 121
Mojito ............................................................ 122
Café Au Cacao ............................................... 122
Italian Blizzard .............................................. 123
Spicy Spiked Slush ........................................ 123
Sangría Blanca ............................................... 124
Hot Christmas Cider ...................................... 124

# FRENCH TOAST SOUFFLÉ

*This easy "do-ahead" breakfast will please you and your guests.*

| | | | |
|---|---|---|---|
| 5 | cups white bread cubes | ⅓ | cup half-and-half |
| 4 | ounces low fat cream cheese, softened | ¼ | cup maple syrup |
| 4 | small eggs | ¼ | teaspoon vanilla extract |
| ¾ | cup milk | 1 | tablespoon confectioners' sugar |

- Place bread cubes in a lightly greased 13x9x2-inch baking pan.
- In a large bowl, beat cream cheese with an electric mixer at medium speed until smooth.
- Add eggs one at a time, mixing well after each addition.
- Stir in milk, half-and-half, maple syrup and vanilla until mixture is smooth.
- Pour cream cheese mixture over bread cubes; cover and refrigerate 8 to 12 hours or overnight.
- Remove soufflé from refrigerator and let stand at room temperature for 30 minutes.
- Preheat oven to 375 degrees.
- Bake for 30 minutes or until set.
- Sprinkle soufflé with powdered sugar and serve warm.

*Yield: 8 servings*

*Note: You may add fresh fruit on top for variety. Baked apples are a delicious addition in the winter.*

---

*A good home must be made, not bought.*

Joyce Maynard

# PANETTONE FRENCH TOAST

*A holiday treat!*

| | | | |
|---|---|---|---|
| 1 | loaf stale panettone, sliced 1¼ to 1½-inch thick | 1-2 | tablespoons orange liqueur |
| 3 | eggs | ¼ | teaspoon cinnamon |
| 1 | cup milk | | Nutmeg |
| 1 | orange, zest and juice | | Butter |
| 1 | teaspoon vanilla or almond extract | | Confectioners' sugar |

- Cut bread into triangles or use a cookie cutter for different shapes.
- In a large bowl, beat together eggs, and milk. Add orange zest, juice, extract, liqueur, cinnamon and nutmeg. Stir well.
- Add the bread one piece at a time and let soak for 2 minutes.
- In a medium-sized skillet, melt 1 tablespoon of butter over medium heat until it stops sizzling.
- Add several slices of bread (make sure you have enough room to turn bread over with a spatula).
- Fry until light brown. Turn and fry on other side until light brown. Remove from pan and keep warm.
- Add 1 tablespoon of butter to the pan for each batch.
- Dust with confectioners' sugar and serve with warm syrup.

*Yield: 6 servings*

---

*It has been said, "If you can't fix it, feed it." There are many times in life when our friends have a difficult time. Events like illness, job loss, death or divorce unfortunately occur. As a friend, there is nothing that you can do to fix the problem. Here in Jackson, we feed the friend in an effort to temporarily relieve their burden. It is a nice tradition that truly shows your friends how you care and allows you to help in some small way.*

# BLUEBERRY AND LEMON SOUFFLÉ PANCAKES

*A delicious alternative to traditional pancakes.
Sure to become your family favorite!*

| | | | |
|---|---|---|---|
| 6 | eggs, separated | 4 | teaspoons fresh squeezed lemon juice |
| 2 | cups low fat cottage cheese (small curd) | 4 | teaspoons baking powder |
| ¼ | cup butter, melted | 1 | cup all-purpose flour |
| 2 | tablespoons maple syrup | 1 | cup fresh blueberries, rinsed and drained |
| ½ | teaspoon salt | | |

- Put egg whites in a cold bowl and beat until stiff but not dry. Reserve.
- In a food processor or blender, combine the cottage cheese, egg yolks, butter, syrup, salt, lemon juice, baking powder, and flour. Blend until smooth.
- Pour cottage cheese mixture into a bowl. Fold in egg whites.
- Heat griddle or large heavy skillet. Lightly oil the griddle.
- Spoon about 3 tablespoons batter for each pancake and cook until bubbles form on top.
- Sprinkle 1 teaspoon blueberries on top of each pancake before turning.
- Turn and cook other side.

*Yield: 6 servings*

*Note: If blueberries are not in season, substitute grated apple, chopped banana, chopped strawberries or other fruit.*

---

*When you know that several people will be bringing food to a friend's house due to a new baby, illness or death consider taking paper goods along with your contribution. At times when friends are too busy or overwhelmed to cook, they do not need to do dishes either! If you do take a meal or dessert, take it in a disposable dish so that your friend does not have to wash and return a dish.*

# GRITS GRUYÈRE

*A new twist on a Southern favorite!*

| | | | |
|---|---|---|---|
| 1 | cup grits, uncooked | ½ | teaspoon pepper |
| 1 | quart milk | 6 | ounces Gruyère cheese, grated |
| ½ | cup butter plus ⅓ cup melted butter | ⅓ | cup grated Parmesan |
| 1 | teaspoon salt | | |

- Heat milk in a large sauce pan over medium heat. Add ½ cup butter and stir until melted. Add grits and cover.
- When grits are thick, remove from heat. Add salt and pepper.
- Remove from heat and beat with electric mixer until creamy, about 5 minutes.
- Pour into an ungreased 13x9x2-inch baking pan. Cover and refrigerate 4 hours or overnight.
- When you are ready to bake grits, preheat oven to 400 degrees.
- Using a sharp knife, cut chilled grits into 1½x2-inch rectangles in the baking pan.
- Pour melted butter over top and sprinkle with Gruyère and Parmesan cheese.
- Bake for 30 to 55 minutes.

*Yield: 8 to 10 servings*

---

*The Battle of Britton Lane was fought near Denmark, Tennessee in 1862. Confederate Cavalry, raiding from North Mississippi, lost nearly 200 men in the battle.*

# ARTICHOKE FRITTATA

*This Italian omelet is sure to satisfy anyone's appetite!*

| | | | |
|---|---|---|---|
| 2 | tablespoons butter | 9 | eggs, lightly beaten |
| 1 | (5-ounce) jar marinated artichokes, coarsely chopped, drained and oil reserved | 2 | cups grated sharp Cheddar cheese |
| | | 1/4 | cup chopped parsley |
| | | 1/8 | teaspoon thyme |
| 1 | bunch green onions, diced | 1/8 | teaspoon oregano |
| 1 | garlic clove, minced | 1/2 | cup spinach, cooked, chopped and squeezed dry of all moisture |
| 1 | medium zucchini, quartered lengthwise and sliced | | |
| 1/2 | cup mushrooms, washed and sliced | | |

- Preheat oven to 350 degrees. Grease a 10-inch pie plate or quiche pan
- Melt butter in a medium saucepan over medium heat.
- Add oil drained from artichoke jar.
- Sauté onions, garlic, zucchini and mushrooms in butter and oil mixture until soft, about 5 minutes; remove from heat and drain.
- Whisk eggs lightly in a large bowl.
- Add cheese, parsley, thyme, and oregano to eggs.
- Fold in drained, cooked vegetables, chopped artichokes, and spinach.
- Pour filling in prepared pan and bake for 45 minutes or until mixture is firm and the edges are slightly golden.

*Yield: 6 to 8 servings*

---

*For interesting lighting for a summer outdoor party, hang can lights from the trees. Save tin cans from canned vegetables, wash the can and remove labels. Punch holes all over the sides of the can with a screwdriver. Use wire to make handle (like a bucket). Place candles in cans and hang from trees.*

# SANTA'S BREAKFAST SURPRISE

*Your guests will love this easy "do ahead" breakfast dish!*

| | | | |
|---|---|---|---|
| 2 | cups water | ½ | teaspoon thyme |
| ½ | teaspoon salt | ⅛ | teaspoon garlic powder |
| ½ | cup quick grits | 3 | shakes red pepper or to taste |
| 4 | cups (16-ounces) shredded medium Cheddar cheese | 2 | pounds sausage, cooked, drained and crumbled |
| 4 | eggs, beaten | | Salsa |
| 1 | cup milk | | |

- Bring water to a boil in a large saucepan over medium-high heat, add salt and grits, cook until water is absorbed, about 5 minutes.
- Add cheese and stir until melted.
- Stir in egg, milk, thyme, garlic powder, red pepper and sausage.
- Pour in a greased 13x9x2-inch glass baking pan; cover and refrigerate overnight.
- Bake (starting in a cold oven) at 350 degrees for about 50 minutes, until lightly browned.
- Serve with salsa spooned over individual servings.

*Yield: 10 to 12 servings*

*Variation: May add fresh mushrooms, sliced and sautéed in butter before placing in baking dish.*

# SAUSAGE MUSHROOM QUICHE WITH PARMESAN

| | | | | |
|---|---|---|---|---|
| 4 | tablespoons butter | 4 | tablespoons lemon juice |
| ¾ | pound fresh mushrooms, thinly sliced | ½ | teaspoon salt |
| | | ½ | teaspoon pepper |
| 1 | pound sausage, cooked and drained | 1 | (9-inch) pastry shell, partially baked |
| 1 | cup heavy cream | ½ | cup freshly grated Parmesan cheese |
| 2 | egg yolks, lightly beaten | | |
| 1 | tablespoon flour | | |

- Preheat oven to 350 degrees.
- Melt butter in a skillet over medium heat. Add mushrooms and sauté until tender. Add sausage and stir to combine.
- Mix cream, egg yolks, flour, lemon juice, salt and pepper in a medium-sized bowl.
- Spread sausage and mushroom mixture evenly over bottom of pastry shell.
- Pour cream mixture over sausage and mushrooms.
- Sprinkle with cheese and bake for 35 minutes or until puffy and lightly browned.

*Yield: 6 servings*

---

*Peace and rest at length have come*

*All the day's long toil is past,*

*And each heart is whispering, "Home, Home at last."*

Thomas Hood (1799-1845)

# BREAKFAST STRATA

*Micajah Autry, a Jackson attorney and poet, was one of the heroes who perished at the Alamo. He was related to cowboy movie star, Gene Autry.*

| | | | |
|---|---|---|---|
| 6 | slices bread, torn into 1-inch pieces | 3 | cups shredded Cheddar cheese, divided |
| 1 | pound bacon, cooked, drained and crumbled | 8 | eggs, lightly beaten |
| | | 1 | cup fresh mushrooms, sliced |
| | | 2 | cups milk |

- Coat a 13x9x2-inch baking pan with cooking spray.
- Place bread pieces in the bottom of the pan. Sprinkle bacon over bread.
- Mix 2 cups cheese, eggs, mushrooms and milk in a medium-sized bowl.
- Pour over bread and bacon.
- Cover and refrigerate overnight.
- Top with remaining cheese.
- Bake at 350 degrees for 45 minutes.

*Yield: 6 servings*

*Note: You may substitute crumbled, cooked sausage or diced ham for bacon.*

# MUSHROOM, TOMATO, AND BACON PUFF

*This delicious "do ahead" dish will be a winner with family and friends!*

| | | | |
|---|---|---|---|
| 4 | cups day old French or white bread cut into cubes | 2 | tablespoons Worcestershire sauce |
| 1 | cup shredded Monterey Jack cheese | 5 | dashes hot pepper sauce |
| 1 | cup shredded sharp Cheddar cheese | 2 | green onions, green part only, chopped |
| 10 | eggs, lightly beaten | 1 | cup fresh mushrooms, sliced |
| 4 | cups milk | ¾ | cup chopped fresh tomatoes |
| 2 | teaspoons dry mustard | 10-12 | slices bacon, cooked, drained, and crumbled |
| 1 | teaspoon salt | | Paprika, to garnish |
| ⅛ | teaspoon black pepper | | Chopped parsley, to garnish, optional |
| ¼ | teaspoon onion powder | | |

- Generously coat a 13x9x2-inch baking pan with cooking spray.
- Arrange bread cubes in pan and sprinkle cheese evenly over top.
- In a large bowl, beat together eggs, milk, dry mustard, salt, pepper, onion powder, Worcestershire sauce, and hot pepper sauce.
- Pour egg mixture evenly over bread and cheese in baking dish.
- Sprinkle with green onion, mushrooms, tomatoes and bacon.
- Sprinkle generously with paprika all over for attractive color.
- Cover and chill overnight.
- Preheat oven to 325 degrees.
- Bake uncovered about 1 hour or until set. If top begins to brown, tent with foil.
- Garnish with chopped parsley and serve.

*Yield: 10 to 12 servings*

*Note: This must be made 1 day ahead. You may add 2 teaspoons of curry for variation if desired.*

# TOM'S FAVORITE FRUIT AND NUT GRANOLA

*What a treat for an overnight guest!
They will think they are staying at a bed and breakfast!*

| | | | |
|---|---|---|---|
| ¼ | cup orange juice | ¼ | cup slivered almonds |
| ¼ | cup brown sugar | ¼ | cup sunflower seeds |
| 1 | tablespoon dark corn syrup or honey | ¼ | cup dried apricots, chopped |
| 3 | cups rolled oats or old-fashioned oatmeal (not quick-cooking) | ¼ | cup golden raisins |
| | | ¼ | cup dark raisins |
| | | ⅓ | cup dried cherries or cranberries |
| ¼ | cup broken walnuts | 1½ | tablespoons sesame seeds |

- Preheat oven to 325 degrees.
- Combine orange juice, brown sugar and corn syrup in a large bowl. Stir in oats.
- Spread mixture evenly on a foil-lined baking sheet. Squeeze into clumps.
- Bake until crisp and thoroughly dry for 25 to 30 minutes. Watch closely to avoid burning. Remove from oven and allow to cool.
- Place walnuts and almonds in a 9-inch baking pan. Bake 10 minutes.
- Add sunflower seeds to pan and bake until just golden, 5 to 10 minutes longer.
- Break up oat mixture with a metal spatula and place in bowl. Add nut and seed mixture, dried apricots, raisins, dried cherries and sesame seeds. Toss to combine.
- Cool completely and store in an airtight container.
- Serve with milk or yogurt.

*Yield: 8 servings or 6 cups*

*Note: This is also a great healthy snack for kids of all ages!*

---

*It is believed that Daniel Boone traveled through the area now known as Jackson with a hunting party in 1776. A beech tree with his name carved on it still stands North of Jackson near Oakfield.*

# CREAM CHEESE SPREADS

*These tasty spreads add zip to bagels, fruit breads, English muffins or toast!*

### Lemon Cream Cheese Spread

- 8 ounces cream cheese, softened at room temperature
- 2 tablespoons fresh lemon juice
- 1 tablespoon grated lemon zest
- 1 tablespoon confectioners' sugar

### Brown Sugar/Cinnamon Cream Cheese Spread

- 8 ounces cream cheese, softened at room temperature
- 3 tablespoons brown sugar
- 1 teaspoon cinnamon

### Vanilla Cream Cheese Spread

- 8 ounces cream cheese, softened at room temperature
- 1 tablespoon vanilla
- 1 tablespoon confectioners' sugar

### Strawberry Cream Cheese Spread

- 8 ounces cream cheese, softened at room temperature
- 1-2 cups strawberries, washed and hulled
- 1 tablespoon confectioners' sugar
- 1 tablespoon frozen orange juice concentrate

- To prepare each cream cheese spread, combine the ingredients in a food processor fitted with a metal blade. Pulse, scraping down the sides of the bowl with a rubber spatula until spread is creamy and smooth.
- Serve spread over fresh baked scones, breads, muffins, or bagels. Keep refrigerated.

*Yield: 1 cup more or less*

---

*The happiest moments of my life have been the few which I have passed at home in the bosom of my family.*

*Thomas Jefferson (1743-1826)*

# SPICED ORANGE BANANA BREAD

*A new twist on an old favorite!*

| | | | |
|---|---|---|---|
| 2 | cups all-purpose flour | ¼ | cup plain yogurt |
| ¾ | cup sugar | 2 | large eggs, lightly beaten |
| ¾ | teaspoon baking soda | 6 | tablespoon butter, melted and cooled to room temperature |
| ½ | teaspoon salt | | |
| 1¼ | cups toasted pecans, chopped coarsely to yield approximately 1 cup | 1½ | teaspoons vanilla |
| | | 2 | tablespoons grated orange zest |
| 3 | very ripe bananas, mashed well to yield approximately 1½ cups | 1 | teaspoon ground cinnamon |
| | | ¼ | teaspoon nutmeg |

- Preheat oven to 350 degrees. Move oven rack to lower middle.
- Grease and flour bottoms and sides of an 8x4x2-inch nonstick loaf pan or 3 (4x2x1-inch) loaf pans.
- Mix first 5 ingredients (flour through pecans) in large bowl and set aside.
- Mix remaining 8 ingredients (banana through nutmeg) in a separate medium-sized bowl with a wooden spoon.
- Gently fold banana mixture into flour mixture with a rubber spatula just until well combined but still lumpy, being careful not to over mix.
- Spoon batter into prepared pan(s) and bake until golden brown and toothpick inserted in the center comes out clean, about 45 minutes for larger pan and 25 minutes for smaller pans.
- Allow to cool in pans for 5 minutes then invert onto cooling rack or plate to continue cooling.

*Yield: 1 large loaf or 3 miniature loaves*

---

*Friends, they are kind to each other's hopes. They cherish each other's dreams.*

*Thoreau*

# RASPBERRY PECAN BREAD

| | | | |
|---|---|---|---|
| 1 | (12-ounce) package frozen raspberries, thawed | ½ | teaspoon salt |
| ½ | cup coarsely chopped pecans, toasted to medium brown and cooled | ½ | teaspoon baking soda |
| | | 2 | eggs, beaten |
| | | ½ | cup vegetable oil |
| 1½ | cups all-purpose flour | ¼ | teaspoon ground cinnamon |
| 1 | cup sugar | ½ | teaspoon vanilla |

- Preheat oven to 350 degrees.
- Allow raspberries to drain in sink in colander.
- Combine flour, sugar, salt and baking soda in a large bowl.
- Add eggs, oil, cinnamon and vanilla.
- Fold in raspberries and pecans and mix thoroughly.
- Spray bottom of 2 (8x4x2-inch) loaf baking pans with non-stick spray containing flour.
- Pour batter into pans half full.
- Bake for 50 to 60 minutes or until toothpick inserted in the middle comes out clean.
- Allow to cool in pans before removing.

*Yield: 2 loaves*

*Note: You may make 3 small loaves using mini loaf pans. Cooking time will be shorter if you use small loaf pans.*

---

*Fielding Hurst, a Yankee Colonel from McNairy County, held Jackson up for ransom in 1864. Even though the ransom was paid, his soldiers burned most of Jackson's downtown business district.*

# CINNAMON STRAWBERRY BREAD

*Strawberries are an unexpected treat in this bread!*

| | | | |
|---|---|---|---|
| 3 | cups all-purpose flour | 2 | (10-ounce) packages frozen sliced strawberries, thawed and undrained |
| 1 | teaspoon salt | | |
| 1 | teaspoon baking soda | 1¼ | cups vegetable oil |
| 4 | teaspoons cinnamon | 1¼ | cups chopped pecans, toasted and cooled (optional) |
| 2 | cups sugar | | |
| 3 | eggs, well beaten | | Cinnamon sugar |

- Preheat oven to 350 degrees. Spray 2 (8x4x2-inch) loaf pans with a non-stick spray containing flour.
- Sift flour, salt, baking soda, cinnamon, and sugar together in a large bowl.
- Make a well in the center and add eggs, strawberries, oil, and pecans (if desired) to the flour mixture.
- Mix, by hand only, until moist and combined, being sure not to over mix.
- Pour batter into pans to ⅔ full.
- Sprinkle top of each loaf moderately with cinnamon sugar.
- Bake for 1 hour if using dark pan or 45 minutes if using shiny pan.
- Allow to cool before inverting out of pans

*Yield: 2 large loaves or 6 mini loaves*

*Note: This bread freezes well.*

---

*There are many things that you can use to hold your flowers in a vase: lemons, strawberries, apples, and cranberries are some examples. Fill a clear vase with the fruit of your choice and add water. Place flower stems in the water allowing the fruit to anchor the stems. Make sure that you coordinate the color of fruit with the flowers in your arrangement.*

# ZESTY ZUCCHINI BREAD

- 3 eggs
- 2 cups sugar
- 1 cup oil
- 1 tablespoon vanilla
- 2 cups loosely packed, coarsely grated zucchini
- 2 cups flour
- 1 teaspoon cinnamon
- 2 teaspoons baking powder
- 1 teaspoon salt
- ¼ teaspoon baking soda
- 1 cup chopped toasted pecans
- Flavored cream cheese (optional)

- Preheat oven to 350 degrees. Grease and flour an 8x4x2-inch loaf pan.
- In a large bowl, combine eggs and sugar beating with an electric mixer until combined.
- Add oil and vanilla, beat until thick and yellow. Add zucchini.
- In a separate bowl, sift together flour, cinnamon, baking powder, salt, and baking soda.
- Add flour mixture to egg mixture, stirring until just combined. Fold in pecans.
- Pour batter into the prepared loaf pan and bake for 1 hour.
- Cool in pan for 10 minutes, then invert onto a serving plate.
- Serve alone or with flavored cream cheese.

Yield: 1 loaf

Note: You may use 3 small loaf pans and bake 45 minutes instead of the large loaf pan.

*Be not forgetful to entertain strangers for thereby some have entertained angels unaware.*

Hebrews 13:2

# CHERRY-LEMON SCONES

*A tasty dish to set before royalty.*

| | | | |
|---|---|---|---|
| 2 | cups all-purpose flour | ½ | cup butter, cut in pieces |
| 1 | tablespoon baking powder | ⅔ | cup buttermilk |
| ½ | teaspoon baking soda | ¾ | cup dried cherries |
| ¼ | teaspoon salt | 1 | tablespoon milk |
| 2 | tablespoons sugar | 1 | tablespoon sugar |
| 1 | teaspoon grated lemon zest | | |

- Preheat oven to 425 degrees.
- Combine first 6 ingredients (flour through zest) in a large bowl. Cut in butter with a pastry knife until mixture is crumbly. Add buttermilk and dried cherries, stirring just until moistened.
- Turn dough out onto a lightly floured surface, then knead 5 or 6 times. Pat into an 8-inch circle. Cut into 8 pie shaped wedges and place 1-inch apart on a lightly greased baking sheet.
- Brush tops with milk and sprinkle with sugar.
- Bake for 15 minutes or until scones are golden brown.

*Yield: 8 servings*

*Note: You may substitute dried cranberries for cherries.*

# ALMOND CREAM CHEESE DANISH

*This easy breakfast dish is perfect to serve for a morning meeting.*

| | | | |
|---|---|---|---|
| 2 | packages (8-count) refrigerated crescent rolls | 1 | egg |
| 12 | ounces cream cheese, softened | 2 | teaspoons almond extract |
| | | ½ | cup butter, melted |
| 1¼ | cups sugar, divided | 1 | teaspoon cinnamon |
| | | 1 | cup sliced almonds |

- Preheat oven to 350 degrees.
- Grease a 13x9x2-inch baking pan.
- Unroll 1 can of crescent rolls and press into bottom of dish, pressing perforations together to form a flat sheet of dough.
- Spread dough to edges of dish and up slightly.
- Beat cream cheese until smooth, add ¾ cup sugar, egg and almond extract and beat until combined.
- Spread evenly over dough.
- Unroll remaining crescent roll dough and place over cream cheese layer. Create a solid layer of dough by pinching perforations closed.
- Combine melted butter, remaining sugar, and cinnamon.
- Sprinkle almonds over dough and spread butter mixture evenly over top layer of dough.
- Bake for 30 minutes or until golden.
- To serve, cut into squares.

*Yield: 16 to 20 servings*

*Note: You can mix the filling together the night and assemble immediately before baking.*

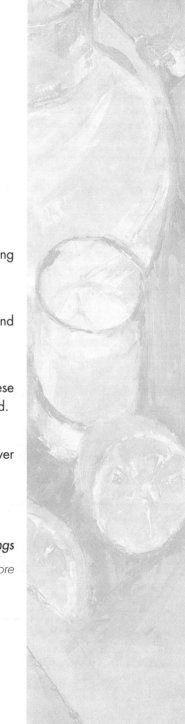

# CINNAMON ROLL UPS

| | | | |
|---|---|---|---|
| 3 | eggs, divided | 5 | tablespoons cinnamon |
| 8 | ounces cream cheese, softened | 1 | loaf day old bread, crusts and ends removed |
| 1½ | cups sugar | | |

- Beat 2 eggs in bowl, set aside.
- Combine 1 egg with cream cheese and beat until smooth, set aside.
- In a separate bowl, combine sugar and cinnamon together, set aside.
- Using a rolling pin, flatten each slice of bread.
- Spread cream cheese mixture on bread; roll each piece up lengthwise.
- Dip bread roll in beaten eggs, then in cinnamon sugar mixture.
- Place bread rolls on cookie sheet, cover, and freeze at least 4 hours.
- Remove from freezer and cut into thirds (while frozen).
- Lay on cookie sheet and bake at 350 degrees for 15 minutes. Do not thaw before baking.

*Yield: Approximately 50*

# MANDARIN ORANGE BRUNCH CAKE

*Keep one in the freezer for unexpected guests! Delicious!*

| | | | |
|---|---|---|---|
| 2 | cups sugar, plus extra ¼ cup for sugaring pan | ½ | teaspoon salt |
| 3 | sticks butter, softened at room temperature | 3 | cups flour |
| | | ½ | cup buttermilk |
| 6 | large egg yolks | 1 | (11-ounce) can Mandarin oranges, drained, syrup reserved |
| 2 | teaspoons orange extract | | |
| 1 | teaspoon vanilla | 1 | tablespoon orange liqueur |
| 1 | teaspoon baking powder | | |

- Preheat oven to 350 degrees.
- Butter and sugar a Bundt pan.
- Cream butter and sugar in a large bowl until smooth.
- Add eggs yolks 3 at a time, beating well.
- Add orange extract and vanilla; beat well.
- Add baking powder and salt.
- Add flour slowly, alternating with buttermilk, beating until just combined.
- With beater on low speed, slowly add Mandarin oranges.
- Pour into prepared pan and bake 55 to 65 minutes, until toothpick inserted in middle of the cake comes out clean.
- Cool for 10 minutes and remove from pan.
- Prepare glaze by combining Mandarin orange syrup and orange liqueur in a small saucepan over medium heat; cook until thickened, about 10 minutes.
- Pour glaze over warm cake.

*Yield: 12 servings*

*Note: This cake is beautiful with a day lily bloom placed in the center.*

---

*Add fruit to your flower arrangement for some additional color! For example, cut a lime in half. Use the pulp side of the lime as you would a flower. Stake the back of the lime and place the stake in the vase. You could do this with a variety of fruits including pomegranates.*

# GINGERBREAD MUFFINS

*Wonderful muffins on a cool fall morning.
Serve with Lemon Curd for a real treat!*

> When measuring flour, place your measuring cup on the counter and spoon the flour into the cup. Fill it to overflowing and level with a knife. Do not shake or tap the cup on the counter to pack the flour, this will add more flour to the recipe than necessary.

**Muffins**

| | | | |
|---|---|---|---|
| 1 | cup butter | ½ | teaspoon ground allspice |
| ½ | cup sugar | ½ | teaspoon ground nutmeg |
| ½ | cup molasses | 1¼ | cups all-purpose flour |
| 1 | large egg | 1 | teaspoon baking soda |
| 1½ | teaspoons ground ginger | ½ | cup boiling water |
| 1 | teaspoon ground cinnamon | | |

- Preheat oven to 350 degrees.
- Butter the muffin tins or use paper liners.
- With an electric mixer, cream butter and sugar until smooth. Add molasses and egg, beat until smooth. Add ginger, cinnamon, allspice, nutmeg, and flour and beat until well blended.
- In a separate cup, dissolve baking soda in the boiling water. Add water mixture to batter and mix until smooth.
- Pour batter into prepared muffin tins. Fill cups as the muffins do not rise very high.
- Bake for 20 minutes, until the muffins are slightly springy to the touch. Cool for 5 minutes, remove from tin and cool on wire racks.

**Lemon Glaze**

| | | | |
|---|---|---|---|
| ¼ | cup sugar | 2 | tablespoons fresh lemon juice |

- For glaze, heat sugar and lemon juice in a nonreactive saucepan on medium, stirring constantly, until sugar dissolves. Remove from heat and brush on tops of muffins.

*Yield: 12 muffins*

# GOOD MORNING GLORY MUFFINS

*These moist muffins are better than those in a bakery!*

| | | | |
|---|---|---|---|
| 2½ | cups sugar | 4 | cups shredded carrots |
| 4 | cups all-purpose flour | 2 | apples, cored, peeled, and shredded |
| 2 | tablespoons cinnamon | 1 | cup chopped pecans |
| 4 | teaspoons baking soda | 6 | eggs, lightly beaten |
| 1 | teaspoon salt | 2 | cups vegetable oil |
| 1 | cup shredded coconut | 2 | tablespoons vanilla |
| 1 | cup raisins | | |

- Preheat oven to 375 degrees.
- Combine the first 5 ingredients (sugar through salt). Add the next 5 ingredients (coconut through pecans) one at a time, mixing well after each addition.
- In a separate bowl, combine eggs, oil and vanilla. Add egg mixture to fruit and carrot mixture, stirring until blended, not beaten.
- Spoon into paper-lined or greased muffin tins. Make sure to fill the muffin tins as these muffins do not rise very much.
- Bake for 20 minutes.

*Yield: 3 dozen*

*Note: This recipe is easily halved, but extras can be given away or frozen!*

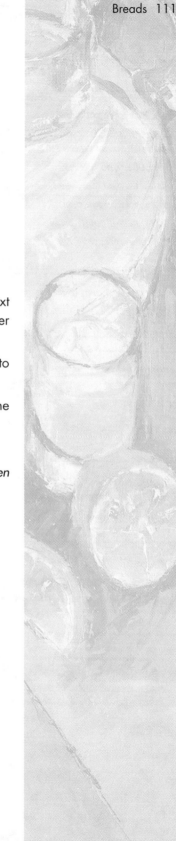

# "GOOD FOR YOU" ORANGE CRANBERRY BRAN MUFFINS

*A must for those who are health conscious.*

| | | | |
|---|---|---|---|
| 1½ | cups whole bran cereal | 2 | tablespoons brown sugar |
| 1½ | cups buttermilk | 2 | teaspoons baking powder |
| ½ | cup orange juice | ½ | teaspoon baking soda |
| ½ | teaspoon orange extract (optional) | ¼ | teaspoon salt |
| 1 | egg, beaten | 1 | tablespoon orange zest, finely grated |
| 2 | tablespoons butter, melted | 1 | cup dried cranberries |
| 1¼ | cups all-purpose flour | | |

- Preheat oven to 400 degrees. Coat muffins tins with cooking spray.
- Combine cereal and buttermilk in a small bowl; let stand 5 minutes.
- Add orange juice, orange extract, egg and melted butter to bran mixture, stirring to combine.
- In a large bowl, combine flour, brown sugar, baking powder, baking soda, salt, orange zest and cranberries.
- Make a well in the center of flour mixture and add bran mixture, stirring just until moistened.
- Spoon batter into tins, filling ⅔ full.
- Bake for 20 to 25 minutes.

*Yield: 12 servings*

*Variation: You can substitute dried cherries and lemon extract.*

---

*If you are short on time when preparing muffins, do not cream the butter and sugar together, melt the butter in the microwave and combine with eggs and the remaining dry ingredients. The muffins will not rise as high as the creamed butter method, but they will taste very good all the same.*

# "READY WHEN YOU NEED THEM" DINNER ROLLS

*This recipe provides easy homemade rolls for any occasion!*

| | | | |
|---|---|---|---|
| 2 | packages dry yeast | 1 | cup cold water |
| ½ | cup lukewarm water (100 to 110 degrees Fahrenheit) | ¾ | cup sugar |
| | | 2 | teaspoons salt |
| ¾ | cup butter | 2 | eggs, lightly beaten |
| 1 | cup boiling water | 8 | cups flour |

- Dissolve yeast in ½ cup lukewarm water for 5 minutes. Set aside.
- Combine butter with boiling water and stir until butter is melted. Cool and place in large bowl.
- Add cold water, sugar, salt, eggs, and dissolved yeast. Mix well. Add flour 1 cup at a time while continuing to mix to make a soft dough. Add enough flour so that when beaten the dough forms. Once the dough forms in a ball, stop adding flour.
- Immediately cover and chill for at least 6 hours or overnight. Dough may be kept in refrigerator for up to 10 days or frozen for several weeks.
- When ready to use dough, remove amount needed. Place on floured board; roll out dough about 1-inch thick and cut into desired size.
- Place rolls 1-inch apart on a greased cookie sheet, cover, and let rise in a warm place 1 to 2 hours or until doubled in bulk.
- Preheat oven to 375 degrees, then bake for 12 to 15 minutes until lightly browned.
- Rub tops of hot rolls with melted butter and serve.

*Yield: 4 to 5 dozen*

*Note: If you freeze the dough, let it thaw completely before placing it on a floured board and rolling it out. We used egg shaped cookie cutters at Easter for egg shaped rolls!*

---

*When reheating left over rolls use this trick. Sprinkle a paper bag with water. Place rolls inside and place in the oven on low heat (250 degrees). The moisture from the bag will help keep the rolls soft.*

# SWEET POTATO BISCUITS

*Make these delightful biscuits for your next large gathering!*

| | | | |
|---|---|---|---|
| 3 | packages active dry yeast | 1¼ | cups sugar |
| ¾ | cup warm water (100 to 110 degrees) | 1½ | cups shortening |
| 7½ | cups all-purpose flour | 3 | cups canned mashed sweet potatoes |
| 1 | tablespoon salt | | Mint jelly or black currant jelly |
| 1 | tablespoon baking powder | | |

- Combine yeast and ¾ cup warm water in a 2 cup liquid measuring cup; let stand 5 minutes.
- Sift together flour, salt, baking powder, and sugar in a large bowl; cut in shortening with a pastry blender until mixture is crumbly.
- Stir in yeast mixture and sweet potatoes just until blended.
- Turn dough out onto a lightly floured surface, and knead until smooth and elastic (about 5 minutes).
- Place dough in a well-greased bowl, turning to grease top of dough.
- Cover and chill 8 hours, if desired (optional).
- Roll dough to ½-inch thickness; cut with a 2-inch round cutter.
- May be frozen at this point for up to 1 month.
- Place biscuits on ungreased baking sheets.
- Thaw if frozen, then cover and let rise in a warm place (85 degrees), free from drafts, 20 minutes or until doubled in size.
- Bake at 400 degrees for 10 to 12 minutes or until lightly browned.
- Serve with jelly.

*Yield: 7½ dozen biscuits*

*Note: You may use this unique biscuit for small ham or turkey sandwiches!*

---

*Jackson's oldest church is First Presbyterian organized in 1823. First Methodist church dates to 1826 with St. Luke's Episcopal following in 1832. First Baptist church was organized in 1837.*

# ARTICHOKE GARLIC BREAD

*Serve this stuffed garlic bread with a light salad.*

| | | | |
|---|---|---|---|
| 1 | loaf French bread | ¼ | cup grated Parmesan cheese |
| 6 | tablespoons butter | 2 | tablespoons minced parsley |
| 2 | cloves garlic, crushed | 2 | teaspoons lemon pepper |
| 7 | teaspoons sesame seeds | 1 | (14-ounce) can artichoke hearts, drained, chopped |
| 1½ | cups sour cream | | |
| 2 | cups Monterey Jack cheese | 1 | cup shredded Cheddar cheese |

- Preheat oven to 350 degrees.
- Cut French bread in half lengthwise, tear out soft center into chunks, leaving crust intact.
- Melt butter in a large saucepan over medium heat. Stir in garlic and sesame seeds. Cook 1 to 2 minutes being careful not to burn the garlic.
- Add bread chunks and cook until butter is absorbed, stirring often. Remove from heat.
- Combine sour cream, Monterey Jack cheese, Parmesan cheese, parsley, and lemon pepper in a large bowl.
- Add artichoke hearts and bread chunks to cheese mixture, stirring well to combine.
- Place mixture in bread shells. Lay bread shells on a cookie sheet.
- Sprinkle bread shells with Cheddar cheese.
- Bake for 30 minutes.

*Yield: 12 servings*

*To cut fresh bread cleanly, use a heated serrated knife.*

# MISS JEANNE'S CORN LIGHT BREAD

*A sweet cornbread which is delicious served with Mexican Chowder (page 84)!*

| | | | |
|---|---|---|---|
| 2 | cups self-rising cornmeal | ½ | cup sugar |
| ¾ | cup self-rising flour or biscuit baking mix | 2 | cups buttermilk |
| | | 1 | egg |
| 1 | teaspoon salt | 1 | tablespoon butter |

- Preheat oven to 325 degrees.
- Combine all dry ingredients (cornmeal through sugar) thoroughly in a medium-sized bowl.
- Add buttermilk.
- Add egg, beat well.
- Put butter in bottom of 9x5-inch loaf pan and put in oven until butter sizzles.
- Tilt pan to evenly distribute butter over bottom of pan and pour in batter.
- Bake for 50 to 60 minutes.
- Turn out on a rack to cool.
- Wrap in aluminum foil to store.

*Yield: 12 to 16 slices*

*Note: This recipe is easily doubled. Mix in a large bowl and bake both loaves at the same time.*

# GUILT FREE POPOVERS

*Serve these wonderful popovers with Old Hickory's Chicken Salad (p. 63) for a wonderful lunch or light dinner. Kids love these!*

| 2 | eggs | 1 | cup skim milk |
|---|---|---|---|
| 1 | cup all-purpose flour | ½ | teaspoon salt |

- Preheat oven to 450 degrees.
- Grease or spray 6 to 8 muffin tins or custard cups.
- Beat eggs slightly in a medium-sized bowl.
- Add flour, milk and salt, beating just until smooth. Do not overbeat.
- Fill muffin tins ½ to ⅓ full.
- Bake 20 minutes or until lightly browned.
- Decrease oven temperature to 350 degrees and bake 20 minutes longer.
- Immediately remove from pans and serve hot.

*Yield: 3 to 4 servings*

---

*When I was a little girl, my mother was a member of the Jackson Service League. My mother would often take her turn volunteering in the Thrift Store. It was a small place with anything that you could imagine – clothes, furniture, and kitchen items. Sometimes I was able to go with her to the store. My favorite place was the toy department. I was never allowed to play with the toys, unless I was a customer and had money. It was never extremely busy, but there were always people shopping. I always remembered those days when I worked my shifts at our annual thrift sale. I wonder what the sustainers would think of the throng of people that run in the door at 7:00 am when we open the doors for shopping.*

## REFRESHING ALMOND TEA

| | | | |
|---|---|---|---|
| 3 | cups boiling water | ½ | cup fresh lemon juice |
| 2 | family-size tea bags | 2 | tablespoons almond extract |
| 1 | cup sugar | 1 | tablespoon vanilla |
| | Ice and water | | |

- Pour water over tea bags, steep to desired strength and remove bags.
- Add sugar and stir until dissolved.
- Add ice and water to make ½ gallon.
- Stir in lemon juice, almond extract, and vanilla.

*Yield: 8 servings*

## FAMOUS ICED TEA

*Cool off on the porch with this Southern favorite.*

| | | | |
|---|---|---|---|
| 6 | regular tea bags | 1 | (6-ounce) can frozen lemonade concentrate, thawed |
| 4 | cups boiling water | | |
| 1½ | cups sugar | | |
| 1 | (6-ounce) can frozen orange juice, thawed | 8-10 | cups water |
| | | | Lemon slices (optional) |
| | | | Mint (optional) |

- Steep tea bags in boiling water for 5 minutes; discard tea bags.
- Add sugar and stir until dissolved.
- Add juices and 8 cups water. Taste.
- Add up to 2 more cups water to desired strength.
- Add lemon and/or mint to glass when served.

*Yield: Approximately 1 gallon*

*Note: Make ahead and store in gallon milk jugs for luncheons or cookouts.*

---

*Mint syrup is a delightful addition to summertime drinks. You can make it by bringing 2 cups water and 2 cups sugar to a boil. Add 1 bunch fresh mint and simmer 5 minutes. Let stand 2 hours, strain, store in airtight container in the refrigerator.*

# COFFEE PUNCH

| | | | |
|---|---|---|---|
| 2 | quarts strong brewed coffee | 2 | quarts vanilla ice cream |
| 1 | pint cold milk | ½ | pint heavy whipping cream |
| 2 | teaspoons vanilla extract | ½ | tablespoon ground nutmeg (optional) |
| ½ | cup sugar | | |

- In a large bowl, combine coffee, milk, vanilla, and sugar. Cover and chill.
- Break ice cream into chunks in a punch bowl just before serving; pour chilled coffee mixture over ice cream.
- Whip cream and spoon into mounds on top of punch.
- Sprinkle with nutmeg, if desired.

*Yield: 18 servings*

---

*If you are serving cocktails in the summer, it is fun to have decorative ice cubes. You can float lemon peel, fruit or flowers in the ice tray before freezing. Making ice out of the drink that you will be serving keeps the drinks from becoming watered down. For example, make ice from the tea or lemonade that you plan to serve.*

---

# AUNT LIZZIE'S PUNCH

*Great for a baby or wedding shower!*

| | | | |
|---|---|---|---|
| 1 | (16-ounce) can orange juice, chilled | 1 | (50-ounce) bottle ginger ale, chilled |
| 1 | (6-ounce) can pineapple juice, chilled | 2 | oranges, thinly sliced |
| | | 1 | lemon, thinly sliced |
| 1 | (32-ounce) jar cranberry juice, chilled | | |

- Combine juices and ginger ale in a large bowl with fruit.
- Add ice to chill.

*Yield: 30 servings*

*The queen is crowned each year in Jackson, Tennessee. Since 1952, contestants have traveled from all over Tennessee to compete in the Miss Tennessee Pageant. The beautiful and talented women vie for the title of Miss Tennessee and the opportunity to represent the state in the Miss America Pageant.*

## QUEEN'S PUNCH

*Elegant enough for Miss Tennessee!*

| | | | |
|---|---|---|---|
| 12 | ounces frozen lemonade concentrate, thawed | 2 | cups white grape juice |
| 1½ | cups confectioners' sugar | 1 | (2-liter) bottle ginger ale, chilled |
| 6 | cups ice cold water (no ice) | | |

- Mix lemonade with confectioners' sugar and water.
- Add white grape juice.
- Freeze in the large gallon container.
- Take out of freezer 3 hours before serving, place in a punch bowl and add ginger ale.
- This should have ice crystals when served.

*Yield: Approximately 20 servings*

## BANANA PUNCH

*This is a delightful punch which always is a hit because of the slushy consistency and wonderful combination of flavors!*

| | | | |
|---|---|---|---|
| 6 | cups water | 3½ | cups sugar |
| 3 | cups pineapple juice | 2 | cups orange juice |
| | Juice of 2 lemons | 2-3 | (50-ounce) bottles ginger ale, chilled |
| 4-5 | bananas, pureed | | |

- Mix all ingredients, except ginger ale, with a wire whisk, until sugar is dissolved.
- Freeze for 24 hours or longer (up to 2 months).
- Take out of freezer 1 hour before serving.
- Mash with a potato masher to turn into a slush.
- Add ginger ale and serve.

*Yield: approximately 30 servings, depending upon size of cups*

*Note: You may make an adult version of this punch by adding light rum to taste.*

# FROZEN WATERMELON MARGARITA

*The taste of summer!*

| | | | |
|---|---|---|---|
| 5 | cups watermelon, cubed | ½ | cup fresh lime juice |
| 1 | cup white tequila | ¼ | cup sugar |

- Freeze watermelon in a sealed plastic bag until firm, about 3 hours.
- Blend frozen watermelon with remaining ingredients in a 6-cup blender until smooth.

*Yield: 6 servings*

*Note: Watermelon may be stored in the freezer for up to 1 week.*

---

*Denmark, Tennessee once rivaled Jackson in size and prominence. A series of fires and failure of the railroad to travel through Denmark caused its demise. Today, less than ten people live there.*

---

# SEA BREEZE IN A PITCHER

| | | | |
|---|---|---|---|
| 1 | (64-ounce) bottle cranberry juice cocktail | 2¼ | cups vodka |
| 1 | (48-ounce) bottle pink grapefruit cocktail | ¼ | cup lime juice |
| | | 1 | lime, sliced |

- Combine first 4 ingredients in a large pitcher, stirring well.
- Chill and serve over ice with a slice of lime.

*Yield: 1 gallon*

## MOJITO

*A refreshingly light cocktail!*

| | | | |
|---|---|---|---|
| 1 | lime, halved | 2 | tablespoons white rum |
| 3 | fresh mint sprigs | | Ice cubes |
| 1 | tablespoon sugar | ⅓ | cup sparkling water |

- Squeeze juice from lime into a 12-ounce highball glass.
- Add lime halves to glass.
- Add mint and sugar, crushing mint with back of a spoon until sugar is dissolved.
- Add rum and stir.
- Add ice, then top off drink with sparkling water and stir well.

*Yield: 1 drink*

## CAFÉ AU CACAO

*A perfect after dinner drink served at a dessert party.*

| | | | |
|---|---|---|---|
| ½ | gallon cold coffee | ½ | cup heavy whipping cream |
| ½ | gallon chocolate ice cream, softened | | Whipped cream, garnish |
| ¾ | cup dark crème de cacao | | Unsweetened cocoa powder, garnish |

- Combine coffee, ice cream and crème de cacao.
- Whip cream and fold into coffee mixture.
- Pour into serving cups and garnish with whipped cream and cocoa powder. Serve immediately.

*Yield: 12 servings*

## ITALIAN BLIZZARD

| | |
|---|---|
| 1½ ounces amaretto | ½ cup crushed ice |
| ¼ ounce cream de banana | ½ ripe banana (optional) |
| 1 scoop vanilla ice cream | |

- Combine all ingredients in a blender. Blend until smooth.

*Yield: 1 to 2 servings*

## SPICY SPIKED SLUSH

*Great on a hot day or for your next backyard barbeque!*

| | |
|---|---|
| 7 cups water | 1 (12-ounce) can frozen lemonade concentrate |
| 2 cups sugar | 2 cups vodka |
| 4 tea bags (herbal blend) | |
| 1 (12-ounce) can frozen limeade concentrate | |

- Combine 7 cups water and 2 cups sugar in a 4 quart sauce pan, boil 1 minute, remove from heat.
- Steep tea bags in 2 cups warm water.
- Combine sugar water and tea, cool.
- Add frozen concentrates and vodka to tea mixture.
- Place spiked tea in a 1 gallon container and freeze for at least 6 hours.
- To serve, allow to thaw a little and scoop into cups.
- Serve with a fruit garnish.

*Yield: 6 to 8 servings*

*Variation: May serve diluted by filling cup ½ full with slush and adding lemon-lime soda to each individual serving. Also, may substitute orange juice for limeade and brandy for vodka.*

---

*When you are having a dinner party, a nice way to get your guests involved with the festivities is to recruit your guests to become the bartenders. Set up an area where all drinks are located. Have a pair of friends serve as bartenders and trade off with other pairs as long as cocktails are being served. This allows your guests to mingle with many more people and saves you the stress of making sure that everyone has a drink.*

*Jackson was originally named Alexandria in honor of Adam Rankin Alexander, a surveyor and one of our first settlers. The founders then discovered that there was another Alexandria, Tennessee in existence and the name was changed. Some of the founding fathers of Jackson were Andrew Jackson's nephews, therefore, Jackson was named for Andrew Jackson, the seventh president of the United States.*

# SANGRÍA BLANCA

*Your guests will surely ask for "una mas, por favor"!*

| | | | |
|---|---|---|---|
| 1 | gallon dry white wine | 1 | (1-liter) bottle club soda, chilled |
| 2 | cups brandy | 1 | quart strawberries, hulled and sliced |
| 1 | cup orange liqueur | 1 | lemon, thinly sliced |
| 3 | oranges, thinly sliced | 1 | lime, thinly sliced |
| 1 | bunch fresh mint leaves | | |

- Combine first 5 ingredients in large bowl.
- Cover and chill 8 hours.
- Add club soda and next 3 ingredients just before serving.

Yield: 1½ gallons

*Note: Strawberries may be kept whole if they are small in size.*

*Variation: Ginger ale may be substituted for club soda.*

# HOT CHRISTMAS CIDER

| | | | |
|---|---|---|---|
| 4 | cups apple cider | 3 | cinnamon sticks |
| 3 | cups cranberry juice | 1 | teaspoon whole cloves |
| ¼ | cup brown sugar | | |

- In a large saucepan over low heat, combine all ingredients.
- Mix well to dissolve sugar.
- Simmer for 10 minutes.
- Strain before serving to remove cinnamon and cloves.

Yield: 10 to 12 servings

*Note: This is a delicious cold weather drink. You may make this in a percolator by placing the sugar, cinnamon and cloves in the basket of the percolator.*

# SIDE DISHES

#  SIDE DISHES

Scalloped Tomatoes and Artichokes ............. 125
Sesame Marinated Asparagus .................... 126
Balsamic Roasted Asparagus ....................... 126
Lemon Garlic Sautéed Artichoke Hearts ......... 127
Asparagus and Prosciutto Bundles ................ 127
Lemon Pepper Broccolini ............................ 128
Everybody's Favorite Green Beans ................ 128
Zesty Garlic Roasted Broccoli
   with Pine Nuts ..................................... 129
Brussels Sprouts in Wine ............................. 130
Lemon Carrot Sticks .................................. 130
Ginger Orange Roasted Carrots ................... 131
Confetti Corn ........................................... 132
Farmers Market Fiesta Corn ........................ 133
Basil Marinated Corn on the Cob ................. 134
Black-Eyed Peas with Caramelized
   Onion and Country Ham ........................ 135
Sweet Potato Soufflé .................................. 136
Grated Cheese Potatoes ............................. 137
Two Potato Roast ..................................... 138
Herb Roasted Potatoes
   with Balsamic Vinegar ............................ 139
Wok Sesame Spinach ................................ 139

Fresh Spinach Crêpes
   with Mushroom Sauce ............................ 140
Grilled Spinach Stuffed Vidalia Onions ......... 142
Italian Spinach and Artichoke Hearts ............ 143
Summer Squash Casserole ......................... 144
Squash Ribbons al Pomodoro ...................... 145
Skillet Tomatoes ....................................... 146
Tomatoes Rockefeller ................................. 147
Tomato Vidalia Stacks ............................... 148
Layered Garden Bake ................................. 149
Grilled Zucchini Boats ................................ 150
Zucchini, Tomato and Onion Bake ............... 151
Roasted Pears with
   Gorgonzola and Pecans ......................... 152
Caramelized Onion and
   Porcini Risotto with Sage ........................ 153
Feta and Vidalia Onion Risotto .................... 154
Spicy Rice Casserole ................................. 155
Angel Hair Pasta Flan ................................ 156
Penne with Pumpkin Sauce ........................ 157
Parmesan Polenta with Wild Mushrooms ....... 158
Almond Jasmine Rice ................................ 159
Mediterranean Couscous ........................... 160

# SCALLOPED TOMATOES AND ARTICHOKES

*An uncommon dish made with common pantry staples! Delicious!*

| | | | |
|---|---|---|---|
| 2 | tablespoons unsalted butter | ½ | teaspoon dried basil |
| ½ | cup julienned white onion | 1 | tablespoon sugar |
| 2 | tablespoons finely chopped shallots | 1 | tablespoon light brown sugar |
| | | | Salt and pepper to taste |
| 1 | (2-pound 3-ounce) can whole peeled plum tomatoes | ½ | cup breadcrumbs |
| 1 | (14-ounce) can artichoke hearts, quartered and drained | ½-1 | cup freshly grated Parmesan cheese |

- Preheat oven to 325 degrees.
- Melt butter in a large saucepan over medium heat. Sauté onions and shallots until tender. Add tomatoes, artichokes and basil. Cook for 3 minutes. Season with sugars, salt and pepper.
- Place in a 13x9-inch greased dish. Top with breadcrumbs, then Parmesan cheese. Bake for 10 to 15 minutes until hot and cheese has melted. Serve warm.

*Yield: 6 to 8 servings*

*Note: May prepare 1 day ahead without topping and keep refrigerated. After returning dish to room temperature, add topping then bake as directed.*

---

*Crush dried herbs between your fingers before adding according to a recipe to release the flavor.*

A fun candleholder can be made using asparagus or green beans. Affix asparagus or fresh green beans vertically around the outside of a candleholder with a rubber band. When you have completely covered the surface of the candleholder with the vegetable, tie raffia, twine or holiday ribbon around the arrangement covering the rubber band.

# SESAME MARINATED ASPARAGUS

*A wonderful infusion of flavors!*

| | |
|---|---|
| 2 | pounds asparagus |
| 1 | teaspoon minced garlic |
| ½ | teaspoon salt |
| ½ | teaspoon white pepper |
| 2 | teaspoons Dijon mustard |
| 1½ | teaspoons fresh lemon juice |
| ¼ | cup sesame oil |
| 1 | tablespoon toasted sesame seeds, for garnish |

- Steam asparagus until just crisp tender, 3 to 5 minutes. Drain and rinse asparagus under cold water. Dry thoroughly and set aside.
- Combine remaining ingredients in blender or food processor and blend until smooth. Pour over asparagus. Sprinkle with toasted sesame seeds.
- Marinate at least 30 minutes before serving, or overnight for more flavorful asparagus. Serve cold.

*Yield: 6 to 8 servings*

# BALSAMIC ROASTED ASPARAGUS

*Great with any meat for an elegant or casual dinner party. Easy to prepare with a lovely presentation!*

| | |
|---|---|
| 1 | pound fresh asparagus, washed and tough ends broken off |
| 3 | tablespoons olive oil |
| 1 | tablespoon balsamic vinegar |
| | Kosher salt, to taste |
| | Fresh ground pepper, to taste |
| | Freshly grated Parmesan cheese, to taste (optional) |

- Preheat oven to 425 degrees.
- Place first 5 ingredients in a roasting pan with sides. Toss well to coat asparagus evenly and spread into a single layer.
- Roast for 15 to 20 minutes or until asparagus is dark and is fork tender. Remove from oven and sprinkle with Parmesan cheese.

*Yield: 3 to 5 servings*

*Note: Tastes great served cold.*

# LEMON GARLIC SAUTÉED ARTICHOKE HEARTS

| | |
|---|---|
| 2 | tablespoons olive oil |
| 1 | (14-ounce) bag frozen artichoke quarters |
| 2 | garlic cloves, minced |
| 3 | tablespoons fresh lemon juice |
| ¼ | teaspoon salt |
| ⅛ | teaspoon pepper |
| | Freshly grated Parmesan cheese, to taste |

- Heat oil in medium saucepan over medium heat. Add artichokes and sauté until tender and cooked through. Add minced garlic and sauté an additional minute. Add lemon juice, salt and pepper. Toss to coat. Sprinkle with Parmesan cheese and serve immediately.

*Yield: 6 to 8 servings*

*Variation: May substitute frozen whole baby artichokes when available.*

*Use fresh garlic when possible. It is readily available and stores well. Fresh garlic is much more flavorful than jarred minced garlic. In order to peel garlic, place garlic clove on a cutting board, crush the garlic with the flat side of a knife by placing the knife blade on the clove and strike the knife with your hand. This will allow you to peel the clove easily.*

# ASPARAGUS AND PROSCIUTTO BUNDLES

*Elegant and easy.*

| | |
|---|---|
| 48 | thin asparagus spears, stalks removed, cut 2 to 3-inches long |
| 2½ | ounces goat cheese, softened at room temperature |
| 2 | tablespoons chopped fresh basil |
| 1 | tablespoon toasted pine nuts, chopped |
| 1 | tablespoon orange zest |
| 1-2 | tablespoons mayonnaise |
| | Salt and pepper to taste |
| 2 | ounces thin prosciutto strips, cut into 24 strips (1x4-inch each) |

- Blanche asparagus until crisp, about 1 minute. Drain and set aside.
- Blend goat cheese, basil, pine nuts, orange zest and mayonnaise in small bowl. Season with salt and pepper.
- Spread a scant teaspoon of filling over each prosciutto strip. Arrange 2 asparagus spears atop filling at short end of prosciutto. Roll up, enclosing the length of the asparagus. Press to seal.
- Serve at room temperature, seam side down.

*Yield: 24 bundles*

*Note: Recipe may be prepared up to a half day ahead, but not overnight.*

*Broccolini is the name of a vegetable that is a cross between broccoli and Chinese kale. It is bright green with long, slender stalks. At the top are tiny buds that resemble miniature broccoli heads. It has a crunchy texture and the flavor is sweet with a slight peppery side.*

# LEMON PEPPER BROCCOLINI

| | | | |
|---|---|---|---|
| 1 | medium bunch of broccolini or broccoli, cut into desired size pieces | 2 | teaspoons lemon zest, finely grated |
| 2 | tablespoons butter or margarine | | Juice of 1 lemon<br>Pinch of salt |
| 1 | (2-ounce) jar diced pimento, drained | | Pinch of cayenne pepper |

- In a 10-inch skillet, place broccolini flat and cover with water. Heat on high and bring to a full boil. Reduce heat to medium and cook for 5 to 7 minutes, until broccolini is bright green and crisp-tender. Do not overcook.
- Drain and set aside.
- In the same skillet, combine remaining ingredients and cook until butter is melted.
- Return broccolini to skillet, tossing with butter mixture. Cook until heated through, approximately 5 minutes.

*Yield: 3 to 4 servings*

# EVERYBODY'S FAVORITE GREEN BEANS

*The tangy blend of flavors will make this one of your favorites too!*

| | | | |
|---|---|---|---|
| 1 | pound bacon, cooked crisp, crumbled and grease reserved | 6 | tablespoons sugar |
| | | ½ | cup white vinegar |
| 3 | cans green beans, drained | ¾ | cup toasted slivered almonds or toasted pecans (optional) |

- Preheat oven to 350 degrees.
- Place half the green beans into an ungreased 13x9-inch baking dish. Sprinkle half the bacon onto the first layer of green beans. Layer the remaining beans, then add remaining bacon bits. Top with nuts, if desired.
- In separate bowl, mix vinegar and sugar with the reserved bacon grease, until sugar is dissolved. Pour liquid mixture on top of the beans. Bake for 30 to 45 minutes, stirring once halfway through cooking time.

*Yield: 8 to 12 servings*

# ZESTY GARLIC ROASTED BROCCOLI WITH PINE NUTS

*Try this recipe, your children are sure to eat their broccoli now!*

| | | | |
|---|---|---|---|
| 1 | pound broccoli florets, rinsed and cut into desired size pieces | 2 | tablespoons unsalted butter |
| | | 1 | teaspoon minced garlic |
| | | 1 | teaspoon grated lemon zest |
| 2 | tablespoons olive oil | 1 | tablespoon fresh lemon juice |
| ½ | teaspoon salt | 2-3 | tablespoons pine nuts, toasted |
| ⅛ | teaspoon freshly ground black pepper | | |

- Preheat oven to 500 degrees.
- Toss broccoli with oil, salt and pepper in large bowl. Arrange in single layer on baking sheet and roast for 6 to 8 minutes. Turn broccoli over and continue roasting until dark brown and crispy, but not scorched, about 6 to 10 more minutes.
- While broccoli is roasting, melt butter in saucepan over medium heat. Add the garlic and lemon zest. Heat and stir for 1 minute. Remove from heat and let cool slightly. Stir in lemon juice.
- Transfer roasted broccoli to serving bowl and pour lemon garlic butter over, tossing to coat. Top with pine nuts. Serve immediately.

*Yield: 4 servings*

---

*When Andrew Jackson visited here in 1840, a huge ashcake weighing 120 pounds was prepared for the occasion. It took more than a bushel of meal to make the cake.*

*Adding ½ teaspoon sugar to vegetables such as corn, peas, beets, broccoli and carrots when cooking brings out flavor and preserves color. Cook vegetables in the least amount of water possible to retain flavor and preserve vitamins. Do not add salt to the water when cooking corn, it will toughen the kernels.*

## BRUSSELS SPROUTS IN WINE

*The combination of flavors elevate this dish to fit any table.*

| | | | |
|---|---|---|---|
| 1½ | pounds fresh Brussels sprouts | | Fresh ground pepper to taste |
| 4 | tablespoons butter | 1 | tablespoon dry white wine |
| | Kosher salt to taste | 1 | tablespoon fresh lemon juice |

- In large bowl of lightly salted water, wash sprouts. Soak sprouts for approximately 10 minutes. Rinse with cold water. Trim and cut each sprout in half lengthwise, then slice thinly crosswise.
- In large skillet, melt butter over medium-high heat, add sprouts and sauté until they begin to turn golden. Season with salt, pepper and wine. Cook for about 4 minutes or until barely limp. Stir in lemon juice and check the seasonings. Serve immediately.

*Yield: 6 to 8 servings*

## LEMON CARROT STICKS

*A simple yet irresistible side dish!*

| | | | |
|---|---|---|---|
| 1½ | pounds carrots, scraped and cut into 3-inch julienne strips | 3 | tablespoons butter, melted |
| ⅓ | cup fresh lemon juice | 2 | tablespoons sugar |
| | | ¼ | teaspoon salt |

- Steam carrots for 1 minute, drain.
- Combine lemon juice and remaining ingredients in a small Dutch oven and bring to a boil. Reduce heat and simmer 1 minute until sugar dissolves.
- Add carrots and cook over medium heat for 3 minutes, or until thoroughly heated. Spoon lemon sauce over carrots frequently.

*Yield: 6 servings*

*Variation: May use baby carrots to save time.*

*Note: For an attractive presentation, tie individual bundles of carrots with a green onion. To make onion pliable for tying, drop into boiling water for 1 to 2 minutes.*

# GINGER ORANGE ROASTED CARROTS

*The ginger adds a wonderful flavor to naturally sweet carrots!*

| | | | |
|---|---|---|---|
| 2 | pounds baby carrots | 2 | tablespoons orange marmalade |
| 2 | tablespoons olive oil | 1 | tablespoon water |
| ½ | teaspoon salt | 1 | teaspoon grated fresh ginger |

- Move oven rack to the middle position of oven and preheat to 475 degrees.
- Place carrots, oil and salt in a roasting pan with sides. Toss well and spread into a single layer.
- In a small saucepan over medium heat, combine orange marmalade, water and ginger, simmer and remove from heat.
- Roast carrots for 10 minutes. Remove carrots from oven and drizzle with orange mixture, tossing well to evenly distribute the sauce. Return carrots to oven, continuing to roast for 10 to 12 more minutes, or until carrots are brown and tender. Serve immediately.

*Yield: 8 servings*

## CONFETTI CORN

*A colorful and tasty side dish that is sure to enhance any entrée!*

| | | | |
|---|---|---|---|
| 1 | pound bacon, cooked crisp, and crumbled | 2 | cups sour cream |
| 1 | stick (8 tablespoons) butter | 4 | cups fresh corn kernels (or 2 pounds frozen corn, thawed) |
| ½ | cup chopped onion | | Salt and pepper to taste |
| ½ | cup chopped celery | 1 | tablespoon fresh chopped parsley (or ¼ tablespoon dried parsley) |
| 1 | red pepper, chopped | | |
| 1 | green pepper, chopped | | |
| 5 | tablespoons all-purpose flour | | |

- Preheat oven to 350 degrees.
- Melt butter in a Dutch Oven over medium heat. Add onion, celery and peppers and sauté until soft. Stir in flour, then sour cream, until well mixed.
- Add the corn and most of the bacon, reserving enough bacon for topping. Season with salt and pepper.
- Pour mixture into a 13x9-inch baking dish and sprinkle the remaining bacon and parsley on top. Bake at 350 degrees for 30 to 45 minutes, until thoroughly heated.

*Yield: 6 to 8 servings*

*Variation: Use half the butter, bacon and flour to reduce fat in this recipe.*

---

Carl Lee Perkins (1932-1998) was born a sharecropper's son in West Tennessee. He always loved music and believed in hard work. He moved to the Jackson area when he was 14 and lived here for the remainder of his life. Perkins wrote Blue Suede Shoes, Daddy Sang Bass, and Silver and Gold. The Beatles recorded more songs written by Perkins than any other songwriter outside of the group. In 1980, Perkins became instrumental in starting a center for child abuse. The center was eventually named the Carl Perkins Center for Child Abuse. Perkins assisted in large measure to raise funds for the center annually. He was happiest surrounded by his family for meals.

# FARMERS MARKET FIESTA CORN

*A delicious blend of vegetables for the summer harvest!*

- 2 tablespoons olive oil
- 1 cup chopped red onion
- 1 medium zucchini, cut into ⅓-inch cubes
- 4 ears fresh corn, kernels cut from ears
- 1 cup coarsely grated Monterey Jack pepper cheese
- 2 tablespoons finely crushed corn tortilla chips

- Preheat oven to 375 degrees.
- Heat oil until very hot (not smoking) in a large skillet over medium-high heat; add onions and sauté until lightly browned. Add zucchini and sauté until tender, about 3 minutes. Remove from skillet with slotted spoon.
- Place corn in skillet and sauté over medium heat until crisp tender, about 5 minutes. Add to zucchini mixture and stir in cheese.
- Spoon into an 8x8-inch baking dish and sprinkle with chips.
- Bake uncovered on upper rack of oven at 375 degrees for about 20 minutes. Serve warm.

*Yield: 4 to 6 servings*

---

*In 1858, a professor from Spring Creek named Isham Walker applied for a patent for an airplane. The machine was named the "Giant Trout". Congress refused to fund the experiment. If Walker had been successful, he would have been 45 years ahead of the Wright brothers!*

*Shuck fresh corn after you buy because the husks and silk draw moisture from the kernels. Place shucked ears in sealed plastic bags and refrigerate until cooking. Fresh corn is best from May through September. When purchasing fresh corn, you should look for bright green ears with tightly fitted husks. The kernels should extend to the tip of the ear and be plump and milky.*

# BASIL MARINATED CORN ON THE COB

*Try this unique corn recipe for your next outdoor party. You will not be disappointed!*

| | | | |
|---|---|---|---|
| ¼ | cup apple cider vinegar or champagne vinegar | 1 | teaspoon salt |
| ½ | cup water | 1 | teaspoon freshly ground pepper |
| 1 | teaspoon lemon juice | ¼ | cup extra virgin olive oil |
| 1 | teaspoon Worcestershire sauce | ½ | cup fresh basil, chopped |
| ½ | cup shallots, chopped | 6-10 | ears of corn (fresh or frozen and cooked as directed) |

- Make marinade by combining all ingredients except basil and corn in a blender or food processor. Process until combined, but not smooth. Remove to a bowl and stir in basil.
- Place warm corn and marinade in a zip-top bag, tossing to coat the corn.
- Refrigerate and marinate corn overnight
- Drain corn and serve at room temperature.

*Yield: 6 to 10 servings*

*Note: Try to use sweet corn as the flavors blend well together. This is a great picnic side dish!*

# BLACK-EYED PEAS WITH CARAMELIZED ONION AND COUNTRY HAM

*Make sure to include these peas on New Year's Day for good luck!*

- 3 (15.8-ounce) cans black-eyed peas
- 1 bay leaf
- 1 (14.5-ounce) can chicken broth
- 2 tablespoons olive oil
- 1 large purple onion, diced
- ¼ pound country ham, diced
- ¼ cup balsamic vinegar
- 1 tablespoon brown sugar
- 1½ teaspoons chopped fresh thyme or ½ teaspoon dried thyme
- ½ teaspoon freshly ground pepper

- Combine first 3 ingredients in a 2 quart saucepan; bring to a boil. Cover, reduce heat, and simmer 10 minutes; drain. Discard bay leaf. Return peas to pan; cover and set aside.

- Heat oil in a large skillet over medium-high heat. Add onion; cook 5 minutes or until golden, stirring often.

- Reduce heat; add ham and brown sugar and cook 10 additional minutes or until ham is crisp and onion is well browned.

- Stir in vinegar, thyme, and pepper. Bring to a boil. Cook, stirring occasionally to loosen any caramelized bits from bottom of pan, 5 minutes or until mixture is a thin syrup.

- Pour syrup over peas and toss well.

*Yield: 8 servings*

# SWEET POTATO SOUFFLÉ

*Don't wait until Thanksgiving to try this favorite Southern dish!*

*Sweet Potato Soufflé is a traditional Southern dish served during the holidays. The presentation of the dish is enhanced if it is placed in orange cups. You can make the cups by cutting an orange in half and removing the pulp. Place the soufflé inside the hollowed out orange peel and sprinkle with topping or orange zest. Place orange cups on a baking sheet and bake according to recipe directions.*

**Potatoes**

| | | | |
|---|---|---|---|
| 3 | cups cooked sweet potatoes (3 to 4 fresh) | ½ | teaspoon salt |
| ½ | cup sugar | 4 | tablespoons butter, melted |
| 2 | eggs, beaten | 1½ | teaspoons vanilla |
| 1 | egg white, beaten | ½ | cup milk |

- Preheat oven to 325 degrees. Grease a shallow 1½-quart baking dish.
- Mash sweet potatoes. Add sugar, eggs, salt, butter, vanilla and milk. Beat with an electric mixer until smooth and fluffy. Spoon mixture into a prepared baking dish.

**Topping**

| | | | |
|---|---|---|---|
| ½ | cup brown sugar | 1 | cup pecans, chopped |
| ⅓ | cup flour | 3 | tablespoons butter, melted |

- To prepare topping, combine brown sugar, flour, pecans and butter. Crumble topping over the sweet potato mixture.
- Bake uncovered for 45 minutes.

*Yield: 6 servings*

# GRATED CHEESE POTATOES

*True comfort food!*

| | |
|---|---|
| 10 medium potatoes | 1½ cups grated sharp Cheddar cheese |
| 1 stick (8 tablespoons) butter, melted | Salt to taste |
| 1 (16-ounce) carton sour cream | White pepper to taste |
| 1 small bunch fresh green onions, chopped | |

- Preheat oven to 300 degrees. Grease a 13x9-inch baking dish.
- In a Dutch oven, boil potatoes with jackets until tender but not done, about 15 minutes. Cool, peel and grate potatoes. Add butter, sour cream, onions, and cheese. Mix well.
- Place mixture in the prepared baking dish and bake uncovered for 45 minutes. Serve warm.

*Yield: 10 to 12 servings*

*Note: May be prepared ahead and chilled overnight; add 5 minutes to the baking time.*

# TWO POTATO ROAST

*A colorful dish that compliments beef or pork beautifully.*

| | | | |
|---|---|---|---|
| 2½ | pounds sweet potatoes, sliced ½-inch thick | ¼ | cup extra virgin olive oil |
| 2 | pounds red potatoes, sliced ½-inch thick | ¼ | cup fresh rosemary, chopped |
| 4 | tablespoons butter | ½ | teaspoon salt |
| | | ½ | teaspoon fresh ground pepper |

- Preheat oven to 450 degrees.
- Heat butter, oil, and rosemary in a small saucepan over medium heat, stirring until butter is melted. Brush ¼ cup of the butter mixture evenly over 2 baking sheets.
- Arrange potato slices in a single layer on the prepared sheets, brushing with remaining butter mixture. Sprinkle with salt and pepper. Bake at 450 degrees for 35 minutes or until potato slices are golden brown.

*Yield: 8 servings*

# HERB ROASTED POTATOES WITH BALSAMIC VINEGAR

- 2 tablespoons olive oil
- 2 pounds potatoes, unpeeled and quartered (Yukon Gold or new potatoes)
- 1 tablespoon minced garlic
- 1 teaspoon dried thyme
- 1 teaspoon dried rosemary
- 3 tablespoons balsamic vinegar
- ½ teaspoon salt, or to taste
- ¼ teaspoon fresh ground pepper, or to taste

- Preheat oven to 425 degrees.
- In large roasting pan, mix first 5 ingredients and toss potatoes to coat.
- Roast in oven for 30 minutes or until potatoes are tender, stirring occasionally.
- Remove from oven, toss with vinegar, salt, and pepper. Serve immediately.

*Yield: 4 to 6 servings*

# WOK SESAME SPINACH

*You can prepare this in a large skillet if you do not have a wok!*

- 2 tablespoons sesame seeds, toasted and divided
- 1 clove garlic, pressed
- 2 tablespoons mirin (rice wine)
- 1 tablespoon soy sauce
- 1 tablespoon dark sesame oil
- 1 teaspoon canola oil
- 2 (9-ounce) bags washed spinach
- Salt to taste

- Mix 1 tablespoon sesame seeds with garlic, mirin, soy sauce, and sesame oil. Set aside.
- Heat canola oil in wok over medium-high heat. Add spinach, turning with tongs until wilted but still bright green. Salt to taste. Drain and remove from wok, leaving any water behind.
- Place spinach in a serving dish. Pour sesame seed mixture over spinach, tossing to coat. Top with remaining sesame seeds.

*Yield: 4 servings*

*Note: May be served warm or at room temperature.*

# FRESH SPINACH CRÊPES WITH MUSHROOM SAUCE

*These tasty crêpes make a wonderful side dish or a light entrée for a memorable meal.*

### Crêpe Batter

- 1½ cups all-purpose flour
- 1½ cups milk
- 6 large eggs
- 5 tablespoons unsalted butter, softened at room temperature
- ⅛ teaspoon salt

- In a large bowl, beat flour, milk, eggs, butter and salt until combined.
- Heat crêpe pan or 6 to 8-inch skillet over medium heat. Lightly butter pan or spray with cooking spray. Do not let pan get hot enough to brown butter or spray.
- Pour about ⅛ cup batter into pan and quickly tilt so batter covers entire bottom of pan. Cook 30 to 45 seconds or until top is dry, being careful not to let get too brown. Flip and cook other side 10 to 15 seconds.
- Remove and put on piece of wax paper. Repeat with remaining batter, layering between pieces of wax paper.

*Yield: 25 crêpes*

*Note: Crêpes may be cooked ahead and placed in a zip-top plastic bag, then refrigerated for up to 1 week or frozen for 2 to 3 months. Remaining Crêpes may be filled with fruit or ice cream for a delicious dessert.*

### Crêpe Filling

- 6 tablespoons unsalted butter
- 1½ cups chopped onion
- 8 ounces fresh mushrooms, sliced
- 12 ounce bag fresh spinach, washed and stems removed
- 4 tablespoons flour
- ½ cup milk
- 1 cup chicken broth

- Melt butter in skillet. Add onions and mushrooms, sauté until tender.
- Add spinach and cook 3 to 5 minutes.
- Add flour, milk, and broth. Whisk to combine. Remove from heat and allow to cool.

---

*Sometimes cream sauces curdle when you are heating them. If your sauce curdles remove it from heat and plunge into a larger pan of ice water to stop the cooking process. Beat the sauce vigorously or pour into a blender and process until smooth.*

## Fresh Spinach Crêpes continued

**Mushroom Sauce**

| | | | |
|---|---|---|---|
| 2 | tablespoons butter | ¾ | cup chicken broth |
| ⅔ | cup fresh mushrooms, sliced | ½ | cup whipping cream |
| 2 | tablespoons flour | ¼ | teaspoon salt |

- Sauté mushrooms in butter until tender. Add flour, broth, and cream stirring until thickened. Season with salt. Serve immediately.

**To Assemble Crêpes**

- Preheat oven to 350 degrees.
- Place ⅓ cup filling on each crêpe. Roll up and place seam-side down in a shallow baking dish. Cover and bake for 25 minutes.
- Prepare Mushroom Sauce while crêpes are baking.
- Place crêpes on individual plates and spoon Mushroom Sauce on top. Serve immediately.

*Yield: 6 servings*

*Note: The assembled crêpes may be made several hours in advance, covered, and refrigerated. Add 5 to 10 minutes on to cooking time if crêpes are cold when placed in the oven.*

---

*Alabama's legendary football coach, Paul "Bear" Bryant, had his first coaching job in Jackson. He was an assistant coach for Union University before moving on to Kentucky and finally Alabama.*

# GRILLED SPINACH STUFFED VIDALIA ONIONS

*Great with grilled meats for a summer supper.*

*One pound of fresh spinach yields 1½ cups cooked spinach.*

| | | | |
|---|---|---|---|
| 6 | medium Vidalia onions | 1 | teaspoon Worcestershire sauce |
| | Salt and pepper to taste | | Salt and pepper to taste |
| 1 | pound fresh spinach | | Dash of cayenne pepper |
| 2 | tablespoons butter | | Grated Parmesan cheese |
| ¼ | cup sour cream | | |

- Peel onions and place in a steamer rack over simmering water. Steam until soft, yet firm, about 5 to 10 minutes. Remove from heat.

- Hollow onion by cutting out inner rings of onion leaving a ¼ inch rim. Remove enough of onion to form a cup. Salt and pepper inside of onion and set aside.

- Wash spinach and remove stems. Pour water from steaming onions over spinach to wilt. Chop spinach.

- Melt butter in a saucepan. Add spinach, sauté and drain. Add sour cream, Worcestershire sauce, salt and pepper. Stir until well combined.

- Fill onions with the spinach mixture. Sprinkle with Parmesan cheese then cayenne pepper. Wrap in foil, sprayed with cooking spray, and grill over low to medium heat for about 20 minutes.

*Yield: 6 servings*

# ITALIAN SPINACH AND ARTICHOKE HEARTS

*Serve this make ahead side dish for your next dinner party!*

- 3 (10-ounce) packages frozen chopped spinach, cooked and drained, ½ cup liquid reserved
- 2 tablespoons unsalted butter
- 4 tablespoons all-purpose flour
- 3 tablespoons yellow or white onion, chopped
- ½ cup evaporated milk
- 1 can artichoke hearts, drained and coarsely chopped
- 1 (6-ounce) roll garlic cheese, cut into chunks
- ½ teaspoon black pepper
- ¾ teaspoon garlic salt
- ¾ teaspoon celery salt
- 1½ teaspoons Worcestershire sauce
- ¼ cup seasoned Italian breadcrumbs
- ¼ cup freshly grated Parmesan cheese

- Preheat oven to 350 degrees. Grease a 2-quart baking pan.
- Melt butter in large pan over medium heat. Add flour and whisk until smooth. Add onion and cook until tender, but not brown. Add ½ cup reserved spinach liquid, then milk, whisking until smooth and mixture thickens.
- Add garlic, cheese, spices and Worcestershire sauce. Stir until melted and smooth. Gently stir in drained spinach and artichoke hearts.
- Spoon spinach mixture into the prepared pan. Top with breadcrumbs and Parmesan cheese. Bake uncovered for 20 to 30 minutes, until cheese is just melted.

Yield: 6 to 8 servings

*Note: May be refrigerated or frozen before baking.*

*A simple artichoke with a name card or picture placed within its leaves is a unique place marker at the dinner table.*

# SUMMER SQUASH CASSEROLE

*Sure to add a Southern accent to any meal!*

| | | | |
|---|---|---|---|
| 2 | pounds yellow squash, sliced | 1 | teaspoon salt |
| 3 | eggs, lightly beaten | ½ | teaspoon pepper |
| ½ | cup heavy cream | 1½ | cups shredded Cheddar cheese, divided |
| 4 | tablespoons butter, divided | 9 | slices cooked bacon, cooked crisp and crumbled |
| 1½ | cups thinly sliced celery | | |
| 1 | cup finely chopped onion | | |

- Preheat oven to 350 degrees.

- Cook the squash until tender, either by steaming or boiling in salted water. Drain well, then mash squash. Transfer squash to large bowl and mix with the eggs and cream. Melt 2 tablespoons butter and add to squash.

- Melt remaining 2 tablespoons butter in a saucepan over medium heat; add celery and onion and sauté until transparent.

- Add celery and onion to the squash, along with the salt, pepper and ¾ cup of the cheese.

- Pour into a 13x9-inch baking dish. Sprinkle with the remaining cheese and top with bacon. Bake uncovered for 45 minutes. Serve immediately.

*Yield: 8 to 10 servings*

---

*When cutting an onion, have a candle or gas burner burning nearby, the flame interacts with the chemical released from the onion which causes your eyes to burn. This interaction decreases the amount of the chemical which reaches your eye.*

# SQUASH RIBBONS AL POMODORO

| | | | | |
|---|---|---|---|---|
| 2 | large zucchini | 1 | green onion, chopped |
| 2 | large yellow squash | 2 | teaspoons minced garlic |
| 1 | cup cherry tomatoes, halved | ½ | teaspoon salt |
| 1 | tablespoon margarine | | |

- Cut off ends of zucchini and discard. Peel skin from zucchini with vegetable peeler and discard.
- Cut long strips from zucchini with peeler until the strips look like ribbons. Cut ribbons until you reach the seeds. Turn zucchini over and continue peeling.
- Repeat same procedure with yellow squash.
- Melt margarine in a large skillet over medium-low heat. Add scallion and garlic, stirring frequently until tender.
- Increase heat to medium and add the zucchini, squash, tomatoes and salt. Sauté for 5 minutes, stirring frequently until ribbons just are tender, but not mushy.

*Yield: 4 to 6 servings*

*Variation: May substitute sliced roasted red peppers for cherry tomatoes.*

# SKILLET TOMATOES

| | | | | |
|---|---|---|---|---|
| 4 | large tomatoes, firm and ripe | 2 | teaspoons salt |
| 1 | teaspoon butter | 2 | teaspoons sugar |
| 1 | tablespoon red wine vinegar | 1 | clove garlic, pressed |
| 2 | tablespoons olive oil | 1 | tablespoon minced parsley |

- Cut tomatoes into halves.
- Melt butter in skillet over medium heat. Sauté tomatoes with the cut surface down until golden brown.
- Blend vinegar, olive oil, salt, sugar, garlic and parsley in a bowl. Turn tomatoes over and add an equal amount of the vinegar mixture to each tomato. Cover skillet and simmer for 15 minutes or until tender. Serve warm.

*Yield: 8 servings*

---

*Heat ripens tomatoes. If they are not ripe when you buy them and you want to eat them soon, place them on the windowsill. If they are ripe, place them on the counter with the least amount of flesh touching the counter (usually upside down). Never put tomatoes on top of each other and do not refrigerate (makes them mealy and blunts their flavor).*

# TOMATOES ROCKEFELLER

*You do not have to be a millionaire to enjoy this combination of flavors!*

| | | | |
|---|---|---|---|
| 12 | tomato slices, 1-inch thick | ½ | cup melted butter |
| 2 | (10-ounce) packages frozen chopped spinach, cooked and well drained | 1½ | teaspoons dried thyme |
| | | ½ | teaspoon dried oregano |
| 1¼ | cups plain breadcrumbs | ¾ | teaspoon salt |
| 1 | cup seasoned breadcrumbs | ¼ | teaspoon pepper |
| ¾ | cup green onions | ½ | teaspoon minced garlic |
| 6 | eggs | 1¼ | cups grated Parmesan cheese |

- Preheat oven to 350 degrees.
- Place sliced tomatoes on lightly greased baking pan.
- Combine spinach with next 10 ingredients. Mix well. Spoon spinach mixture on top of each tomato and form into mound. Top with Parmesan cheese.
- Bake at 350 degrees for 12 to 15 minutes or until spinach has set and cheese is melted. Serve warm.

*Yield: 12 servings*

# TOMATO VIDALIA STACKS

| | | | |
|---|---|---|---|
| 2 | Vidalia onions, sliced 1-inch thick | 6 | slices bacon, cut into 2 to 3-inch lengths |
| 6 | fresh tomatoes, sliced 1-inch to 1½-inch thick | ¼ | cup ketchup |
| | | | Salt and pepper to taste |

- Preheat oven to 350 degrees.
- Place 6 slices of onions on bottom of greased 13x9-inch baking dish. Stack a tomato slice on top of each onion. Repeat onion and tomato layering, ending with tomato layer.
- Place 3 pieces of bacon on top of each tomato. Season generously with salt and pepper. Spread thin layer of ketchup over bacon.
- Cover with foil. Bake for 1 hour. Remove foil and bake for 1 more hour. Serve hot.

*Yield: 6 servings*

*Variation: May substitute yellow onions for Vidalia onions if sweet onions are unavailable. Also may substitute seasoned salt for salt and pepper.*

---

*Buy tomatoes from the farmer's market when they are in season if you cannot grow your own. The flavor is incredible! Fresh "home grown" tomatoes will make any recipe zing with flavor.*

# LAYERED GARDEN BAKE

| | | | |
|---|---|---|---|
| 1 | pound yellow squash, sliced | 1 | large green pepper, seeded and sliced |
| 1 | large Vidalia onion, sliced | | Salt and pepper to taste |
| 4 | medium or large tomatoes, sliced | 1-2 | tablespoons butter or margarine |

- Preheat oven to 350 degrees. Grease a 3-quart baking dish.
- Layer ½ of squash, onion, tomato and pepper in the prepared baking dish. Salt and pepper the squash and tomato layers.
- Repeat layering and seasoning with the remaining vegetables. Dot the top with butter or margarine.
- Cover and bake for 1 hour.

*Yield: 4 to 6 servings*

*Variation: May substitute red or yellow pepper for the green pepper. If Vidalia onions are not available, you may substitute yellow onions.*

# GRILLED ZUCCHINI BOATS

| | | | |
|---|---|---|---|
| 2 | medium zucchini squash | 2 | heaping tablespoons minced fresh basil |
| | Salt to taste | 1 | cup fresh corn kernels |
| | Fresh black pepper to taste | ½ | cup shredded Monterey Jack cheese |
| 1 | tablespoon butter | | |
| 1 | Roma tomato, diced | ¼ | cup Parmesan cheese, shredded (plus enough to sprinkle on top of dish) |
| ⅓ | cup finely chopped green pepper | | |
| 1 | tablespoon finely chopped red onion | | |

- Preheat grill to medium heat. Cut zucchini in half lengthwise. Scoop pulp out with spoon, leaving about a quarter-inch rim. Reserve the pulp. Lightly salt and pepper the zucchini boats and microwave in a glass dish on high for 4 minutes. Chop the reserved pulp.

- Melt butter in skillet over medium heat. Add chopped pulp, tomato, green pepper, onion, basil and corn and sauté for 5 minutes.

- Remove from heat, adding Monterey Jack and Parmesan cheese. Add salt and pepper to taste.

- Fill zucchini boats with the squash mixture and sprinkle with remaining Parmesan cheese. Grill for 10 to 15 minutes or until heated through and cheese is melted.

*Yield: 4 servings*

*Note: Watch bottom of boats carefully so they do not burn. You may prepare this recipe 6 to 10 hours in advance, cover, and chill until ready to grill. If prepared ahead, add 5 to 10 minutes to the grilling time.*

# ZUCCHINI, TOMATO AND ONION BAKE

| | | | |
|---|---|---|---|
| 4 | medium zucchini, cut in 1-inch cubes | ¼ | cup Worcestershire sauce, or more to taste |
| 3 | medium tomatoes, cut in 1-inch cubes | ½ | cup fresh Parmesan cheese, divided |
| 2 | medium onions, cut in 1-inch cubes | | Salt to taste |
| ½ | cup bottled vinaigrette dressing, or more to taste | | Pepper to taste |

- Preheat oven to 400 degrees. Grease a 13x9-inch baking dish.
- Combine vegetables in a bowl; add dressing and Worcestershire sauce. Stir to coat vegetables. Add ¼ cup Parmesan cheese and salt and pepper.
- Place vegetable mixture in a prepared baking dish. Bake for 45 minutes.
- Sprinkle with remaining Parmesan cheese before serving.

*Yield: 6 to 8 servings*

Note: May use low fat or fat-free vinaigrette dressing.

---

*Robert Cartmell, a Civil War soldier and citizen of Jackson, kept a diary from his 21st birthday until his death 65 years later. It is our best record of life in Jackson during the Civil War.*

# ROASTED PEARS WITH GORGONZOLA AND PECANS

*Ripe, sweet pears make this side dish unexpected, but extra special! Gourmet taste with little effort!*

| | | | |
|---|---|---|---|
| ¼ | cup water | 1½ | cups Gorgonzola cheese, crumbled |
| ¼ | cup sugar | ½ | cup chopped, lightly toasted pecans |
| 4 | fresh pears, peeled, cored, and halved lengthwise | | |

- Preheat oven to 425 degrees.
- Mix water and sugar in a large baking dish. Place pears in dish, cut sides down and bake 15 minutes.
- Remove from oven and turn pears over. Place crumbled Gorgonzola and pecans on top of each pear. Return to oven for 5 minutes or until cheese is melted.

*Yield: 8 servings*

# CARAMELIZED ONION AND PORCINI RISOTTO WITH SAGE

- ¾ ounce dried porcini mushrooms
- 1 cup hot water
- 5½ cups chicken or vegetable broth
- 2 tablespoons unsalted butter
- 2 tablespoons extra virgin olive oil
- 2 onions, sliced and halved
- 2 cups Arborio or medium grain rice
- ¾ cup dry white wine
- 1 tablespoons finely chopped sage or 1 teaspoon dried sage
- 1½ cups freshly grated Parmesan cheese
- Salt and fresh ground pepper, to taste
- Fresh sage leaves, optional

- In a small bowl, combine mushrooms and hot water, soak for 30 minutes to soften. Drain mushrooms, and reserve soaking liquid. Strain soaking liquid to remove any sediment. Chop mushrooms and set aside.
- In a small saucepan over high heat, bring broth to a simmer. Reduce heat to low and keep liquid hot.
- In a medium saucepan over medium-high heat, melt butter with olive oil. Add onions and sauté, stirring frequently, until caramelized. Keep onions moist by adding small amounts of water to pan while sautéing.
- Add rice and mushrooms to onions. Stir until a white spot appears in the center of the grain, about 1 minute. Add wine and stir until absorbed, about 2 minutes. Add chopped sage, reserved mushroom liquid, and ¾ cup of warm broth.
- Adjust the heat under the rice to simmer. Stir until liquid is absorbed.
- Continue cooking adding ¾ cup warm broth at a time, stirring almost constantly until rice starts to soften, about 10 minutes.
- Continue cooking and adding warm broth ½ cup at a time until rice is tender but slightly firm in the center and mixture is creamy, about 10 more minutes.
- Add Parmesan cheese, season with salt and pepper. Mix well.
- Garnish with sage leaves and serve immediately.

*Yield: 6 servings*

---

*Tennessee was the 16th state to join the Union in 1769. The name Tennessee comes from a Cherokee village named Tanasie. The lonely pioneer with a flintrock and a coonskin cap is a symbol of Tennessee's past.*

# FETA AND VIDALIA ONION RISOTTO

*Be sure to prepare this wonderful side dish immediately before serving!*

| | | | |
|---|---|---|---|
| 2 | (14.5-ounce) cans chicken broth | ½ | cup (2-ounces) crumbled feta cheese, divided |
| 2 | cups sliced and halved Vidalia onions | ⅓ | cup chopped flat leaf parsley, plus extra to garnish |
| 3 | tablespoons vegetable oil, divided | ¼ | cup grated fresh Parmesan cheese |
| 2 | large garlic cloves, minced | | Fresh ground pepper to taste |
| 1½ | cups Arborio rice | | |

- Warm broth in a medium saucepan over medium heat. Leave on low heat.

- In an 8 to 10-inch skillet, sauté onions in 1 tablespoon vegetable oil on low heat until caramelized. Keep onions moist while sautéing by occasionally adding water.

- In a 2 quart saucepan, heat remaining 2 tablespoons oil over medium heat. Add caramelized onions and garlic; sauté 1 minute. Stir in rice.

- Add ½ cup warmed broth to rice. Cook until liquid is nearly absorbed, stirring constantly. Add remaining warmed broth, ½ cup at a time waiting until each portion of broth is nearly absorbed before adding more liquid, continuing to stir constantly. (This process takes approximately 20 minutes).

- Remove from heat. Stir in feta cheese, parsley, and Parmesan. Top with black pepper and garnish with parsley. Serve immediately.

*Yield: 5 servings*

# SPICY RICE CASSEROLE

*Good with grilled meats!*

| | | | |
|---|---|---|---|
| 3 | cups cooked rice | 1 | cup (8-ounces) pepper jack cheese, grated |
| 2 | cups sour cream | 1 | tablespoon butter |
| | Salt to taste | | |
| 1 | (6-ounce) can green chilies, chopped | | |

- Preheat oven to 350 degrees.
- Combine cooked rice and sour cream and season with salt. Spread ½ rice mixture into bottom of buttered 1½-quart casserole dish.
- Spread green chilies over the rice and layer with cheese. Top with remaining rice and dot with butter.
- Bake uncovered for 30 minutes. Serve immediately.

*Yield: 6 to 8 servings*

*Variation: May substitute light sour cream to reduce fat in this recipe. Also may substitute Monterey Jack or Cheddar cheese for the pepper jack cheese.*

---

*When you are in a fabric store, buy yards of fabric (remnants) after season to use as tablecloths for next year's holiday season. Think bright colors, holiday themes or gingham. If you do not have time to hem the edges, bunch the fabric up near the center with the unfinished edges tucked under. You can place your simple centerpiece on the fabric.*

# ANGEL HAIR PASTA FLAN

*Lovely for a dinner party or anytime.*

| | | | |
|---|---|---|---|
| 3 | ounces angel hair pasta, cooked | ¼ | teaspoon ground nutmeg |
| 1 | cup whipping cream | ¾ | cup freshly grated Parmesan cheese, divided |
| 3 | large eggs | ⅛ | teaspoon pepper |
| 3 | teaspoons minced fresh thyme | ⅛ | teaspoon salt |

- Preheat oven to 350 degrees.
- Spray 8 ramekins with cooking spray. Divide pasta evenly among ramekins.
- Whisk together next 4 ingredients and ½ cup of the Parmesan cheese. Add salt and pepper, whisking again to combine.
- Pour sauce over pasta, dividing evenly between ramekins. Top with remaining ¼ cup Parmesan cheese.
- Bake 20 to 30 minutes until lightly brown. Run knife around edges to unmold. Serve immediately.

*Yield: 8 servings*

*Note: This may be prepared in advance and refrigerated prior to baking. If chilled, add 5 minutes to the baking time.*

# PENNE WITH PUMPKIN SAUCE

*Those adventurous enough to try this side dish will not be disappointed.*

| | | | | |
|---|---|---|---|---|
| 2 | tablespoons unsalted butter | | | Freshly grated nutmeg to taste |
| 1 | onion, chopped fine | | | |
| 1 | red bell pepper, chopped fine | | ¼ | teaspoon ginger |
| 2 | garlic cloves, minced | | ⅛ | teaspoon cinnamon |
| ½ | cup canned solid-packed pumpkin | | | Salt and pepper to taste |
| | | | ½ | pound penne pasta |
| 1 | cup chicken broth | | 3 | tablespoons minced fresh parsley |
| ½ | cup water | | | |
| 2 | tablespoons heavy cream | | | Freshly grated Parmesan cheese |

- Over moderate heat, melt butter in a large deep skillet. Add onion, pepper and garlic, stirring until softened. Stir in pumpkin, broth, water, cream, nutmeg, ginger, cinnamon, salt and pepper, stirring occasionally for 10 minutes.

- While the sauce is simmering, cook the penne in salted boiling water until al dente. Drain pasta, reserving 1 cup of the cooking water.

- Add penne to the sauce, cook the mixture over moderate heat for 1 to 2 minutes, stirring and thinning the sauce as desired with the reserved cooking water. Stir in parsley.

- Remove from heat. Divide between 2 plates and top with Parmesan cheese. Serve immediately.

*Yield: 2 servings*

*Note: To decrease fat content, may use whole milk instead of heavy cream.*

---

*Pinson Mounds is the largest Middle Woodland mound group in the United States and dates from 200 B.C. to 500 A.D. There are 17 mounds in the 400-acre site. One of the mounds, the Sauls Mound, is 72 feet high and is the second largest Indian mound in the United States.*

# PARMESAN POLENTA WITH WILD MUSHROOMS

*Serve this as a meatless entrée or side dish! It is full of flavor!*

| | | | |
|---|---|---|---|
| 1 | cup polenta | 1 | tablespoon olive oil |
| 4 | cups chicken broth | 1 | pound assorted wild mushrooms, cleaned and chopped |
| 1½ | cups freshly grated Parmesan cheese | | |
| ½ | teaspoon salt | 2 | tablespoons chopped fresh thyme |
| ¼ | teaspoon freshly ground black pepper | | |

- Stir polenta into 1 cup of chicken broth, mixing well. Bring remaining 3 cups broth to boil in a large saucepan. Reduce heat and slowly mix in polenta. Simmer and stir until polenta thickens. Add cheese, salt and pepper, stirring to combine.

- In separate pan, heat oil until hot, add mushrooms; reduce heat to medium high. Sauté mushrooms with thyme just until liquid begins to evaporate (do not let evaporate). Season with salt and pepper.

- Place Polenta in a serving dish or divide on individual plates.

- Pour mushroom mixture over polenta, including the mushroom juices. Top with freshly grated Parmesan cheese. Serve warm.

*Yield: 6 side dishes or 4 main dish servings*

*Note: To prepare ahead, prepare polenta and cover in refrigerator. Prepare mushrooms and store separately. Reheat polenta in a baking pan at 350 degrees for 30 minutes. Reheat mushrooms on stove over low heat, then pour over polenta.*

# ALMOND JASMINE RICE

*Serve this sweet rice with a spicy entrée!*

| | | | |
|---|---|---|---|
| 1¾ | cups water | 2 | tablespoons brown sugar |
| ½ | cup orange juice | ½ | cup almonds, sliced |
| ½ | teaspoon salt | 1 | teaspoon crystallized minced ginger |
| 1 | cup jasmine rice, uncooked | ¼ | teaspoon grated orange zest |
| 2 | tablespoons butter or margarine | | |

- Bring water, juice and salt to boil in medium saucepan, gradually adding rice. Stir constantly. Cover, reduce heat and simmer for 20 to 25 minutes or until rice is tender and liquid is absorbed.

- Melt butter and brown sugar in small skillet over medium heat. Add almonds and ginger, sautéing 2 minutes or until almonds are lightly browned.

- Add almond mixture and grated orange zest to rice, stirring gently to combine.

*Yield: 4 servings*

*Variation: May use brown rice instead of jasmine rice, but cooking time will be longer.*

# MEDITERRANEAN COUSCOUS

*Fresh, crunchy and colorful! An easy dish, great for a picnic!*

| | | | |
|---|---|---|---|
| 1 | box plain couscous | 1 | cup golden raisins |
| 1/4 | cup red onion, minced | 1/2 | cup chopped walnuts, toasted |
| 1 | cup dried cranberries | 2 | apples diced |
| 1/2 | cup yellow bell pepper, diced | | Honey-Lime Vinaigrette |

- Cook couscous according to package directions. Transfer to a large bowl and fluff with fork. Add the next 6 ingredients.
- Pour the Honey-Lime Vinaigrette over the couscous mixture and toss. Serve cold or at room temperature.

### Honey-Lime Vinaigrette

| | | | |
|---|---|---|---|
| 1 | tablespoon honey | 1/2 | teaspoon coriander |
| 2 | tablespoons lime juice | 1/2 | teaspoon salt |
| 1/2 | teaspoon cumin | 1 | tablespoon olive oil |

- In small bowl, whisk together all ingredients.

*Yield: 6 to 8 servings*

*Variation: May add fresh mint. May substitute 1 cup toasted pine nuts for the walnuts and diced nectarines for the apples.*

---

*Wonderful bushes and trees to plant in your yard to use in impromptu arrangements: Cherry Laurel, Nandina, Holly, Rose, Magnolia, and Pine. Many times, centerpieces do not need to include flowers, fresh greenery and berries add a special touch.*

# ENTRÉES

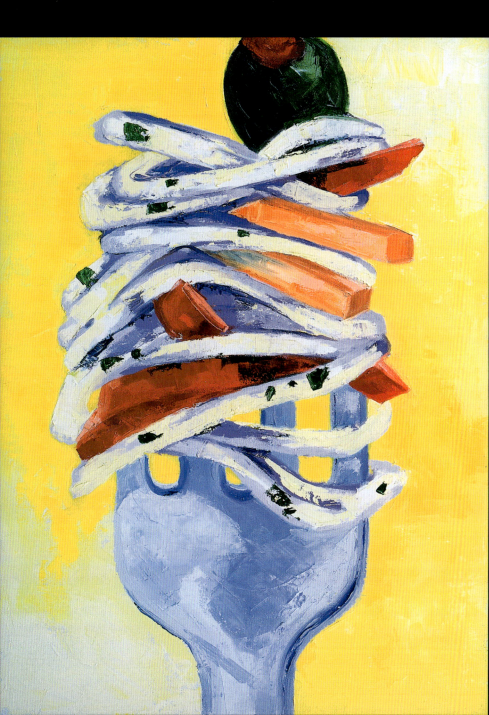

# ENTRÉES

Maple Mustard Pork Tenderloin with Caramelized Apples ....... 161
Marinated Pork Tenderloin with Celebration Sauce ........... 162
Pork Chops with Apples and Raisins ............. 163
Spiced Pork Tenderloin with Jalapeño Honey Sauce .................... 164
Marinated Pork Roast ............................. 165
Pork Tenderloin with Red, Yellow, and Green Peppers ..................... 166
Tennessee Whiskey Spareribs ....................... 167
Roasted Chicken with Goat Cheese and Pine Nuts over Fettuccine ................ 168
Picnic Chicken with Cumin and a Pine Nut Crust .................... 169
Mushroom Chicken Crêpes with Sherry Cream Sauce ...................... 170
Grilled Lime Chicken with Tropical Fruit Salsa ......................... 172
Chicken, Sausage and Tasso Sauce Piquant ................................ 173
Spinach Parmesan Chicken ........................ 174
Chicken Curry ............................................. 175
Grilled Chicken with Creamy Grits and Mushroom Sauce ..................... 176
Pecan Buttermilk Chicken ............................ 177
Chicken Jambalaya ...................................... 178
Soccer Night Chicken ................................. 179
Mushroom Glazed Chicken Breast ................ 180
Greek Chicken Breasts ................................ 181
Family Favorite Barbecue Chicken .............. 181
Crockpot Chicken with Mushroom Sauce ....... 182
Chicken Breasts Sauté with Tarragon Cream Sauce ..................... 183
Lemon Thyme Grilled Chicken ...................... 184
Turkey Burgers with Smoked Gouda and Granny Smith Apples ..................... 185
Apricot-Glazed Cornish Hens Stuffed with Wild Rice ........................ 186
Pecan Encrusted Rack of Lamb .................. 187
Chipotle Baked Brisket ............................. 188

English Roast Beef with Whiskey and Ale ...... 189
Flank Steak with Summer Salsa .................... 190
Garlic and Brandy Glazed Fillet of Beef ........ 191
Italian Stuffed Fillets ................................. 191
Italian Roast Beef ...................................... 192
Spicy Grilled Steak .................................... 192
Marinated Beef Tenderloin with Horseradish Sauce ........................ 193
Mushroom-Stuffed Tenderloin ..................... 194
Steak au Poivre .......................................... 195
Bacon-Wrapped Meatloaf ............................ 196
Shrimp and Crabmeat au Gratin ................... 197
New Orleans Style Shrimp 'n Grits ............... 198
Shrimp Creole with Saffron Rice .................. 199
Shrimp with Spinach and Pine Nuts .............. 200
Citrus Basil Grilled Shrimp ........................... 201
Spicy Baked Barbecue Shrimp ..................... 202
Mahi Mahi with Pineapple Papaya Salsa ...... 203
Wasabi-Glazed Salmon over Wilted Fresh Spinach ..................... 204
Salmon Wellington ..................................... 205
Baked Salmon with Roasted Tomatoes .......... 206
Maple-Glazed Salmon ................................. 207
Pasta with Garlic Shrimp and Zucchini ......... 208
Seafood Fettuccine .................................... 209
Mediterranean Shrimp with Angel Hair Pasta ........................ 210
Sicilian Spaghetti Sauce ............................. 211
Burgundy Lasagna ...................................... 212
Pasta with Ale ............................................ 213
Penne with Corn, Bacon, Leeks and Tomatoes ............................. 213
Prosciutto Vodka Sauce .............................. 214
Spinach Lasagna ........................................ 215
Greek Pasta ............................................... 216
Spinach, Gorgonzola, and Walnuts over Fettuccine ...................... 217
Spicy Tomato Thyme Sauce ......................... 218

# MAPLE MUSTARD PORK TENDERLOIN WITH CARAMELIZED APPLES

*Serve with Spinach Salad with Cranberries (page 74).*

| | | | |
|---|---|---|---|
| 2 | (about ½-pound each) pork tenderloins, silver skin removed | ½ | teaspoon salt |
| ¼ | cup Dijon mustard | ¼ | teaspoon pepper |
| 6 | tablespoons maple syrup, divided | 1 | tablespoon butter |
| 1 | tablespoon chopped fresh rosemary (or 1 teaspoon dried) | 4 | medium Granny Smith apples, peeled, cored, and cut into small wedges |

- Preheat oven to 425 degrees.
- Trim fat from pork. Place pork on a broiler pan coated with cooking spray.
- Combine mustard, 2 tablespoons syrup, rosemary, salt, and pepper in a small bowl. Brush mixture over pork.
- Insert a meat thermometer into thickest part of pork, and roast for 25 minutes or until thermometer registers 160 degrees (slightly pink). Remove pork from heat, and let rest for 5 minutes.
- Meanwhile, melt butter in a nonstick skillet over medium-high heat until hot. Sauté apples for 5 minutes, or until lightly browned; reduce heat to low, and add remaining 4 tablespoons syrup. Simmer for 10 minutes or until apples are tender, stirring occasionally.
- Cut pork crosswise into 1-inch thick pieces, and top with cooked apples.

*Yield: 6 servings*

---

*The Southern Engine and Boiler Works was the biggest business in Jackson at the turn of the century. From 1922 to 1926, W. H. Collier owned the business and manufactured a "Marathon" automobile for a short period of time.*

# MARINATED PORK TENDERLOIN WITH CELEBRATION SAUCE

*This is a wonderful entrée to serve guests for any type of celebration!*

| | | | |
|---|---|---|---|
| 1 | cup lite (low-sodium) soy sauce | 2 | tablespoons dried tarragon |
| 2 | tablespoons fresh lemon juice | 2 | tablespoons dried basil |
| 1 | tablespoon garlic, finely chopped | 1-3 | pork tenderloins, silver skin removed |
| | | | Celebration Sauce |

- In a large bowl, combine all ingredients, except pork, and mix well.
- Place pork in a zip-top plastic bag, and pour marinade over pork. Marinate in refrigerator at least 5 hours.
- Grill pork over medium heat 7 to 10 minutes each side or until meat thermometer reaches 160 degrees; remove from grill. Cover with foil, and let pork stand for 10 to 15 minutes. Pork will continue cooking once removed from grill, so do not over cook.
- Slice pork crosswise (against the grain) and serve with Celebration Sauce.

### Celebration Sauce

| | | | |
|---|---|---|---|
| ¾ | cup peach preserves | ¾ | tablespoon prepared horseradish |
| ½ | cup apple jelly | | |
| 2 | tablespoons Dijon mustard | | |

- Combine all ingredients, mixing well.

*Yield: 2 to 3 servings per tenderloin*

*Note: Be sure to use low-sodium soy sauce or the tenderloin will be very salty. The tenderloin can be served hot or at room temperature. Increase the horseradish in the sauce for a little more kick!*

---

*Store basil in the refrigerator wrapped in a damp paper towel inside of a plastic bag. It will keep in this manner for up to four days.*

# PORK CHOPS WITH APPLES AND RAISINS

*Delicious with Everybody's Favorite Green Beans (page 128)*

| | | | |
|---|---|---|---|
| 6 | boneless pork loin chops (4-ounces each) | ½ | teaspoon pepper |
| 2 | teaspoons olive oil, plus enough to rub pork chops | 1 | medium-sized Red Delicious apple, peeled, cored, and chopped |
| 1 | tablespoon dried rosemary | 1 | cup golden raisins |
| ½ | teaspoon salt | ¾ | cup apple juice or Marsala wine |

- Rub pork chops evenly on both sides with olive oil.
- Combine rosemary, salt, and pepper. Rub mixture evenly on both sides of pork; set aside.
- Heat oil in a large skillet over medium high heat. Add apples and raisins and cook for 5 minutes, stirring often.
- Add ¼ cup juice or wine, stirring constantly, until most of the liquid has evaporated.
- Add remaining juice or wine and cook for 15 minutes or until mixture is thickened. Set aside and keep warm.
- In a large skillet coated with cooking spray, cook pork chops over medium-high heat for 5 to 10 minutes on each side until done.
- Top with apple mixture, and serve immediately.

*Yield: 6 servings*

# SPICED PORK TENDERLOIN WITH JALAPEÑO HONEY SAUCE

*Do not let the long list of ingredients frighten you! This is very easy and will bring rave reviews from your guests. It is spectacular!*

*If you have extra dry rub left over after preparing your tenderloin, you can place it in a zip-top bag to give to a friend. Be sure to include the entire recipe so that your friend will be able to fully enjoy the tenderloin!*

**Spiced Pork Tenderloin**

| | |
|---|---|
| ½ cup brown sugar | ½ teaspoon ground allspice |
| 1½ tablespoons salt | ¼ teaspoon ground cloves |
| 1 tablespoon dried thyme | ¼ teaspoon ground cinnamon |
| ½ tablespoon ground cumin | 1 tablespoon ground cardamom |
| 1 tablespoon crushed bay leaf | 2 pounds pork tenderloin, silver skin removed |
| 1 teaspoon freshly ground black pepper | Basting Sauce |
| 1 teaspoon ground oregano | Jalapeño Honey Sauce |

- In a small bowl, mix together brown sugar and next 10 spices.
- Place tenderloin in a 1-gallon zip-top plastic bag, and add spice mixture, coating tenderloin completely. Place sealed bag in refrigerator overnight or at least 6 hours.
- Grill tenderloin over a hot fire, turning and basting with the Basting Sauce every 3 minutes. Grill for a total of 18 to 20 minutes, until the tenderloin reaches an internal temperature of 160 degrees.
- Remove from grill and place on a carving board, letting tenderloin rest for 10 minutes.
- Slice on the bias and arrange on a platter. Serve tenderloin with Jalapeño Honey Sauce.

*Yield: 4 to 6 servings*

**Basting Sauce**

| | |
|---|---|
| 1 cup apple juice | 2 tablespoons chili powder |
| 3 tablespoons brown sugar | |

- Whisk together ingredients in a small bowl.

## Spiced Pork Tenderloin continued

**Jalapeño Honey Sauce**

| | | | |
|---|---|---|---|
| 2 | jalapeño peppers, seeded and deveined | ½ | teaspoon allspice |
| ¼ | cup honey | ½ | teaspoon cumin |
| 1 | tablespoon garlic | 2 | teaspoons olive oil |
| 1 | tablespoon fresh cilantro | 2 | teaspoons balsamic vinegar |
| | | 2 | teaspoons Dijon mustard |

- Blend all ingredients in a blender or a food processor until smooth.

*Yield: ½ cup*

*Riverside is our oldest cemetery, dating back to 1824. For sixty years it was Jackson's primary cemetery. Most of our founding fathers and early settlers are buried there, including Mexican war heroes and a Civil War general.*

# MARINATED PORK ROAST

*Serve with our Sweet Potato Soufflé (page 136) and Zucchini Tomato Onion Bake (page 151)*

| | | | |
|---|---|---|---|
| 1 | cup unsulphured molasses | 8 | pounds boneless pork loin roast |
| 1 | cup Dijon mustard | | |
| ½ | cup tarragon vinegar | | |

- In a large nonmetal bowl, combine all marinade ingredients, mixing well.
- Add pork to marinade mixture, turning to coat all sides. Marinate 2 hours to overnight in refrigerator, turning pork several times.
- Preheat oven to 325 degrees.
- Remove pork, reserving marinade, and place in a shallow roasting pan. Insert a meat thermometer into center of thickest part of meat; roast for 2 to 3 hours or until thermometer reaches 170 degrees. Baste with marinade every 30 minutes.

*Yield: 8 servings*

# PORK TENDERLOIN WITH RED, YELLOW, AND GREEN PEPPERS

*This entrée is sure to please the eye as well as the palette!*

| | | | |
|---|---|---|---|
| 2 | teaspoons dried rosemary | 1½ | tablespoons olive oil |
| 2 | cloves garlic, minced | ¼ | cup extra virgin olive oil |
| 1 | tablespoon Dijon mustard | 2 | tablespoons balsamic vinegar |
| 2 | teaspoons salt | 1 | each red, yellow, and green pepper, seeded and cut in 1-inch pieces |
| 2 | teaspoons pepper | | Salt and pepper to taste |
| 2 | (12-ounce) pork tenderloins, silver skin removed | | |

- Mix rosemary, garlic, mustard, salt, and pepper in a small bowl. Rub mixture evenly over pork, and place in a shallow dish.
- Let pork stand at room temperature for 15 minutes or in the refrigerator for up to 2 hours.
- Preheat oven to 400 degrees.
- Heat 1½ tablespoons olive oil in skillet over medium-high heat. Add pork to the skillet, and brown pork on all sides. Place in a roasting pan, and roast for 20 to 30 minutes or until internal temperature registers 160 to 165 degrees.
- Meanwhile, heat ¼ cup oil and vinegar in a skillet over medium heat. Add peppers and sauté for 5 minutes, adding salt and pepper to taste.
- Serve tenderloin on a large platter surrounded by peppers.

*Yield: 8 servings*

*Variation: Before roasting, you may add new potatoes, cut in halves, to the roasting pan, and cook as called for in the recipe.*

---

*Think summertime fun when creating centerpieces for your next warm weather party. Pots or buckets filled with jellybeans, chocolate candies or nuts with a flag, pinwheel, or fresh flowers (stuck in florist foam and covered with plastic with candy on top of the plastic) sticking out of the top would be a conversation starter.*

# TENNESSEE WHISKEY SPARERIBS

*Try these wonderful Tennessee style ribs with Grilled Zucchini boats (page 150).*

| | | | |
|---|---|---|---|
| 2 | cups ketchup | 2 | tablespoons soy sauce |
| ⅔ | cup Tennessee Whiskey | 1 | tablespoon dry mustard |
| ½ | cup molasses | 1 | teaspoon pepper |
| ½ | cup vinegar | 2 | cloves garlic, minced |
| 2 | tablespoons lemon juice | 6 | pounds lean spare ribs |

- Preheat oven to 425 degrees.
- Combine all ingredients, except ribs; set aside.
- Place ribs in a roasting pan, bake for 45 minutes; reduce oven temperature to 325 degrees.
- Remove from oven and drain excess fat from pan. Pour half of sauce over the ribs.
- Cover ribs, and return to oven for 45 minutes.
- Dip ribs in remaining sauce, and grill for 30 minutes over low fire.

*Yield: 6 servings*

---

*Patriotic Party –* While this party can be held any time of the year, the holiday season is a good time to get friends together to provide needed care packages to those who are serving overseas. Your guests can bring a variety of items that would be appreciated by men and women ages 18 to 20. The local recruiting office will provide you with a list of items that you can include in the packages as well as a list of the addresses to send the care packages.

---

# ROASTED CHICKEN WITH GOAT CHEESE AND PINE NUTS OVER FETTUCCINE

*Prom Progressive Dinner –* Consider throwing a dinner party for your teenager when it is prom season. You can organize the dinner with the parents of your child's friends. A limousine can be rented to transport the prom-goers from house to house. Each parent can be responsible for a different course. This will allow all parents to have peace of mind and enjoy the prom night almost as much as the teenagers.

| | |
|---|---|
| ¾ cup pine nuts | Pinch of nutmeg |
| 3 tablespoons unsalted butter | 1 roasted chicken, skinned, deboned and cut into ¼-inch strips |
| 2 medium shallots, finely chopped | 1 pound fettuccine, cooked |
| 1 cup heavy cream | 3 tablespoons chopped fresh chives |
| ½ pound goat cheese, cut into chunks | |

- Preheat oven to 450 degrees.
- Spread pine nuts on a baking sheet and toast in oven, until golden brown, about 5 minutes. Watch nuts carefully to prevent burning.
- Meanwhile, melt butter in a medium saucepan over moderate heat. Add shallots and sauté until tender, about 2 to 3 minutes. Add cream and bring to a boil. Add goat cheese and nutmeg.
- Reduce heat, and simmer, stirring continuously until cheese just melts.
- Stir in chicken pieces, and simmer about 5 minutes more, until chicken is warm.
- Spoon sauce over cooked fettuccine.
- Sprinkle with pine nuts and chives and serve immediately.

*Yield: 4 to 6 servings*

*Variation: May substitute toasted, chopped walnuts for pine nuts.*

# PICNIC CHICKEN WITH CUMIN AND A PINE NUT CRUST

*This is a delicious updated version of the traditional Southern Fried Chicken.*

| | | | |
|---|---|---|---|
| 8 | chicken breast halves, skinned and boned | 1 | cup finely chopped pine nuts |
| 1 | cup flour | 1 | tablespoon ground cumin |
| 2 | eggs | 1 | teaspoon oregano |
| ½ | cup milk | | Kosher salt to taste |
| 1½ | cups dry breadcrumbs | | Fresh ground pepper to taste |
| | | | Vegetable oil for frying |

- Wash chicken pieces and pat dry on paper towels.
- Place flour in a shallow dish.
- In another shallow dish, whisk together eggs and milk.
- In a third shallow dish, combine breadcrumbs, pine nuts, cumin, oregano, salt, and pepper.
- Dip each chicken piece first into flour, then egg mixture, and then breadcrumb mixture, coating chicken well.
- In a large heavy skillet, add oil to the depth of 1-inch, and heat over medium high heat until hot, but not smoking.
- Place chicken in hot oil, leaving plenty of space between pieces.
- Fry chicken, turning once, until fully cooked, approximately 10 to 15 minutes.
- Drain chicken on paper towels; cool slightly.
- Slice each piece crosswise into 5 pieces, and arrange on a serving platter.
- This may be served warm or cold.

*Yield: 8 servings*

Note: May also be served warm.

---

*Jackson's most famous outlaw was John A. Murrell. Adept at stealing slaves and horses, he headed up a gang of thieves who operated throughout 8 states. His home was near Denmark, TN and today treasure hunters search there for gold.*

# MUSHROOM CHICKEN CRÊPES WITH SHERRY CREAM SAUCE

*An elegant dish to serve for a luncheon or dinner party.*

**Crêpes**

| | | | |
|---|---|---|---|
| ⅔ | cups all-purpose flour | 3 | tablespoons melted butter, cooled |
| 2 | eggs | 3⅛ | teaspoons salt |
| | | 1 | cup milk |

- Prepare crêpes by beating all ingredients together until smooth.
- Coat 6-inch pan with cooking spray and heat over medium heat. Pour 3 tablespoons of batter in the pan, making a thin pancake. Cook until slightly brown, turn, and cook on other side. Repeat until all crêpes are made.
- Place crêpes, individually, between wax paper. Set aside.

*Hint: The crêpes may be made up to 3 days ahead and stored in stacks in zip-top plastic bag.*

**Mushroom Chicken Filling**

| | | | |
|---|---|---|---|
| ¼ | cup butter | ½ | cup sherry |
| 10-12 | ounces fresh mushrooms, sliced | ½ | teaspoon salt |
| | | ¼ | teaspoon black pepper |
| ½ | cup chopped green onions | ¼ | cup chopped fresh parsley |
| 2½ | cups chopped cooked chicken | 1 | tablespoon chopped fresh thyme |

- Melt butter in a medium-sized saucepan. Add mushrooms and onions and sauté for 10 minutes. Add other ingredients, and cook over medium-high heat, until liquid has evaporated. Set aside.
- After you have prepared the Sherry Cream Sauce, add ½ of the sauce to the filling; stir to combine.

*Variation: May substitute shrimp for the chicken.*

---

*Fresh herbs make all the difference in a recipe so grow your own! If you garden produces more herbs than you and your friends can use, dry them. Place cut herbs between 2 layers of paper towels or napkins. Let them remain there until they can be crumbled. Crumble them and store in plastic bags or containers, making sure to label the bag. Dried herbs have a more concentrated flavor than fresh. Use one teaspoon dried herbs for each tablespoon fresh. Store in a cool dry place to preserve flavors.*

## Mushroom Chicken Crêpes continued

**Sherry Cream Sauce**

| | | | |
|---|---|---|---|
| ¼ | cup flour | ½ | teaspoon salt |
| ⅔ | cup sherry | ⅛ | teaspoon black pepper |
| 1 | (10.5-ounce) can chicken broth | ⅔ | cup grated Parmesan cheese |
| 1 | cup half-and-half | | Paprika to taste |
| 1 | cup whipping cream | | Parsley to taste |

- Blend flour and sherry in a saucepan over medium-high heat. Stir in next 5 ingredients (chicken broth through pepper). Bring to a boil, stirring constantly. Reduce heat, and simmer 2 minutes. The sauce will be thin.

**Assembling Mushroom Chicken Crêpes**

- Preheat oven to 425 degrees. Grease a 13x9-inch baking pan.
- Place ¼ cup of the filling in each crêpe, and roll up. Arrange seam-side down in a single layer in prepared pan.
- Pour remaining Sherry Cream Sauce over Crêpes and sprinkle with Parmesan cheese. Garnish with paprika and parsley.
- Bake 15 to 20 minutes or until cheese is slightly browned.

*Yield: 4 to 6 servings*

# GRILLED LIME CHICKEN WITH TROPICAL FRUIT SALSA

*While you are grilling the chicken, try a Mojito cocktail (page 122), Shrimp Quesadillas (page 45) and Monterey Salsa (page 51)!*

| | | | |
|---|---|---|---|
| 2 | limes, zest and juice | 4 | boneless, skinless chicken breasts |
| 2 | cloves garlic, crushed | | |
| 1 | teaspoon chili powder | | Salt and pepper to taste |
| ¼ | teaspoon red pepper flakes | | Tropical Fruit Salsa |

- Make marinade by mixing first 4 ingredients in a bowl.
- Flatten chicken breasts using a meat mallet.
- Place marinade and chicken in a large zip-top plastic bag and chill for 2 hours or up to 1 day.
- Heat grill to very hot.
- Remove chicken from bag and place on grill. Cook for about 5 minutes on each side.
- Season with salt and pepper.
- Serve chicken with Tropical Fruit Salsa.

**Tropical Fruit Salsa**

| | | | |
|---|---|---|---|
| ½ | cup peeled, cored, and diced pineapple | 1 | tablespoon finely minced ginger |
| ½ | cup peeled, cored, and diced Granny Smith apple | 1 | jalapeño, roasted under broiler, then peeled, seeded and minced |
| ½ | cup peeled, pitted, and diced mango | 1 | ripe tomato, peeled, seeded, and diced |
| 2 | tablespoons Vidalia onion (or red onion) | 2 | limes, juice only |
| ¼ | cup chopped fresh cilantro | | |

- Gently combine all ingredients in a mixing bowl, then chill in refrigerator.

*Yield: 4 servings*

*Variation: May substitute peaches for mangoes in salsa. This salsa is also delicious with grilled pork and fish.*

---

Mangoes are originally from India where many consider them sacred. Mangoes are ripe when the skin turns yellow with red mottling and they yield to gentle pressure in the hand. They are in season from May through September. Ripe mangoes may be stored in a plastic bag in the refrigerator for up to 5 days. To ripen a mango, place it in a paper bag at room temperature.

# CHICKEN, SAUSAGE AND TASSO SAUCE PIQUANT

*A very spicy one dish meal!*

| | | | | |
|---|---|---|---|---|
| 4 | tablespoons oil | | 2 | (10-ounce) cans chopped tomatoes with green chilies |
| 4 | tablespoons flour | | 1 | (8-ounce) package fresh mushroom, sliced |
| 1 | tablespoon butter | | 3 | bay leaves |
| 3 | pounds boneless, skinless chicken breasts, cubed | | ½ | teaspoon Worcestershire sauce |
| 1 | pound tasso, chopped into small cubes (or ham) | | 1 | teaspoon hot sauce |
| 1 | pound smoked sausage, sliced | | 2 | cups chicken stock |
| 3 | onions, chopped | | 1 | slice of lemon |
| 2 | bell peppers, chopped | | 2 | tablespoons Cajun seasoning |
| 4 | ribs celery, chopped | | | Cooked white rice |
| 2 | teaspoons garlic, minced | | | |

- Make roux by heating oil and flour in a heavy bottom Dutch Oven. Stir constantly until medium brown. Set aside.
- In a large pot, melt butter and brown chicken, tasso, and sausage.
- Add onion, bell pepper, celery, and garlic; simmer for 5 minutes, stirring often.
- Add roux and all remaining ingredients; simmer for 1 hour.
- Remove bay leaves and lemon slice. Serve over rice.

*Yield: 10 to 12 servings*

---

*Piquant, pronounced Pee-Kahn, is a French term for flavor that can be spicy, tart, or pungent. In the case of this dish it means spicy. You will find this term used in French and Cajun cooking.*

# SPINACH PARMESAN CHICKEN

*Terrific for the working mother!*

*Chicken cooks more evenly and quickly if it is uniform in thickness. Remove fresh boneless, skinless chicken breasts from the package (rinse with water) and place inside a zip top plastic bag. Pound them with a meat tenderizer until they reach a uniform thickness. You can do this before you cook them or before you freeze them.*

- 3-4 (10-ounce) packages frozen chopped spinach, thawed and patted dry
- ½ cup flour
- ½ stick butter, melted
- 4 boneless, skinless chicken breasts
- ⅓ teaspoon garlic salt
- ¼ teaspoon pepper
- 1 (8-ounce) carton heavy whipping cream
- 1 (6-ounce) package shredded Parmesan cheese
- ½ cup Parmesan cheese, grated
- 1 teaspoon paprika

- Preheat oven to 350 degrees.
- Press spinach into a buttered 13x9-inch baking pan. Pour flour and butter into separate small bowls.
- Dip chicken in flour then butter. Arrange chicken over spinach.
- Season with garlic salt and pepper.
- Pour cream over chicken and spinach.
- Sprinkle Parmesan cheese and paprika over chicken
- Bake uncovered for 45 minutes.

*Yield: 4 servings*

# CHICKEN CURRY

*This dish is great to prepare ahead and reheat before serving.*

| | | | |
|---|---|---|---|
| 6 | tablespoons butter | ½ | cup cream |
| 1 | cup chopped onion | 2 | tablespoons chutney |
| ½ | clove garlic, minced | ¼ | cup chopped almonds |
| 1¼ | tablespoons curry | 1 | (3-pound) chicken, boned, stewed and cut into bite-sized pieces |
| 8 | whole peppercorns | | |
| 1½ | teaspoons ginger | | Juice of 1 lemon |
| 2 | teaspoons sugar | | Salt to taste |
| ½ | cup raisins | | |
| 1½ | cups chicken stock | | |

- Melt butter in a large skillet. Add onions and garlic, cooking over medium heat until onion is soft.
- Add curry and next 4 ingredients to the onion mixture, stirring over low heat until smooth. Slowly add stock and cream, stirring until smooth.
- Add chutney and almonds, cooking for 2 more minutes.
- Add chicken; heat to boiling point.
- Remove from heat and add lemon juice and salt. Serve over rice with desired toppings.

**Suggested Toppings for Chicken Curry**
   **Chopped hard-boiled egg**
   **Chopped onion**
   **Raisins**
   **Peanuts**
   **Sliced cucumbers**
   **Crumbled bacon**
   **Olives**
   **Green pepper**

*Yield: 6 servings*

# GRILLED CHICKEN WITH CREAMY GRITS AND MUSHROOM SAUCE

*Delicious and very filling, serve with a simple salad.*

**Grilled Chicken**

| | | | |
|---|---|---|---|
| ½ | cup olive oil | 4 | large chicken breasts |
| ½ | cup white wine | | Salt and pepper to taste |
| 2 | tablespoons chopped garlic | | Mushroom Sauce |
| 2 | tablespoons chopped rosemary or 1 tablespoon dried rosemary | | Creamy Grits |

- Mix oil, wine, garlic, and rosemary in an 8x8-inch glass baking dish. Sprinkle chicken with salt and pepper. Place chicken in baking dish and toss to coat with oil mixture. Cover and refrigerate for at least 4 hours or overnight.

- Remove chicken from marinade and grill until cooked through, about 30 minutes. Chicken should be placed on grill while Mushroom Sauce is cooking.

- To serve, spoon equal portions of Creamy Grits on each plate. Top grits with Grilled Chicken and Mushroom Sauce

*Yield: 4 servings*

*Variation: Chicken may also be baked in oven at 350 degrees for 1 hour, if grilling is not an option.*

**Mushroom Sauce**

| | | | |
|---|---|---|---|
| 1 | cup beef broth | 8 | ounces mushrooms, sliced |
| 1 | cup chicken broth | ¾ | cup heavy cream |
| ½ | cup dry white wine | 1 | tablespoon fresh sage or ½ tablespoon dried sage |
| 3 | ounces bacon, cut into matchstick-size strips | | Salt and pepper to taste |

- Combine broths and wine in a medium saucepan over medium high heat. Boil until liquid is reduced to 1 cup, about 15 minutes. Remove from heat.

- Cook bacon in a large skillet over medium-high heat until crisp, about 3 minutes. Transfer to a bowl.

- Add mushrooms to the skillet, and sauté about 4 minutes. Add broth mixture and cream to the skillet, and simmer until reduced to sauce consistency, about 5 minutes. Mix in bacon and sage. Season to taste with salt and pepper.

---

*How do you know when your grill has reached the correct temperature? When you can hold your hand at the grilling level and count 6 seconds, your grill is at low heat (approximately 250 degrees). If you can count 4 seconds, you grill is at medium heat (approximately 300 degrees). If you can only count 2 seconds your grill is hot (approximately 350 degrees or hotter).*

## Grilled Chicken continued

**Creamy Grits**

| | | | |
|---|---|---|---|
| 3 | cups chicken broth | 1 | cup quick-cooking grits |
| 1 | cup heavy cream | | Salt and pepper to taste |
| 4 | tablespoons butter | | |

- Combine broth, cream, and butter in a saucepan, and simmer over medium heat; gradually whisk in grits. Reduce heat to low, cover, and cook until creamy and tender, about 6 minutes. Season to taste with salt and pepper.

# PECAN BUTTERMILK CHICKEN

*Delicious hot or cold! Serve for a picnic with Mediterranean Couscous (page 160) and Four-Pound Brownies (page 250)!*

| | | | |
|---|---|---|---|
| ½ | cup butter | 1 | tablespoon salt |
| 1 | cup buttermilk | ⅛ | teaspoon pepper |
| 1 | egg, slightly beaten | ¼ | cup sesame seeds |
| 1 | cup flour | 8 | chicken breast halves with skin |
| 1 | cup ground pecans | | |
| 1 | tablespoon paprika | ¼ | cup pecan halves |

- Preheat oven to 350 degrees.
- Melt butter in a large baking dish.
- Mix buttermilk with egg in a shallow dish.
- Mix flour, ground pecans, paprika, salt, pepper, and sesame seeds in another shallow dish.
- Dip chicken in buttermilk mixture, then in flour mixture. Roll each chicken piece in the melted butter in baking dish, and place skin side up.
- Place pecan halves on each piece of chicken; bake for 1 hour and 15 minutes until tender and golden brown.

*Yield: 8 servings*

*Note: This can be prepared with skinless, boneless chicken breasts.*

---

*Immortalized in a ballad, Casey Jones was a railroad engineer from Jackson. He was killed in a train wreck near Vaughn, Mississippi on April 30, 1900. He was able to warn others of the impending collision by blowing the famous "Whippoorwill Whistle". Casey was the only fatality in the accident. His home has been moved to the Casey Jones Village, a shopping and restaurant area in Jackson.*

# CHICKEN JAMBALAYA

*A meal in itself! After you have eaten this you will swear you transported your kitchen to New Orleans!*

| | | | |
|---|---|---|---|
| 1 | medium onion, peeled, ends trimmed, and quartered lengthwise | 1½ | cups (10-ounces) long-grain white rice |
| 1 | medium celery rib, cut crosswise into quarters | 1 | teaspoon salt |
| | | ½ | teaspoon minced fresh thyme leaves |
| 1 | medium red bell pepper, stem removed, seeded, and quartered lengthwise | 1 | tablespoon Cajun seasoning |
| | | 1 | (14.5-ounce) can diced tomatoes, drained, ¼ cup juice reserved |
| 5 | medium garlic cloves, peeled | | |
| 2 | teaspoons vegetable oil | 2½ | cups canned low-sodium chicken broth |
| 4 | bone-in chicken thighs | | |
| 8 | ounces smoked sausage, halved lengthwise, and cut into ¼-inch pieces | 2 | large bay leaves |
| | | 2 | tablespoons minced fresh parsley leaves |

- In a food processor, pulse onion, celery, red pepper, and garlic until chopped fine, about six 1-second pulses, stopping to scrape down the sides of the bowl once or twice. Do not over process; vegetables should not be pureed.

- Heat oil in a large heavy-bottomed Dutch oven over medium high heat until shimmering, but not smoking, about 2 minutes. Add chicken skin side down, and cook until golden brown, about 5 minutes. Using tongs, turn chicken and cook until golden brown on second side, about 3 minutes longer. Transfer chicken to a plate and set aside.

- Reduce heat to medium and add sausage. Cook, stirring frequently, until browned, about 3 minutes. Using a slotted spoon, transfer sausage to a paper towel-lined plate and set aside.

- Reduce heat to medium-low, add vegetables and cook, stirring occasionally and scraping bottom of the pot with the wooden spoon, until vegetables have softened, about 4 minutes.

- Add rice, salt, thyme, and Cajun seasoning. Cook, stirring frequently, until rice is coated with fat, about 1 minute. Add tomatoes, tomato juice, chicken broth, bay leaves, and browned sausage to the pot; stir to combine.

---

*Descriptions of different types of pans:*

**shallow baking dish** *allows food to cook quickly and brown evenly*

**11x17-inch dish** *is commonly called a 2-quart shallow baking dish*

**roasting pan** *designed for cooking large cuts of meat. Usually a heavy pan with 2 to 4 inch high straight sides, some pans may have a roasting rack to elevate the meat above the drippings while cooking)*

**Dutch oven** *is a deep pot with a tight fitting lid that can be used in both the oven and on the stove top. It usually holds 3 to 6 quarts of liquid.*

## Chicken Jambalaya continued

- Remove and discard skin from chicken; place chicken skinned-side down, on rice. Bring to a boil and reduce heat to low. Cover and simmer for 15 minutes. Stir once, keeping chicken on top, skinned side down. Continue simmering until chicken is no longer pink when cut into with a paring knife, about 10 minutes more. Transfer chicken to a clean plate and set aside.
- Cook rice about 5 more minutes until rice is fully tender.
- Shred chicken.
- Remove rice from heat, discard bay leaves, stir in parsley and chicken. Serve immediately.

*Yield: 4 to 6 servings*

# SOCCER NIGHT CHICKEN

*This quick and easy entrée for the busy family!*

| | | | |
|---|---|---|---|
| 4 | boneless, skinless chicken breasts | ¼ | cup chopped green onions |
| ½ | teaspoon salt | 1 | tablespoon lime or lemon juice |
| ½ | teaspoon pepper | 2 | tablespoons dried parsley or 3 tablespoons fresh parsley |
| 2 | tablespoons olive oil, divided | 1-2 | teaspoons Dijon mustard |
| 2 | tablespoons margarine, divided | ¼ | cup chicken broth |

- Place chicken in a zip top bag and pound lightly with a mallet to flatten. Remove from bag and sprinkle with salt and pepper.
- Heat 1 tablespoon of oil and 1 tablespoon margarine in a large skillet over medium-high heat. Cook chicken for 3 minutes on each side, being careful not to overcook. Transfer chicken to a casserole dish, and keep warm.
- Add green onions, juice, parsley, and mustard to the skillet, whisking constantly for 15 seconds.
- Whisk in broth until sauce is smooth. Whisk in remaining butter and oil.
- Pour sauce over chicken, and serve immediately.

*Yield: 4 servings*

# MUSHROOM GLAZED CHICKEN BREAST

*Sautéing chicken breasts is a wonderful way to prepare chicken. Reduce your heat for thicker cuts of chicken to allow the center to cook thoroughly.*

- 1 stick (½ cup) butter
- Salt and pepper to taste
- 2 pounds boneless, skinless chicken breasts or tenders
- 1 (8-ounce) package fresh sliced mushrooms
- 2 tablespoons Worcestershire sauce
- 1 bay leaf
- 1 tablespoon lemon juice
- 1 (10.5-ounce) can beef broth
- 1 tablespoon flour
- 1 tablespoon water

- Preheat oven to 350 degrees.
- Melt butter in a skillet. Salt and pepper chicken, place chicken in the skillet and cook turning once until lightly browned about 4 minutes per side. Transfer chicken to a large casserole dish.
- Brown mushrooms in the same butter, then spoon over chicken.
- Combine Worcestershire sauce, bay leaf, lemon juice, and broth in a saucepan over medium heat and simmer.
- Mix flour with water; whisk into the sauce to thicken.
- Pour sauce over chicken, and bake uncovered for 1 hour.

*Yield: 4 to 6 servings*

# GREEK CHICKEN BREASTS

*Serve with a pasta salad.*

| | | | |
|---|---|---|---|
| 1 | cup low-fat plain yogurt | 4 | boneless, skinless chicken breasts |
| 1 | large garlic clove, minced | | |
| ½ | teaspoon oregano | ⅓ | cup feta cheese, crumbled |
| ¼ | teaspoon black pepper | | |

- Combine first 4 ingredients. Marinate chicken in the mixture for at least 30 minutes.
- Preheat broiler. Line the broiler pan with foil, if desired.
- Remove chicken from marinade and place smooth-side down on pan. Broil chicken for 6 to 8 minutes, or until slightly brown at edges.
- Turn chicken, and broil 4 minutes more. Sprinkle with feta cheese, and broil until cheese is melted and chicken is cooked through, approximately 2 to 4 minutes.

*Yield: 4 servings*

*Variation: May use feta cheese with basil and sun-dried tomatoes.*

*On September 12, 1985, a large cache of gold coins was unearthed on West Main Street in downtown Jackson. These coins came from a robbery of the Jackson branch of the Union Bank in 1859.*

# FAMILY FAVORITE BARBECUE CHICKEN

| | | | |
|---|---|---|---|
| ½ | cup butter | ½ | cup chopped onions |
| ¼ | cup vinegar | ¼ | teaspoon pepper |
| ¼ | cup Worcestershire sauce | 1 | cup brown sugar |
| 1 | tablespoon dry mustard | 4 | chicken breasts |
| ½ | cup ketchup | | |

- Preheat oven to 350 degrees.
- Bring all ingredients, except chicken, to a boil in a saucepan over high heat. Reduce heat, and simmer for 30 minutes.
- Place chicken in a 13x9-inch casserole dish, and pour sauce over chicken.
- Bake covered for 45 minutes. Uncover and cook for 30 minutes or until slightly browned.

*Yield: 4 servings*

# CROCKPOT CHICKEN WITH MUSHROOM SAUCE

*Wonderful for the working mom, whether you work outside of the home or not!*

| | |
|---|---|
| 1 | fryer chicken, cut into pieces, or 4 chicken breasts |
| | Salt and pepper to taste |
| 2 | tablespoons butter, melted |
| 2 | tablespoons dry Italian salad dressing mix |
| 1 | (10.5-ounce) can condensed mushroom soup, undiluted |
| 2 | (3-ounce) packages cream cheese, cubed (do not substitute with fat-free) |
| ½ | cup sherry (optional) |
| 1 | tablespoon chopped onion |

- Sprinkle chicken with salt and pepper, and brush with butter; then place in a crock pot.
- Sprinkle with salad dressing mix.
- Cover and cook on low for 5 to 6 hours.
- About 45 minutes before serving, heat the canned soup, cream cheese, sherry and onion in a small saucepan over medium heat until smooth stirring occasionally. Pour sauce over chicken in a crock pot, and replace the lid. Cook for 30 more minutes.
- Serve with rice or pasta.

*Yield: 6 servings*

# CHICKEN BREASTS SAUTÉ WITH TARRAGON CREAM SAUCE

| | | | |
|---|---|---|---|
| 2 | tablespoons butter | 1 | tablespoon chopped fresh tarragon or 1 teaspoon dried tarragon |
| 1 | tablespoon vegetable oil | | |
| 4 | boneless, skinless chicken breasts | 1/8 | teaspoon salt |
| | | | Freshly ground pepper to taste |
| 3/4 | cup dry white wine | | |
| 2 | teaspoons Dijon mustard | 3/4 | cup heavy cream |

- In a large skillet, melt butter in oil over medium heat. Add chicken breasts, and cook, turning once, until lightly browned, about 4 minutes per side. Remove and set aside.

- Add wine to the skillet. Bring to a boil, scraping up brown bits from bottom of the pan with a wooden spoon. Stir in mustard, tarragon, salt, and pepper. Whisk in cream and boil until mixture slightly thickens, about 3 minutes.

- Return chicken to pan, turning to coat with sauce. Simmer for 5 to 10 minutes until chicken is tender.

- Remove chicken to a serving platter and spoon sauce over all.

- Serve immediately with rice or pasta.

*Yield: 4 servings*

---

*In order to mince parsley or fresh herbs, bunch leafy tops together, hold herbs over a measuring cup and cut with scissors. To mince more finely, put scissors in cup and cut until you have minced as finely as you wish. To keep herbs fresh leave a little moisture on the leaves after washing, wrap in a paper towel and place in a plastic bag. The herbs can be stored up to one week using this method.*

# LEMON THYME GRILLED CHICKEN

*This easy grilled chicken is light and delicious any time of year!*

|   |   |   |   |
|---|---|---|---|
|  | Juice of 4 lemons | 1 | teaspoon dried thyme or 1 tablespoon fresh thyme |
| 2 | teaspoons kosher salt | ¾ | cup extra virgin olive oil |
| 2 | teaspoons freshly ground black pepper | 2-3 | pounds boneless, skinless chicken breasts |

- Combine lemon juice, salt, black pepper, and thyme in a large, non-reactive bowl.
- Slowly add oil, while whisking mixture to create an emulsion.
- Add chicken breasts, making sure each is covered in marinade.
- Cover and refrigerate for 2 hours to overnight. (You may also place chicken and marinade in a large resealable bag to marinate.)
- Grill over medium high heat for 10 minutes on each side, or until cooked through.

*Yield: 6 servings*

*Note: This may be sliced crosswise and layered on top of Summer Strawberry Salad page 76. It is also very good to add to chicken salad or a casserole.*

---

*To juice lemons, roll them on the counter applying pressure or roll between your hands to warm and soften and therefore to get more juice. If the lemons come from the refrigerator before juicing, place in hot water or microwave for 10 to 20 seconds until warm. The warm lemon will release juice easily. Also, remember, if your recipe calls for zest and juice, make sure that you zest the fruit first. It is very difficult to zest the rind of the fruit if it has been juiced.*

# TURKEY BURGERS WITH SMOKED GOUDA AND GRANNY SMITH APPLES

*The tangy apples and smoked Gouda add marvelous texture and flavor to the ordinary turkey burger!*

| | | | |
|---|---|---|---|
| 1 | pound ground turkey | 1 | Granny Smith apple, cored, seeded, and sliced into ¼-inch slices |
| 2 | slices smoked Gouda, approximately ⅛-inch thick | 4 | hamburger buns |
| | Light olive oil | | |
| | Salt and pepper to taste | | |

- Divide turkey into 4 portions.
- Cut each gouda slice into quarters.
- Put 2 quarters of gouda on top of each other, and place on one portion of turkey. Form the turkey into a ball enclosing gouda in meat. Form the ball into a patty. Repeat with remaining cheese and turkey, making sure that cheese is fully enclosed.
- Toss apple slices in a bowl with enough olive oil to coat.
- Grill burgers over medium-high heat, turning over only once (about 5 to 7 minutes each side). When burgers are first turned, start grilling apples by placing them in a single layer directly on the grill for about 2 minutes on each side.
- Serve burgers on warmed buns with 2 apple slices each.

*Yield: 4 servings*

*Note: Apples should be soft when cooked, but should stay together.*

---

*One of the community agencies that Service League supports is WRAP- WO/Men's Resource & Rape Assistance Program (WRAP). WRAP provides crisis intervention and long term assistance to victims of domestic violence, sexual assault, and child abuse. JSL members aid WRAP by donating supplies for the shelters, baking cookies for the "Cookies for Cops" program and providing holiday presents for families in crisis. One member of the League serves on the board of WRAP.*

*Though many famous politicians have come to Jackson, Bill Clinton is the only President to visit here while he was in office.*

# APRICOT-GLAZED CORNISH HENS STUFFED WITH WILD RICE

*This elegant dish is easy to prepare!*

### Cornish Game Hen

- 1 (6-ounce) package long grain wild rice
- 2 teaspoons dried tarragon leaves
- Salt and freshly ground pepper to taste
- 4-6 Cornish game hens
- Apricot Glaze

- Prepare rice according to package directions. Add tarragon and season with salt and pepper.
- Preheat oven to 350 degrees.
- Wash hens, inside and out, and pat dry. Loosely stuff hens with cooked rice.
- Fold wings back and tie legs together. Season outside with salt and pepper. Place hens, breast side up, in a shallow roasting pan.
- Baste hens with Apricot Glaze.
- Bake uncovered for 1 hour and 15 minutes to 1 hour and 30 minutes, basting frequently. Remove when meat thermometer reaches 180 degrees when inserted into thigh of hen.
- Remove hens to a serving platter. Serve immediately.

### Apricot Glaze

- 1 (12-ounce) jar apricot preserves
- 4 tablespoons butter
- ⅓ cup orange-flavored liqueur, such as Triple Sec or Grand Marnier

- Heat preserves, butter and liqueur in a saucepan until well blended.

*Yield: 4 to 6 servings*

*Note: Remaining portion of Apricot Glaze is delicious served with pork or chicken.*

# PECAN ENCRUSTED RACK OF LAMB

| | |
|---|---|
| 2 tablespoons Dijon mustard | 2 (1½ to 3 pounds each) lamb rib roasts (Frenched) |
| 3 tablespoons fresh lemon juice, divided | 1 cup pecan pieces |
| 2 tablespoons olive oil | ¼ teaspoon salt |
| ½ teaspoon salt | ½ teaspoon freshly ground pepper |
| ½ teaspoon minced garlic | 2 tablespoons melted butter |
| 1 tablespoon dried tarragon | Mint jelly (optional) |
| 1½ teaspoons dried oregano | |

- Preheat oven to 425 degrees.
- Combine mustard, 2 tablespoons lemon juice and next 5 ingredients in a small bowl, stirring well. Spread mustard mixture over meaty portion of lamb racks; set aside.
- Process pecans in a food processor until ground. Combine pecans, salt, pepper, butter, and remaining 1 tablespoon lemon juice. Pat pecan mixture over the mustard-coated lamb.
- Place rack of lamb on a rack in a roasting pan, fat side scored and ribs crossed; for 35 to 40 minutes for rare; add additional 20 more minutes for well done. If roasts get too brown, cover loosely with foil for remaining cook time.
- Remove from oven and let rest 10 minutes before slicing. Serve with mint jelly, if desired.

*Yield: 4 to 6 servings*

# CHIPOTLE BAKED BRISKET

*Chipolte peppers add a smoky spicy flavor to this brisket.*

| | |
|---|---|
| 5 pound beef brisket, trimmed | 3-4 canned chipotle peppers in Adobo sauce, chopped |
| Salt and pepper to taste | ½ cup packed brown sugar |
| Garlic powder to taste | ½ cup Worcestershire sauce |
| 2 cups chunky salsa | Hamburger buns |

- Season brisket with salt, pepper and garlic powder, place in a 3-quart shallow baking dish fat side up.
- Mix salsa, peppers, sugar and Worcestershire sauce; spread over brisket. Cover and refrigerate overnight.
- Preheat oven to 300 degrees.
- Tightly cover and bake brisket 4½ to 5 hours, until tender. Cooking time will vary depending on thickness of brisket.
- Slice or shred brisket and serve with barbeque sauce on warm hamburger buns.

*Yield: 10 servings*

*Note: Add more chipotle peppers for more spice.*

---

*Many times you cannot use all of the chipotle peppers in a can before they go bad. You can freeze them by placing wax paper on top of a cookie sheet. Place peppers individually on the wax paper. Spoon the excess adobo sauce on each pepper and place in the freezer. When they are frozen, you can remove them from the freezer, place them in a zip-top storage bag, and return them to the freezer. This way you will have individual chipotle peppers ready when you need them!*

# ENGLISH ROAST BEEF WITH WHISKEY AND ALE

*Try this make it and forget it entrée with Ginger Orange Roasted Carrots (page 131) and potatoes!*

- 2½-3½ pounds English shoulder roast
- 1 (15½-ounce) can undiluted cream of onion soup
- 1 envelope dry onion soup mix
- 1 tablespoon minced garlic
- 1 (12-ounce) can beer
- 1 tablespoon Worcestershire sauce
- 2 shots of whiskey
- ¼ cup cornstarch
- ¼ cup cold water

- Place beef in a Dutch oven over medium heat turning until well browned on all sides.
- Remove from pan and place in a crock pot.
- Pour soup, soup mix, garlic, beer, Worcestershire sauce, and whiskey over beef. Stir to combine.
- Turn crockpot on medium or low and cook for 8 hours or until fork tender.
- Remove beef, skim fat from top of sauce. Slice beef and keep warm.
- Combine cornstarch and water in small bowl. Add to sauce in crock pot, turn crock pot on high and stir until thickened. Serve with sliced meat.

*Yield: 10 to 12 servings*

Note: The sauce is excellent over mashed potatoes. The roast is great for sandwiches too! If meat is to be used for sandwiches, set sauce aside and shred the meat.

---

*To skim the fat from a sauce or soup, place several ice cubes in the liquid. They will float on top and chill the sauce causing the grease to harden slightly. This will allow you to skim the fat easily from the sauce.*

# FLANK STEAK WITH SUMMER SALSA

*This easy to prepare steak has a gorgeous presentation!*

**Grilled Flank Steak**

| | | | |
|---|---|---|---|
| 2 | pounds flank steak | 1 | tablespoon Creole seasoning |
| ¼ | cup olive oil | | |

- Rub flank steak with olive oil, and season with Creole seasoning. Cover and refrigerate, marinating for 4 hours to overnight.
- Bring flank steak to room temperature. Grill over high heat to medium rare, about 6 minutes each side or longer if desired.
- Slice the steak thinly on the bias and against the grain. Fan the slices on each plate, and top with Summer Salsa.

*Yield: 4 servings*

**Summer Salsa**

| | | | |
|---|---|---|---|
| ½ | cantaloupe, peeled, seeded, and diced | ½ | cup diced red onion |
| | | | Juice of ½ lemon |
| 1 | fresh jalapeño, seeded, deveined and minced | ¼ | cup chopped fresh parsley |
| | | ¼ | cup chopped fresh cilantro |
| 1 | cup blackberries or blueberries | ¼ | cup chopped green onions |
| | | | Kosher salt to taste |
| ½ | cup diced red bell pepper | | Fresh ground pepper to taste |

- Combine all ingredients in large bowl, season with salt and pepper to taste. Cover and chill until ready to serve.

*Yield: 4 servings*

# GARLIC AND BRANDY GLAZED FILLET OF BEEF

| | | | |
|---|---|---|---|
| 4 | (6 to 7-ounce) beef tenderloin fillets, 1-inch thick | 2 | tablespoons chopped fresh parsley |
| | Salt and pepper to taste | 3 | large garlic cloves, chopped |
| 1 | tablespoon olive oil | ⅔ | cup beef broth |
| | | 2 | tablespoons brandy |

- Season fillets with salt and pepper.
- Heat oil in a large skillet over medium-high heat. Add fillets, and cook to desired doneness, about 5 minutes per side for medium-rare. Transfer fillets to serving platter and keep warm.
- Add parsley and garlic to skillet, stirring for 30 seconds, scraping the bottom of the pan to loosen browned bits from bottom of the pan. Stir in broth. Add brandy. Boil until juices are reduced to a glaze, usually about 6 minutes.
- Spoon glaze over fillets and serve immediately.

*Yield: 4 servings*

*Have you ever forgotten chill the white wine before your company arrives? You chill the wine in about an hour by placing it in container filled ½ ice and ½ water. If the wine is not completely covered by the cold water, invert the wine into the water for a few minutes before serving.*

# ITALIAN STUFFED FILLETS

*Men will enjoy this hearty entrée!*

| | | | |
|---|---|---|---|
| 4 | beef fillets (1½-inch thick) | 1 | teaspoon black pepper |
| 4 | thin slices prosciutto ham | ¼ | cup all-purpose flour |
| 4 | slices Gruyère cheese (or Swiss cheese) | 2 | eggs, whisked |
| 1 | teaspoon salt | ⅓ | cup seasoned breadcrumbs |
| | | 5 | tablespoons butter |

- Cut a slit horizontally ¾ of the way through fillets.
- Place 1 slice ham and 1 slice of cheese in center of each fillet, then close and press edges together, securing with a wooden pick, if necessary.
- Season each fillet with salt and pepper.
- Coat thoroughly with flour, dip in egg, and roll in breadcrumbs.
- Sauté fillet in butter for 5 minutes per side or to desired doneness. Remove pick before serving.

*Yield: 4 servings*

*Tom Gaston was Jackson's famous police chief. He was shot so many times, a Memphis paper simply reported, "Gaston shot again!"*

## ITALIAN ROAST BEEF

| | | | |
|---|---|---|---|
| 1 | (5 to 6-pound) rump roast | 1 | teaspoon dried oregano |
| 2-3 | cups water | 1 | teaspoon dried marjoram |
| 3 | beef bouillon cubes | | Salt and pepper to taste |
| 2 | tablespoons Worcestershire sauce | 2 | green bell peppers, seeded and sliced |
| 1 | teaspoon dried thyme | | |

- Preheat oven to 325 degrees.
- Place roast in a shallow roasting pan and bake for 40 minutes per pound.
- In saucepan, over medium heat, add bouillon cubes to water and heat until dissolved. Add pan drippings and all other ingredients; simmer 15 minutes.
- Slice roast thinly and lay in a large pan. Pour broth over the roast and cover. Refrigerate 4 to 5 hours to allow meat to marinate.
- Before serving, reheat meat but do not boil marinade. Alternately, the roast may be placed in a slow cooker on low instead of refrigerator for 4 to 5 hours to eliminate reheating step.

*Yield: 10 to 12 servings*

*Note: This is excellent served on French bread with broth as a dip.*

## SPICY GRILLED STEAK

*In a pinch for a new barbeque rub?
Try this next time you are grilling steaks!*

| | | | |
|---|---|---|---|
| 1½ | teaspoons freshly ground black pepper | 1 | tablespoon minced onion |
| ½ | teaspoon paprika | ¼ | teaspoon salt |
| ¼ | teaspoon cayenne pepper | 1 | tablespoon olive oil |
| 1 | teaspoon minced garlic | 4-6 | steaks of your choice (sirloin, fillet or t-bone) |
| ½ | teaspoon crumbled dried thyme | 1 | tablespoon unsalted butter, melted |

- In a bowl, combine first 8 ingredients to form a paste; rub on steaks.
- Grill steaks to desired doneness.
- Pour butter over steaks before serving.

*Yield: 4 to 6 servings*

*Variation: Try this spice rub on salmon!*

# MARINATED BEEF TENDERLOIN WITH HORSERADISH SAUCE

*Serve this with Herb Roasted Potatoes (page 139) and Orange Walnut Salad (page 67).*

| | | | |
|---|---|---|---|
| 1 | bottle steak marinade (such as Allegro) | 1 | tablespoon ground pepper |
| 1½ | cups vegetable oil | 2 | tablespoons dry mustard |
| ½ | cup wine vinegar | ¼ | teaspoon garlic powder |
| ¾ | cup soy sauce | 1½ | teaspoons dried parsley |
| ¼ | cup Worcestershire sauce | 1 | (2-pound) beef tenderloin, trimmed |
| ⅓ | cup lemon juice | | Horseradish Sauce |

- Combine first 10 ingredients in a large bowl; stir well. Add tenderloin to marinade, cover and refrigerate 2 hours to overnight, turning occasionally to allow meat to marinate.
- Remove tenderloin from marinade and place in a roasting pan. Roast at 450 degrees until thermometer registers 140 degrees (rare), 160 degrees (medium) or 170 degrees (well-done). Allow approximately 15 minutes per pound, depending on desired degree of doneness.
- Let stand 15 minutes before serving with Horseradish Sauce.

**Horseradish Sauce**

| | | | |
|---|---|---|---|
| ½ | cup heavy cream, whipped | 6 | tablespoons prepared horseradish |
| ½ | cup mayonnaise | 1 | teaspoon dry mustard |

- Combine all Horseradish Sauce ingredients in a bowl; stir well. Cover and chill.

*Yield: 4 servings*

*Note: You may marinate the tenderloin in a zip top bag instead of the large bowl, if desired.*

# MUSHROOM-STUFFED TENDERLOIN

*For a terrific dinner party menu serve this tenderloin with Ginger Orange Roasted Carrots (page 131), Risotto (page 154) and dinner rolls. This is an elegant entrée for the holidays!*

| | | | |
|---|---|---|---|
| 3 | bacon strips, cooked crisp and crumbled, reserving 1 tablespoon drippings | 2 | tablespoons minced fresh parsley |
| 1 | cup chopped fresh mushrooms | 1 | (2-pound) beef tenderloin, trimmed |
| 2 | tablespoons chopped onion | 1 | tablespoon butter, softened |
| 1 | garlic clove, minced | 1 | tablespoon grated Parmesan cheese |
| ¾ | cup dry breadcrumbs, divided | | Salt and pepper to taste |

- Preheat oven to 350 degrees.
- Sauté mushrooms, onion, and garlic in bacon drippings in a skillet. Remove from heat; stir in ½ cup breadcrumbs, parsley, and bacon.
- Cut a slit horizontally ¾ of the way through the tenderloin. Lightly place bread crumb mixture in the pocket; close with toothpicks or truss with cooking twine.
- Combine butter and Parmesan cheese; spread over top and sides of meat. Press remaining breadcrumbs into butter mixture.
- Place meat on a rack in a shallow roasting pan. Bake uncovered for 15 minutes. Cover and bake for 1 hour or until thermometer registers 145 degrees (medium-rare), 160 degrees (medium) or 170 degrees (well-done). Let stand for 10 minutes. Remove toothpicks before slicing.

*Yield: 6 to 8 servings*

---

*When is it done? This is a very important question when you are cooking meat. Using a meat thermometer, insert the probe into the thickest part of the meat (but not close to the bone). For beef and lamb look for an internal temperature of 130 degrees (rare), 140 degrees (medium), and 150 degrees (well done). For chicken, the temperature should reach 170 degrees (thigh meat) or 160 degrees if only cooking the breast. For pork, the temperature should be reach 150 to 160 degrees. When cooking a turkey the breast should reach 170 degrees and the thigh 180 degrees.*

# STEAK AU POIVRE

*If you love pepper, this steak is for you!*

- 2 tablespoons whole white peppercorns, crushed
- 2 tablespoons whole black peppercorns, crushed
- 4 (7-ounce) beef fillets, 1½-inches thick
- Sea salt or kosher salt
- 1 tablespoon olive oil
- 4 tablespoons butter, divided
- ⅓ cup cognac or brandy
- 1 cup half-and-half

- Press peppercorns firmly into each side of each fillet, using the heel of your hand. Season to taste with salt.

- Heat oil in a heavy skillet over medium-high heat until shimmering. Add fillets, and cook 7 minutes, or until a thick crust has formed. Turn fillets, and reduce heat to medium. Add 2 tablespoons butter, and cook fillets 6 minutes more (medium-rare), basting often with the buttery juices. Transfer fillets to 4 plates.

- Increase heat to medium-high. Add cognac to skillet, and cook approximately 1 minute to burn off alcohol.

- Whisk in half-and-half and add remaining 2 tablespoons butter. Continue whisking until sauce thickens then boil for 1 minute.

- Spoon sauce over fillets to serve.

*Yield: 4 servings*

---

*To crush peppercorns, place them in a zip top freezer bag and crush them with the bottom of a heavy skillet or a meat mallet.*

# BACON-WRAPPED MEATLOAF

*A flavorful and hearty meatloaf that your husband will enjoy.
Serve with our Grated Cheese Potatoes (page 137).*

| | | | |
|---|---|---|---|
| ½ | cup diced onions | 3 | eggs |
| ½ | cup diced celery | ¾ | cup half-and-half |
| ½ | cup diced red bell peppers | 1¼ | cups oatmeal |
| 1 | tablespoon butter | 2 | teaspoons salt |
| 2 | pounds ground sirloin | 1 | teaspoon red pepper flakes |
| ¾ | cup ketchup | 1 | pound bacon |

- Sauté onions, celery, and bell peppers in butter in small pan over medium heat. Remove from heat and allow to cool. Place cooled vegetables into a mixing bowl with remaining ingredients, except bacon; mix well.

- Line a loaf pan with bacon strips; add meat mixture to the pan. Cover with plastic wrap and place in refrigerator overnight.

- Preheat oven to 350 degrees.

- To bake, cover with foil and place loaf pan on top of a roasting pan; bake in oven for 60 minutes.

- Uncover and bake an additional 20 minutes to allow top to brown.

- Turn the loaf pan upside down to remove meatloaf onto the roasting pan, and cook an additional 20 minutes to brown bacon.

- Remove from oven and let rest for 15 to 20 minutes. Slice with a sharp knife.

*Yield: 8 servings*

# SHRIMP AND CRABMEAT AU GRATIN

*A wonderfully rich seafood dish!*

| | | | | |
|---|---|---|---|---|
| ½ | cup butter | | 1 | pound shrimp, peeled, deveined, and cooked |
| 1 | medium onion, chopped | | 2 | tablespoons grated Romano cheese |
| 2 | green onions, chopped | | 5 | ounces grated Cheddar cheese |
| 1 | rib celery, chopped | | | |
| ¼ | cup flour | | 1 | teaspoon salt |
| 1 | cup half-and-half | | ¼ | teaspoon black pepper |
| ¼ | cup dry white wine | | ¼ | teaspoon red pepper |
| 1 | tablespoon fresh parsley | | 1½ | teaspoons lemon juice |
| 1 | egg, beaten | | 1 | cup breadcrumbs |
| 1 | pound crabmeat | | | |

- Preheat oven to 350 degrees.
- Melt butter in a Dutch oven over medium heat. Add onions and celery and sauté until soft.
- Stir in flour and half-and-half slowly to make a smooth sauce. Remove from heat.
- Stir in white wine; add remaining ingredients, except breadcrumbs, blending carefully.
- Place mixture in a 1½-quart casserole dish, and top with breadcrumbs.
- Bake for 20 minutes.

*Yield: 6 to 8 servings*

---

*Two of America's most notorious criminals have come through Jackson. George "Machine Gun" Kelly was arrested here in 1922, and spent sixty days in jail. Al Capone came through Jackson in 1947, on an Illinois Central train, in his coffin.*

# NEW ORLEANS STYLE SHRIMP 'N GRITS

*Grits is the first truly American food.*

*Turner Catledge*

**Grits**

| | | | |
|---|---|---|---|
| 1½ | cups chicken broth | ¼ | teaspoon salt |
| 1½ | cups milk | 1 | cup shredded Cheddar cheese |
| ¾ | cup quick grits | | |

- Bring broth and milk to a boil in a saucepan. Stir in grits and salt; return to a boil.
- Cover and reduce heat to low.
- Cook until thick, about 5 minutes, then add cheese. Stir until cheese is melted.

**Shrimp**

| | | | |
|---|---|---|---|
| 2 | tablespoons oil | 2 | teaspoons hot pepper sauce |
| ½ | cup chopped onion | 1 | cup cooked and crumbled bacon, for garnish |
| ½ | cup chopped green pepper | | Sliced green onions, for garnish |
| ½ | cup chopped red pepper | | |
| 1 | pound medium shrimp, peeled and deveined | | Shredded Cheddar cheese, for garnish |

- Heat oil in large saucepan over medium heat. Lightly sauté onion and pepper in oil. Add shrimp and cook until pink, about 5 minutes. Season with hot pepper sauce.
- Serve shrimp over grits, and garnish with bacon, green onions, and cheese, as desired.

*Yield: 4 servings*

*Note: The grits cannot be made in advance.*

# SHRIMP CREOLE WITH SAFFRON RICE

- ¼ cup bacon drippings
- ¼ cup all-purpose flour
- 2 cups chopped onion
- 1 cup chopped celery
- 1 cup chopped green bell pepper
- 2 cloves garlic, minced
- 1 (16-ounce) can chopped tomatoes, undrained
- 1 (8-ounce) can tomato sauce
- 1 (6-ounce) can tomato paste
- 1 cup water
- 1½ teaspoons salt
- 1 teaspoon ground black pepper
- ½ teaspoon ground red pepper
- 2 bay leaves
- 1 tablespoon lemon juice
- 1 teaspoon Worcestershire sauce
- ⅛ teaspoon hot sauce
- 5 pounds jumbo shrimp, peeled, deveined, and cooked
- ½ cup finely chopped parsley
- 4 (10-ounce) packages saffron rice mix, prepared according to package directions

- Combine bacon drippings and flour in a heavy skillet. Cook over medium heat, stirring constantly, about 15 minutes, or until roux is chocolate colored.
- Stir in onions, celery, bell pepper, and garlic; cook 15 minutes, stirring often. Transfer mixture to a large Dutch oven.
- Add tomatoes and next 10 ingredients (tomato sauce through hot sauce); bring to a boil.
- Cover, reduce heat, and simmer 1 hour, stirring occasionally.
- Add shrimp to tomato mixture stirring to combine. Heating until shrimp are heated through.
- Remove bay leaves.
- Sprinkle with finely chopped parsley and serve over saffron rice.

*Yield: 12 servings*

*Note: Sauce may be frozen before the shrimp is added.*

# SHRIMP WITH SPINACH AND PINE NUTS

| | |
|---|---|
| 2 tablespoons olive oil, divided | 2 (9-ounce) bags fresh spinach |
| 2 tablespoons butter, divided | 1 pound shrimp, peeled (tails intact), deveined, and butterflied |
| 2 teaspoons blackening seasoning | |
| 8 ounces fresh mushrooms, sliced | 1 (2-ounce) bag pine nuts, toasted |
| 1 clove garlic, minced | ¼ cup crumbled blue cheese |
| 6 green onions, chopped | |

- Heat 1 tablespoon olive oil and 1 tablespoon butter with blackening seasoning in a sauté pan over medium heat. Add mushrooms and sauté until soft. Add garlic and green onions, stirring constantly being careful not to burn, about 1 to 2 minutes. Add spinach and sauté until spinach is wilted. Remove from heat and drain liquid.

- In a separate pan, sauté shrimp in remaining oil and butter over medium heat until pink, about 3 to 4 minutes.

- Spread wilted spinach evenly over a serving platter. Top with shrimp. Sprinkle with pine nuts, and blue cheese, if desired.

*Yield: 6 servings*

# CITRUS BASIL GRILLED SHRIMP

*An excellent dish to add to your summer outdoor fun! Serve with a Watermelon Margarita (page 121)!*

| | | | |
|---|---|---|---|
| ½ | cup olive oil | 2 | garlic cloves, minced |
| | Juice of 1 large lemon | 1 | teaspoon salt |
| | Juice of 1 lime | ½ | teaspoon pepper |
| 2 | tablespoons balsamic vinegar | 2 | pounds fresh shrimp, peeled (tails intact) and deveined |
| 2 | shallots, diced | | |
| 4 | large basil leaves, chopped | | |

- Whisk oil and remaining ingredients together (except shrimp) in a bowl. Pour over shrimp. Cover, chill, and marinate for 2 hours.
- Place shrimp on skewers, and grill for 10 minutes, or until just done, basting occasionally with marinade.

Yield: 4 to 6 servings

*Note: Do not overcook shrimp or it will be dry.*

---

*The first laws of Jackson were passed in January 1823. Some of these laws include: "any person or persons who shall be found guilty of the mischievous and dangerous practice of fastening matches or other combustible substances to dogs or other animals, within said town- shall forfeit and pay $5.00 for each offense." And "Any person or persons who shall run a horse race or run a horse at full speed within the incorporated limits of said town shall for each offense forfeit and pay the sum of $20.00 for each offense."*

# SPICY BAKED BARBECUE SHRIMP

*Your friends will certainly beg for this recipe when you prepare it for your next get together!*

| | | | |
|---|---|---|---|
| 1 | cup butter | ⅛ | teaspoon ground red pepper |
| ½ | cup lemon juice | 1 | tablespoon hot sauce |
| ¾ | cup Worcestershire sauce | 3 | cloves garlic, minced |
| 1 | tablespoon salt | 2½ | pounds shrimp, shells on |
| 1 | tablespoon coarsely ground pepper | 2 | lemons, sliced |
| 1 | teaspoon dried rosemary | 1 | medium onion, sliced into rings |

- Preheat oven to 400 degrees.
- Melt butter in a saucepan. Add next 8 ingredients (lemon juice through garlic), stirring to combine.
- Layer shrimp in a 3-quart baking dish. Layer lemon slices next, then onion slices on top.
- Pour butter sauce on top.
- Bake for 10 minutes, uncovered. Remove from oven and stir. Return to oven and cook 5 more minutes or until shrimp are pink.
- Serve with French bread and use remaining butter sauce for dipping.

*Yield: 8 servings*

---

*Provide guests with a variety of wines when hosting a dinner party. Think of the party as an opportunity to introduce your friends to a new variety or vineyard. Make sure that you speak with the wine merchant and explain your menu. It is also fun to pick out a bottle of wine that you have never tasted before to serve guests. Sometime, just go on a whim and pick one because the label is interesting. You never know what new wonderful vineyard you will discover!*

# MAHI MAHI WITH PINEAPPLE PAPAYA SALSA

| | | |
|---|---|---|
| 4 | mahi mahi fillets | Salt and pepper to taste |
| | Extra virgin olive oil | Pineapple Papaya Salsa |

- Preheat oven on broil.
- Rub fillets with olive oil; sprinkle with salt and pepper.
- Place fillets in a broiling pan and broil approximately 5 minutes on each side, or grill over medium hot coals until cooked through.
- Make a bed of Pineapple Papaya Salsa on each of 4 plates. Place a fillet over the salsa. Serve immediately.

*Yield: 4 servings*

**Pineapple Papaya Salsa**

| | | | | |
|---|---|---|---|---|
| 1 | tomato, chopped | | 1 | jalapeño, seeded and minced |
| 1 | cup chopped fresh pineapple | | 1 | tablespoon lemon juice |
| 1 | cup chopped fresh papaya | | 1 | teaspoon minced garlic |
| 4 | green onions, chopped | | ½ | teaspoon sea salt or kosher salt |
| ¼ | cup chopped cilantro | | | |

- Combine ingredients and chill.

*Yield: 4 servings*

# WASABI-GLAZED SALMON OVER WILTED FRESH SPINACH

*A terrific taste combination. Serve with Almond Jasmine Rice (page 159) for a trip to the Orient without your passport!*

| | | | |
|---|---|---|---|
| ½ | teaspoon wasabi powder | ⅛ | teaspoon salt |
| 1½ | teaspoons Dijon mustard | | Freshly ground pepper |
| 1 | tablespoon oil | 2 | (8-ounce) salmon fillets, preferably center cut |
| 1 | teaspoon rice wine vinegar or white wine vinegar | | Wilted Fresh Spinach |
| ½ | teaspoon sugar | | |

- Preheat oven to 450 degrees.
- In a bowl, stir together first 7 ingredients (wasabi powder through pepper); spread mixture over salmon.
- Place salmon on a greased baking sheet, and roast in oven until salmon flakes easily, approximately 10 to 15 minutes.
- Make a bed of Wilted Fresh Spinach on 2 plates. Lay the salmon fillet over the spinach.

*Note: You may substitute prepared horseradish for wasabi powder.*

**Wilted Fresh Spinach**

| | | |
|---|---|---|
| 3 | cups baby spinach leaves | Salt and pepper to taste |
| 1 | tablespoon butter | |

- Wash spinach leaves and shake off excess water.
- Melt butter in a skillet over medium heat.
- Cook spinach until leaves are just wilted. Drain, add salt and pepper to taste.

*Yield: 2 servings*

# SALMON WELLINGTON

*An elegant presentation! Serve with Herb Roasted Potatoes (page 139) and Lemon Pepper Broccolini (page 128).*

| | | | |
|---|---|---|---|
| 1 | (17.3-ounce) package frozen puff pastry (2 sheets), thawed | 4 | tablespoons, plus 2 teaspoons chopped fresh tarragon |
| 4 | (6-ounce) salmon fillets, ¾-inch thick | | Salt and pepper to taste |
| | | 1 | egg, beaten |
| 6 | tablespoons minced shallots, divided | ½ | cup dry white wine |
| | | ½ | cup white wine vinegar |
| | | ½ | cup chilled butter, diced |

- Preheat oven to 425 degrees.
- Roll out each pastry sheet on a lightly floured surface to 12-inch square. Cut each square in half to make 4 rectangles.
- Place 1 salmon fillet in the center of each sheet. Sprinkle each fillet with 1 tablespoon shallot and 1 tablespoon tarragon, add salt and pepper, as desired.
- Brush edges of rectangles with egg; fold long sides of pastry over fillets. Fold short edge of pastry over fillets and roll up pastry, enclosing fillets. Seal edges of pastry; place pastries, seam side down, on a baking sheet.
- Brush pastries with egg; bake until dough is golden brown, about 20 minutes.
- Remove from oven and let stand 10 minutes.
- Meanwhile, boil wine, vinegar, remaining 2 tablespoons shallots, and 2 teaspoons tarragon in a small saucepan until liquid is reduced to 6 tablespoons, about 8 minutes. Remove the pan from heat; whisk in 1 piece of butter at a time, letting each piece melt before adding the next. Season with salt and pepper.
- Cut pastries into thirds, and serve on plates with sauce.

*Yield: 4 servings*

---

*'Mid pleasures and palaces though we may roam, Be it ever so humble, there's no place like home.*

John Howard Payne; "Home, Sweet Home", from the opera Clari the Maid of Milan (1823).

# BAKED SALMON WITH ROASTED TOMATOES

*Add a simple rice on the side and
you will have a delicious and complete meal!*

| | | | |
|---|---|---|---|
| 6 | large plum tomatoes, cut into ⅓-inch slices | 3 | tablespoons Worcestershire sauce |
| 2 | tablespoons olive oil | 1 | tablespoon balsamic vinegar |
| ½ | teaspoon salt | ½ | teaspoon soy sauce |
| ½ | teaspoon sugar | 6 | cups baby spinach leaves, without stems |
| ½ | teaspoon freshly ground pepper | 2 | tablespoons chives |
| 6 | (6-ounce) salmon fillets | | |

- Preheat oven to 400 degrees.

- Place tomatoes in a 13x9-inch baking pan. Gently toss with oil; sprinkle with salt and sugar. Spread tomatoes in a single layer in the pan, sprinkle with pepper.

- Roast tomatoes, uncovered, until blistered, but not browned or falling apart, about 20 to 25 minutes. Transfer hot slices to baking sheet to cool.

- Increase oven heat to 450 degrees. Rinse salmon quickly; pat dry. Arrange in a single layer on a foil-lined shallow roasting pan.

- Combine Worcestershire sauce, vinegar, and soy sauce in a small bowl, setting aside 2 tablespoons of the sauce. Brush sauce over salmon and sprinkle lightly with pepper.

- Bake salmon, uncovered, until salmon flakes easily, about 10 to 15 minutes.

- Arrange spinach on a platter. Use spatula to separate fillets from skin, and transfer to the platter. Arrange tomatoes on salmon; drizzle 2 tablespoons of reserved sauce over salmon and spinach. Sprinkle with chives. Serve immediately

*Yield: 6 servings*

*Variation: May prepare the tomatoes and marinate salmon with sauce several hours ahead of serving time and refrigerate.*

# MAPLE-GLAZED SALMON

*Partner this Salmon with Angel Hair Pasta Flan (page 156) and Balsamic Roasted Asparagus (page 126) for a delicious meal.*

| | | | |
|---|---|---|---|
| 2 | tablespoons maple syrup | 1½ | teaspoons grated peeled ginger |
| 1½ | tablespoons apple juice | 1½ | teaspoons country-style Dijon mustard |
| 1½ | tablespoons lemon juice | ¼ | teaspoon five-spice powder |
| 2 | teaspoons hoisin sauce | 4 | (6-ounce) salmon fillets |

- Combine first 7 ingredients (maple syrup through five-spice powder) in a large zip-top plastic bag. Add salmon to bag and seal. Marinate in refrigerator for 30 minutes.
- Preheat broiler.
- Remove salmon from bag, reserving marinade.
- Place salmon fillets, skin side down, on a broiler rack coated with cooking spray.
- Broil 12 minutes, basting frequently with reserved marinade.

*Yield: 4 servings*

---

Fresh fish should not smell when first purchased. Odor will become more pronounced over time. Thaw frozen fish in the refrigerator and never refreeze thawed fish.

Hoisin sauce can be found in the Asian food section of your supermarket.

# PASTA WITH GARLIC SHRIMP AND ZUCCHINI

*Serve this easy dish with a Caesar salad and French bread!*

| | | | |
|---|---|---|---|
| 3 | tablespoons olive oil | 1 | pound medium shrimp, peeled (tails intact) and deveined |
| 1 | medium onion, finely chopped | 3 | garlic cloves, minced |
| 3 | medium zucchini, halved lengthwise, sliced crosswise | 3 | ripe plum tomatoes, seeded and chopped fine |
| | Salt to taste | ½ | cup basil |
| | Freshly ground pepper to taste | 1 | pound fettuccine, cooked and drained |
| 2 | tablespoons unsalted butter | | Olive oil, to taste |

- Heat olive oil in a large skillet. Add onion and zucchini, season with salt and pepper. Sauté over medium heat until tender, about 8 minutes.
- In another skillet, melt butter, add shrimp and garlic; season with salt and pepper. Sauté over high heat, about 3 minutes, until shrimp are tender and barely pink. Add tomatoes and basil. Sauté for 1 more minute.
- Combine zucchini and shrimp mixtures with the cooked fettuccine; drizzle with olive oil.
- Toss well, adjust seasonings, and serve immediately.

*Yield: 4 servings*

---

*At dinner, instead of serving butter, you can make your own oil and herb mixture as many restaurants do. In a small bowl combine one tablespoon each of crushed red pepper, dried parsley and fresh Parmesan cheese. Add one clove of minced garlic and a dash of salt. Stir to combine thoroughly. Place a small amount of the mixture in a dish with a slight rim or a bread plate at each place setting. Add extra-virgin olive oil and allow to stand at room temperature for several minutes before seating your guests. Serve with very fresh bread.*

# SEAFOOD FETTUCCINE

*Elegant and rich!*

| | | | |
|---|---|---|---|
| 4 | tablespoons butter, divided | 1 | cup sliced fresh mushrooms (optional) |
| 3 | tablespoons flour | 1 | egg yolk |
| 1 | pint heavy whipping cream | 2 | tablespoons red wine sherry |
| ¼ | pound bay scallops | 1 | pound fettuccine, cooked and drained |
| ¼ | pound crabmeat | | |
| ¼ | pound shrimp, peeled and deveined | | |

- Make a cream sauce by melting 2 tablespoons butter in saucepan; stir in flour. Whisk in heavy cream, remove from heat and set aside.
- In a large nonstick skillet, over medium heat, sauté the seafood and mushrooms in 2 tablespoons butter for 3 to 4 minutes until shrimp turn pink.
- Whisk egg yolk and sherry together and pour over seafood and mushrooms.
- Add cream sauce to seafood mixture, stirring constantly until heated through.
- Serve immediately over cooked fettuccine.

*Yield: 6 servings*

*Variation: May use more than 1 pound of fettuccine, if desired. You may also serve the sauce over 2 cups cooked rice.*

# MEDITERRANEAN SHRIMP WITH ANGEL HAIR PASTA

*Put fresh black olives in a few tablespoons of vodka or vinegar; this will keep them fresh longer. This method works well with pimentos too.*

- 3 tablespoons olive oil, divided
- 1½ pounds large shrimp, peeled (tails intact), deveined
- 1 medium onion, chopped
- 2 cloves garlic, crushed
- 2 (28-ounce) cans whole tomatoes, drained
- ¾ cup large pitted black olives, sliced
- 2 teaspoons dried oregano
- ¼ teaspoon plus 1 tablespoon salt, divided
- ¼ teaspoon freshly ground black pepper
- 1 (12-ounce) package angel hair pasta
- ½ cup feta cheese
- 2 tablespoons chopped fresh parsley

- Bring 4 quarts water to a boil in a large pot for cooking pasta.
- In a 12-inch skillet over medium-high heat, heat 2 tablespoons oil. Add shrimp, and cook 4 minutes, stirring frequently until shrimp are tender and barely pink. Use slotted spoon to transfer shrimp to a plate.
- Add remaining 1 tablespoon oil to the skillet. Sauté onion and garlic stirring frequently until onion is softened, about 3 minutes.
- Stir in tomatoes, olives, oregano, ¼ teaspoon salt, and pepper. Bring sauce to a boil, then reduce heat to low. Simmer 8 to 10 minutes until sauce has thickened, stirring occasionally to break up tomatoes.
- Meanwhile, add 1 tablespoon salt and pasta to boiling water, cook pasta according to package directions. Drain pasta.
- Return shrimp to skillet, and cook about 1 minute longer, until heated through.
- Arrange warm pasta on a serving platter. Spoon shrimp and sauce over pasta. Sprinkle with feta cheese and chopped parsley.

*Yield: 6 servings*

# SICILIAN SPAGHETTI SAUCE

*Cinnamon adds a terrific twist to this sauce.*

- 2 tablespoons olive oil
- 1 large onion, finely chopped
- 2 cloves garlic, finely chopped
- ½ pound ground pork, browned and drained
- ½ pound ground beef, browned and drained
- 2 (28-ounce) cans whole tomatoes with juice, mashed
- 2 (8-ounce) cans tomato sauce
- 1 (6.5-ounce) can tomato paste
- 2 tablespoons dried basil
- 2 tablespoons dried oregano
- 1 teaspoon cinnamon
- Salt to taste
- 1 pound pasta noodles, such as vermicelli, fettuccine or angel hair, cooked and drained
- Freshly grated Parmesan cheese, to taste

- In a stock pot, heat olive oil over medium heat. Add onion and garlic and sauté until transparent, about 5 minutes.
- Add meats, tomatoes, sauce, paste, basil, oregano, cinnamon, and salt.
- Simmer on low for at least 1 hour.
- Serve over cooked and drained pasta with Parmesan cheese on top.

*Yield: 8 servings*

*Variation: May substitute ground turkey for beef. Also, may add 1 cup sliced mushrooms (include when adding tomatoes). This sauce may also be used over eggplant, chicken, or veal as well.*

*Where there is room in the heart, there is room in the house.*

*Danish Proverb*

# BURGUNDY LASAGNA

*Enjoy the other half of the bottle of wine with dinner!*

| | | | |
|---|---|---|---|
| 1½ | pounds Italian sausage | ½ | teaspoon pepper |
| 1 | small onion, chopped very fine | ½ | bottle burgundy wine |
| 1 | small (6-ounce) can tomato paste | 1 | pound ricotta cheese |
| 1 | tablespoon sugar | 1 | (10-ounce) package frozen spinach, thawed and drained |
| ¼ | teaspoon garlic powder or ½ clove garlic, chopped | 4 | eggs |
| 2 | small (8-ounce) cans tomato sauce | 9-12 | lasagna noodles, cooked, drained, and patted dry |
| 1 | teaspoon dried oregano | 12 | slices mozzarella cheese |
| 1 | teaspoon dried basil | ½ | cup fresh grated Parmesan cheese |
| 1 | teaspoon salt | | |

- Brown sausage and onion; drain. Add next 9 ingredients and simmer for 1 hour.
- Preheat oven to 350 degrees.
- Mix ricotta, spinach, and eggs.
- Layer noodles, mozzarella cheese, ricotta mixture, and sauce in a 13x9-inch lasagna/baking pan. Repeat 2 more layers.
- Bake until bubbling, approximately 40 minutes. Top with foil if top begins to cook too rapidly. Add Parmesan cheese to top of lasagna during last few minutes of baking time. Return to oven and bake until cheese melts, approximately 5 minutes.

*Yield: 8 servings*

---

*In preparing for a big meal, it is a good idea to create place cards for the food. Write the name of each dish that you are going to serve during the meal. Place the card in the dish that you are going to use to serve the food. If you are serving the meal family style, you can arrange the dishes on the table in advance. This allows you to visualize the table, know if you need additional serving dishes and serves as a reminder to put all of the food on the table. Even seasoned hostesses forget to take something out of the oven in the rush to get the meal served.*

# PASTA WITH ALE

*Quick and easy, your whole family will enjoy this dish!*

| | | | |
|---|---|---|---|
| 2 | tablespoons butter | 1 | package (4 links) Italian sausage, cut into bite-size pieces |
| 2-3 | cloves garlic, crushed | | |
| 1 | can chicken broth | | |
| 1 | (12-ounce) bottle beer | 1 | pound tubular shaped pasta, cooked |
| 1 | (8-ounce) jar sun-dried tomatoes, drained and julienned | 4 | ounces goat cheese, crumbled |
| | | | Fresh basil, to taste |

- In a stock post over medium heat, melt butter. Add garlic and sauté until soft. Add broth, beer, tomatoes and sausage.
- Bring to a boil; simmer until reduced by half.
- Pour over cooked pasta.
- Stir in cheese and top with fresh basil.

*Yield: 4 servings*

*One way to cook pasta al dente is to bring water to a boil (add salt or oil if desired), add pasta, bring to a boil again and boil 1 minute. Remove from heat, and let stand for 12 minutes then drain. This should produce pasta al dente and will reduce your concern about "boil-overs".*

# PENNE WITH CORN, BACON, LEEKS AND TOMATOES

*A wonderful combination of flavors!*

| | | | |
|---|---|---|---|
| ½ | pound bacon, cut into ½-inch pieces | 2 | cups heavy cream |
| 3 | cups thinly sliced leeks | 1 | cup grated Parmesan cheese |
| 2 | cups chopped tomatoes | 1 | (16-ounce) package penne pasta, cooked and drained |
| 3 | cups fresh or frozen corn kernels | 1 | teaspoon red pepper flakes |
| 1 | cup chicken stock | 2 | teaspoons salt |
| | | ½ | cup freshly chopped parsley |

- Heat a large saucepan over medium-high heat. Add bacon, and sauté until ⅔ cooked. Discard drippings, leaving 2 tablespoons in the pan along with partially cooked bacon.
- Add leeks and tomatoes, sautéing for 3 minutes. Stir in corn, stock, and cream; simmer for 3 minutes.
- Remove from heat. Add Parmesan cheese and pasta. Season with red pepper, salt, and parsley. Toss to combine.
- Serve immediately.

*Yield: 6 servings*

# PROSCIUTTO VODKA SAUCE

*Don't be intimidated by the vodka,
this is a unique sauce sure to bring rave reviews from anyone!*

| | | | |
|---|---|---|---|
| 1 | teaspoon olive oil | ¼ | teaspoon salt |
| 1 | cup chopped onion | ½ | teaspoon black pepper |
| ½ | cup chopped prosciutto | 2 | tablespoons tomato paste |
| 4 | garlic cloves, minced | 2 | (14.5 ounce) cans diced tomatoes, undrained |
| 2 | tablespoons balsamic vinegar | | |
| ⅓ | cup vodka | ½ | cup half-and-half |
| 4 | teaspoons sugar | 2 | tablespoons fresh parsley, chopped |

- In a medium saucepan, heat oil over medium heat. Add onions, prosciutto, and garlic and sauté for 5 minutes.

- Stir in vinegar and next 6 ingredients (vodka through diced tomatoes); bring to a boil.

- Reduce heat to medium; cook uncovered for 30 minutes.

- Remove from heat; stir in half-and-half and parsley.

- Serve over penne or rigatoni pasta.

*Yield: 5 cups*

*Note: You may use fat free half-and-half, but the consistency of the cause will be thinner.*

# SPINACH LASAGNA

*A very rich and creamy lasagna!*

| | | | |
|---|---|---|---|
| 2 | pounds cottage cheese | 8 | ounces lasagna noodles, cooked, drained, and patted dry |
| 2 | eggs | | |
| 1 | tablespoon chopped fresh parsley | 1 | pound Monterey Jack cheese, grated |
| ½ | cup butter, softened | 2 | (10-ounce) packages frozen chopped spinach, cooked and drained |
| | Salt to taste | | |
| | Pepper to taste | | |
| | Garlic powder to taste | 1 | cup grated Parmesan cheese |

- Preheat oven to 350 degrees. Grease a lasagna pan (approximately 13x9x2-inch).
- In a large bowl, combine cottage cheese and next 6 ingredients (eggs through garlic powder).
- Cover bottom of the pan with 1 layer of noodles.
- Layer in order approximately ½ of cottage cheese mixture, ½ of Monterey Jack, ½ of spinach, and ½ of Parmesan cheese. Repeat layers.
- Bake for 30 minutes.

*Yield: 6 to 8 servings*

---

*Many times when we are dining with people that we do not know well or those that we think that we know well, we need a little help getting the conversation flowing. Here are some suggestions for questions that you can ask that each guest should be able to answer: Where in the U.S. would you live and why? How did you meet your spouse (date)? What was your most interesting vacation? What other profession would you chose if you could change professions?*

# GREEK PASTA

*Great meatless main dish!*

| | | | |
|---|---|---|---|
| ⅓ | cup sun-dried tomatoes | 1 | (28-ounce) can diced tomatoes, drained |
| 3 | tablespoons olive oil | 1 | tablespoon capers, drained |
| 1 | small sweet onion, diced | | Salt to taste |
| 2 | cloves garlic, minced | | Fresh ground pepper to taste |
| ¼ | cup pitted kalamata olives, sliced | 1 | (12-ounce) package pasta (penne, bow tie or ziti), cooked and drained |
| 1 | tablespoon dried basil or 2 tablespoons fresh, chopped basil | 4 | ounces goat cheese or feta cheese, crumbled |

- Soak sun-dried tomatoes for 5 minutes in hot water to reconstitute, drain and sliver with shears.

- Heat olive oil in a large skillet over medium heat; add onion, and sauté until tender; add garlic, and cook for 1 to 2 more minutes.

- Add olives, sun-dried tomatoes, basil, diced tomatoes, capers, salt, and pepper.

- Simmer sauce for 5 to 10 minutes.

- Toss pasta with sauce.

- Serve immediately with goat or feta cheese sprinkled on top along with fresh ground pepper.

*Yield: 4 servings*

---

*Kalamata olives are a dark eggplant color and have a flavor that can be rich and fruity. They range in length from ½ to 1-inch. When they are packaged, they are often slit to allow the wine vinegar marinade in which they are soaked to penetrate the flesh.*

# SPINACH, GORGONZOLA, AND WALNUTS OVER FETTUCCINE

| | | | |
|---|---|---|---|
| 2 | tablespoons olive oil | ¼ | cup coarsely chopped walnuts |
| 2 | large garlic cloves, minced | | Salt and pepper to taste |
| 4 | ounces fresh spinach, torn into small pieces | 8 | ounces fettuccine, cooked and drained |
| ½ | cup crumbled Gorgonzola cheese | ¼ | cup roasted marinated peppers, julienned (optional) |

- Heat olive oil in skillet; add garlic and sauté 5 minutes over low heat.
- Add spinach and cook for 5 minutes, stirring frequently. May add additional spinach, as desired.
- Stir in cheese and walnuts.
- Remove from heat, and season with salt and pepper. Serve over fettuccine. Top with roasted peppers if desired.

*Yield: 2 servings*

*Love cannot remain by itself-it has no meaning. Love has to be put into action and that action is service.*

Mother Teresa

# SPICY TOMATO THYME SAUCE

| | | | |
|---|---|---|---|
| 2 | tablespoons olive oil | ½ | cup heavy whipping cream |
| 5 | green onions, white part only, sliced thin | ½ | teaspoon salt |
| 3 | garlic cloves, minced | ¾ | teaspoon dried thyme |
| 3 | large tomatoes, peeled, seeded, and diced | ½ | teaspoon ground red pepper |

- Heat olive oil in a skillet over medium heat, add green onions and sauté for 5 minutes or until soft. Add garlic and sauté for an additional 3 minutes.
- Add tomatoes, reduce heat; simmer, stirring regularly for 10 minutes.
- Stir in cream and remaining ingredients. Simmer until slightly thickened.
- Serve over pasta, fish or chicken.

*Yield: 2 cups*

*Hint: Sauce is best when made a day ahead to allow the flavors to thoroughly blend.*

---

*After the holidays, collect all of the pictures from the Christmas cards that you receive. Place each picture on a separate page of a scrap book. If you do this every year you will have a wonderful book to remember your friends and loved ones.*

# DESSERTS

# DESSERTS

Miss Bess' Famous
   New York Cheesecake ............................ 219
Crowd Pleasing Carrot Cake
   with Cream Cheese Frosting .................... 220
Banana Delight Layer Cake ......................... 222
Mama Nell's Strawberry Nut Cake ............... 223
Golden Circle Pound Cake ......................... 224
Spiced Fresh Apple Cake ........................... 225
Banana Bundt Cake .................................. 226
No Guilt Apricot Lemon Cake ...................... 227
Chocolate Truffle Cake
   with Raspberry Sauce ............................ 228
Tunnel of Love Cupcakes ........................... 230
Chocolate Walnut Fudge Pie ....................... 231
Black and White Chess Tarts ....................... 232
New Baby Peanut Butter Pie ....................... 233
Almond Apricot Tartlets .............................. 234
Apple Cream Pie ...................................... 235
Tennessee Peach Pie ................................. 236
Farmers Market Blackberry Cobbler ............. 237
Gingered Peach Raspberry Crisp ................. 238
Brownie Trifle .......................................... 239
Chocolate Cloud Roll ................................ 240
Orange Curd Tartlets ................................ 242
Creole Bread Pudding
   with Bourbon Sauce .............................. 243

Bread Pudding with
   Tennessee Whiskey Sauce ...................... 244
Baked Apples in Puff Pastry
   with Rum Sauce ................................... 245
Crème Brûlée .......................................... 246
Warm Chocolate Soufflés ........................... 247
Toasted Almond Semi-Freddo with
   Warm Chocolate Sauce .......................... 248
Brandy Chocolate Mousse ......................... 249
Four-Pound Brownies ............................... 250
Mocha Fudge Brownies ............................. 251
Raspberry Oatmeal Bars ............................ 252
Easy Coconut Macaroons .......................... 253
Ginger Cookies ....................................... 254
Triple Threat Chocolate Chip Cookies .......... 255
Last Minute Cookies ................................. 255
Almond Cream Cheese Cookies .................. 256
Lemon Melt-Away Cookies ........................ 257
Graham Cracker Sandwiches ..................... 258
Pecan Wafers .......................................... 259
Grape Sherbet ........................................ 259
Espresso Ice Cream Sundaes ..................... 260
Hot Fudge Sauce ..................................... 261
Balsamic Glazed Strawberries
   over Ice Cream .................................... 262
Pinot Granita .......................................... 263
Almond Toffee ........................................ 264

# MISS BESS' FAMOUS NEW YORK CHEESECAKE

*The unique preparation of this fabulous cheesecake will insure no cracks in the top!*

| | | | |
|---|---|---|---|
| 4 | (8-ounce) packages cream cheese | 2 | heaping tablespoons cornstarch |
| ½ | cup (1 stick) butter | 1¼ | cups sugar |
| 16 | ounces sour cream | 1¼ | teaspoons vanilla |
| 5 | eggs | 1 | teaspoon lemon juice |

- Let cream cheese, butter, sour cream, and eggs stand at room temperature for approximately 1 hour.
- Preheat oven to 350 degrees. Grease bottom and sides of a 9-inch springform pan.
- Blend cream cheese, butter, and sour cream with an electric mixer on medium speed until smooth. Add cornstarch, sugar, vanilla and lemon juice. Increase mixer to high speed and beat until well blended.
- Beat in 1 egg at a time, continuing to beat until well incorporated.
- Pour cream cheese mixture into the prepared pan. Tap pan lightly on countertop to smooth out the top. Place in a larger roasting pan filled with enough warm water to come halfway up side of springform pan.
- Bake for 1 hour, or until top is golden. If it browns too quickly, use foil to tent.
- Turn off oven, and open door; let cheesecake cool in oven with open door for 1 hour.
- Remove cheesecake from water bath, and let cool on a wire rack. Cover and refrigerate for at least 6 hours before serving. Remove sides of springform pan just before serving.

*Yield: 12 to 16 servings*

*Note: This cheesecake is delicious served with the Raspberry Sauce on page 229.*

---

*Each new friend represents a world in us, a world possibly not born until they arrive, and it is only by this meeting that a new world is born.*

*Anaïs Nin*

# CROWD PLEASING CARROT CAKE WITH CREAM CHEESE FROSTING

*It is hard to resist this moist and delicious cake!*

*Add one teaspoon of water to egg yolks before beating (they will beat better and combine with a hot mixture better). To remove any yolk that falls into the white when separating, remove with a little of the shell or with a cold damp cloth or cotton swab.*

**Cake**

| | | | |
|---|---|---|---|
| 2 | cups sifted all-purpose flour | 2 | cups grated carrots, packed |
| 2 | teaspoons baking powder | 1 | (8-ounce) can crushed pineapple |
| 1½ | teaspoons baking soda | 1½ | cups chopped walnuts or pecans |
| 1 | teaspoon salt | 1½ | teaspoons vanilla |
| 2 | teaspoons cinnamon | | Cream Cheese Frosting Supreme |
| 1½ | cups vegetable oil | | |
| 2 | cups sugar | | |
| 4 | eggs | | |

- Preheat oven to 350 degrees. Grease and flour 3 (8-inch) round cake pans.
- Sift together flour, baking powder, soda, salt, and cinnamon; set aside.
- Combine oil and sugar in a large mixing bowl; mix well at medium speed.
- Add eggs, one at a time, beating well with each addition.
- Add flour mixture to egg mixture and continue to beat, at low speed until blended.
- Stir in carrots, pineapple, nuts, and vanilla until combined.
- Pour batter into prepared pans.
- Bake for 30 to 35 minutes or until wooden pick inserted in center comes out clean.
- Cool cake in pans on wire racks for 10 minutes. Invert onto racks and cool completely before frosting.
- Spread Cream Cheese Frosting Supreme between layers and on top and sides of cake. Store in the refrigerator.

*Crowd Pleasing Carrot Cake continued*

**Cream Cheese Frosting Supreme**

| | | | |
|---|---|---|---|
| ½ | cup (1 stick) butter, softened | 1 | (1-pound) box confectioners' sugar |
| 1 | (8-ounce) package cream cheese, softened | 1 | teaspoon vanilla |

- Beat butter and cream cheese with an electric mixer until light and fluffy, about 2 minutes.
- Add confectioners' sugar and continue to beat. Add vanilla and beat until combined.

*Yield: 10 servings*

# BANANA DELIGHT LAYER CAKE

*Banana cake with banana frosting, what a delight!*

*If your muffins, cakes or breads stick to bottom of pan, place pan on a cold damp towel for about thirty seconds then try removing.*

### Cake

| | | | |
|---|---|---|---|
| 1½ | cups sugar | 2 | cups cake flour (or self-rising flour, just omit soda) |
| ½ | cup (1 stick) butter, softened at room temperature | 1 | teaspoon soda |
| 2 | eggs | ¼ | cup buttermilk |
| 3 | ripe bananas, mashed | ½ | cup chopped pecans |
| 1 | teaspoon vanilla extract | | Banana Nut Frosting |

- Preheat oven to 325 degrees. Grease and flour 2 cake pans, 8-inch round.
- Cream sugar and butter in a large bowl with an electric mixer on medium speed.
- Add eggs, bananas, and vanilla, mixing well.
- In a separate bowl, sift together flour and soda.
- Add flour mixture, alternating with buttermilk, to the batter and mix on low speed.
- Fold in pecans.
- Pour batter into prepared pans and bake for 25 minutes, or until toothpick inserted in the middle comes out clean. Do not overcook.
- Cool cake in pans on wire rack before inverting.
- Using a small fork, prick holes for frosting to penetrate cake.
- Frost bottom layer, add top layer, and frost top and sides.
- Store in the refrigerator.

### Banana Nut Frosting

| | | | |
|---|---|---|---|
| ½ | cup (1 stick) butter, softened at room temperature | 1 | (1-pound) box confectioners' sugar |
| 3 | ripe bananas, mashed | 1 | teaspoon lemon juice |
| | | 2 | cups chopped pecans |

- Beat butter and bananas well with electric mixer until smooth. Add sugar, juice, and pecans. Mix until well combined.
- Chilled to thicken if necessary. (There will be more icing than needed.)

*Yield: 10 servings*

# MAMA NELL'S STRAWBERRY NUT CAKE

**Cake**

| | | | |
|---|---|---|---|
| 1 | box white cake mix | 1 | cup pecan pieces |
| 1 | (3-ounce) package strawberry gelatin | 4 | eggs |
| | | 1 | cup vegetable oil |
| 1 | cup sliced fresh or frozen strawberries | ½ | cup milk |
| | | | Strawberry Frosting |
| 1 | cup coconut | | |

- Preheat oven to 350 degrees. Grease and flour a 13x9x2-inch baking pan.
- Combine all cake ingredients in a mixing bowl. Beat with an electric mixer on medium speed until smooth.
- Pour into prepared pan and bake for 35 to 40 minutes or until a wooden pick inserted in middle of cake comes out clean.
- Cool in pan on wire rack.
- When cool, spread frosting over cake.
- Cover and chill.

**Strawberry Frosting**

| | | | |
|---|---|---|---|
| 1 | (1-pound) box confectioners' sugar | ½ | cup coconut |
| | | ½ | cup pecan pieces |
| ½ | cup (1 stick) margarine, melted | 2 | tablespoons milk |
| ½ | cup sliced strawberries | | |

- Combine all frosting ingredients together in a large bowl and beat with an electric mixer until smooth.

*Yield: 12 servings*

---

*Use flowers from your garden to garnish your trays, cakes or dinner plates. A simple day lily bloom in the middle of a Bundt cake is very elegant. Make sure that you shake all of the critters off of the flower before adding it to the top of the cake!*

# GOLDEN CIRCLE POUND CAKE

*This cake is enjoyed in Jackson, the "Golden Circle," and beyond!*

| | | | |
|---|---|---|---|
| 1 | pound (4 sticks) butter, softened at room temperature | 1 | (1-ounce) bottle of lemon extract |
| 3 | cups sugar | 3 | cups sifted flour |
| 10 | eggs | 1 | cup chopped pecans |

- Preheat oven to 300 degrees. Spray a large tube pan with non-stick cooking spray.
- Cream butter and sugar with an electric mixer until fluffy.
- Add eggs one at a time, beating well with each addition.
- Mix in extract on low speed; stir in flour.
- Fold in pecans.
- Pour batter into prepared pan. After baking for 45 minutes, reduce oven temperature to 250 degrees, and continue baking for another 1½ hours.
- Cool in the pan until cake loosens from sides. Invert cake onto serving plate.

*Yield: 16 servings*

---

*The true Southern watermelon is chief of this world's luxuries, king by the grace of God over all the fruits of the earth. When one has tasted it, he knows what the angels eat.*

Mark Twain

# SPICED FRESH APPLE CAKE

*Great for the holiday season!*

| | | | |
|---|---|---|---|
| 2 | cups sugar | 1 | teaspoon salt |
| 2 | eggs | 1½ | teaspoons baking soda |
| 1¼ | cups vegetable oil | 1 | cup broken (not chopped) pecans |
| 3 | cups all-purpose flour | 5 | large fresh Rome apples, peeled, cored, and cut into 1-inch pieces |
| 1½ | teaspoons cinnamon | | |
| 2 | teaspoons freshly ground nutmeg | | |

- Preheat oven to 325 degrees. Spray Bundt pan with non-stick cooking spray.
- Mix sugar, eggs, and vegetable oil in a medium bowl with a wooden spoon only, and set aside.
- In a large separate bowl, mix flour, cinnamon, nutmeg, salt, and baking soda.
- Fold flour mixture into egg mixture; batter will be thick.
- Fold in pecans and apples. (There will be more apples than batter.)
- Pour into Bundt pan.
- Bake for 1 hour and 15 to 25 minutes until toothpick inserted in middle of cake comes out clean.
- Let cool for 20 minutes.

*Yield: 10 to 12 servings*

---

*This cake is delicious served with vanilla whipped cream and freshly grated nutmeg. To make whipped cream, add 1 tablespoon vanilla to heavy cream and whip.*

# BANANA BUNDT CAKE

*This cake will melt in your mouth!*

**Banana Cake**

| | | | |
|---|---|---|---|
| 1 | box yellow cake mix | 3 | ripe bananas, mashed |
| 1 | (3.4-ounce) box instant vanilla pudding mix | 1/3 | cup water |
| 1/3 | cup vegetable oil | 1 | tablespoon sour cream |
| 4 | eggs | | Buttery Glaze |
| | | | Easy Cream Cheese Frosting |

- Preheat oven to 325 degrees. Grease and flour a Bundt pan.
- Mix all Banana Cake ingredients (cake mix through sour cream) in a large bowl and pour into a prepared pan.
- Bake for 50 to 55 minutes.
- Pour Buttery Glaze over cake, and bake another 5 minutes or until a toothpick inserted in middle comes out clean.
- Cool and invert onto cake plate.
- Spread Easy Cream Cheese Frosting over the cake.
- Cover and chill until ready to serve.

**Buttery Glaze**

| | | | |
|---|---|---|---|
| 1/2 | stick butter or margarine | 1/4 | cup water |
| 1/2 | cup sugar | | |

- Melt butter, sugar, and water in a small saucepan. Bring to a boil.

**Easy Cream Cheese Frosting**

| | | | |
|---|---|---|---|
| 1 | (8-ounce) package cream cheese, softened | 1 | teaspoon vanilla |
| 1/2 | stick (4 tablespoons) butter or margarine, softened at room temperature | 1 | (1-pound) box confectioners' sugar |

- Mix cream cheese, butter and vanilla with an electric mixer on medium speed until light and fluffy.
- Slowly add confectioners' sugar, continuing to beat until frosting is spreadable.

*Yield: 10 to 12 servings*

*Note: You may garnish this cake with slices of bananas immediately before serving.*

---

*You can freeze cakes for up to 4 months. It is best to freeze them before icing. Wrap the layers individually in plastic wrap once they cool to room temperature. Then wrap them in aluminum foil. Thaw the cake for 2 to 4 hours at room temperature before unwrapping.*

# NO GUILT APRICOT LEMON CAKE

*You will not be able to tell that is dessert is low-fat! Terrific for the calorie counter!*

| | | | |
|---|---|---|---|
| 1 | box lemon cake mix | ½ | cup sugar |
| 1 | carton egg substitute, or 2 eggs | 1½ | cups apricot nectar (1 small can), divided |
| 1 | individual package Butter Buds | | Grated zest of 1 lemon (optional) |

- Preheat oven to 350 degrees.
- Grease and flour a Bundt pan.
- With an electric mixer, beat cake mix, egg substitute, butter buds, sugar, 1 cup of the apricot nectar, and grated zest until smooth.
- Pour into the Bundt pan.
- Bake for 40 to 45 minutes.
- Poke holes in cake with a fork
- Pour remaining ½ cup nectar over cake.
- Let cake cool in the pan.
- Invert cake onto serving plate.

*Yield: 12 servings*

---

*My grandmother always taught me, "never return a dish empty". If a neighbor was kind enough to bring over a cake or casserole, my grandmother and mother would return the dish with cookies or another casserole inside as a thank you. I try to continue this tradition that I learned at home.*

# CHOCOLATE TRUFFLE CAKE WITH RASPBERRY SAUCE

*An excellent way to end an elegant meal!*

*Jackson is in the South, but we are lucky enough to have one "good" snow each year, sometimes more than that. But, since we are in the South, everything shuts down if it does snow. Therefore, there is no school on snow days. This recipe for "Snow" Cream will give you something to create inside (where it is warm) with the snow that you collect. Take one 12-ounce can of sweetened condensed milk, one can evaporated milk, two teaspoons vanilla and a bowlful of snow. Mix the milks and the vanilla. Gradually beat in the snow and mix until the cream is the consistency of ice cream.*

**Chocolate Truffle Cake**

| | | | |
|---|---|---|---|
| ½ | cup water | 1 | cup unsalted butter, softened |
| 1⅓ | cups sugar, divided | 5 | extra large eggs |
| 1 | cup semi-sweet chocolate chips | | Glaze |
| | | | Raspberry Sauce |
| 8 | ounces unsweetened chocolate, chopped | | Fresh Raspberries to garnish (optional) |

- Preheat oven to 350 degrees; position rack in center of oven.
- Butter a 9-inch cake pan, and line bottom with wax paper, buttering paper on both sides.
- In a medium saucepan, bring water and 1 cup of sugar to a rolling boil, turn off heat.
- Add chocolate chips and unsweetened chocolate, stirring until melted.
- Add butter to chocolate mixture, whisk to combine.
- In a large bowl, whisk eggs with remaining ⅓ cup of sugar until slightly thickened.
- Fold chocolate mixture into egg mixture, and pour into prepared pan.
- Place pan inside a roasting pan, so that the sides do not touch.
- Pour hot water in outer pan to level of ½-inch up the wall of the pan
- Bake 30 minutes. Cake should be dry but not firm.
- Remove from oven and cool 15 to 20 minutes. Cover cake with plastic wrap.
- Invert onto a flat plate. Peel off wax paper.
- Place a flat plate on top of cake, and invert again. Remove plastic, and cool completely.
- Drizzle glaze over cake.
- To serve, spoon Raspberry Sauce onto dessert plates. Place a slice of cake on each plate on top of sauce and garnish with fresh raspberries.

## Chocolate Truffle Cake continued

**Glaze**

| | | | |
|---|---|---|---|
| ½ | cup confectioners' sugar | 2 | tablespoons milk |

- For glaze, mix ingredients until smooth. Glaze will be thin enough to drizzle.

**Raspberry Sauce**

| | | | |
|---|---|---|---|
| 2½ | cups fresh raspberries, or 1 (10-ounce) box frozen raspberries, thawed | ½ | cup confectioners' sugar |
| | | ¼ | cup raspberry liqueur (optional) |

- Puree ingredients in a blender or a processor. Pour through mesh strainer.

*Yield: 1½ cups*

*Variation: You may make a blackberry sauce by substituting blackberries and blackberry liqueur in the sauce.*

*Yield: 10 to 12 servings*

---

*You don't have to cook fancy or complicated masterpieces-just good food from fresh ingredients.*

Julia Child

# TUNNEL OF LOVE CUPCAKES

*Once you bite into this cupcake, you will fall in love!*

| | | | |
|---|---|---|---|
| 1 | box chocolate cake mix | 1 | teaspoon vanilla |
| 1¼ | cups water | | Dash of salt |
| 4 | eggs, divided | 1 | cup (6-ounces) chocolate chips |
| ⅓ | cup sugar | | Grand Mariner Buttercream Frosting |
| 1 | (8-ounce) package cream cheese, softened | | |

- Preheat oven to 350 degrees. Place cupcake liners in muffin pans.
- Prepare cake according to directions on package using water and 3 eggs.
- Fill muffin tins ⅔ full with prepared cake mix.
- Cream sugar and cream cheese at medium speed with an electric mixer. Beat in remaining egg, vanilla and salt; stir in chocolate chips.
- Drop 1 teaspoon of cream cheese mixture on top of each cupcake.
- Bake according to directions on package for cupcakes, approximately 18 to 23 minutes.
- Cool cupcakes and frost with Grand Marnier Buttercream Frosting.

*Yield: 24 cupcakes*

**Grand Marnier Buttercream Frosting**

| | | | |
|---|---|---|---|
| 1 | cup (2 sticks) unsalted butter, softened | ¼ | teaspoon salt |
| | | ½ | tablespoon vanilla extract |
| 4 | cups (1-pound) confectioners' sugar | 1 | tablespoon Grand Marnier (or more to taste) |

- Cream butter and sugar with an electric mixer on medium speed until light and fluffy. Add salt, vanilla, and Grand Marnier and beat until creamy and fluffy, about 1 minute.

*Yield: 3 cups frosting (enough to frost 24 cupcakes)*

*Note: In frosting, you may omit liqueur by increasing vanilla to 1½ tablespoons. Any frosting you have left over is delicious sandwiched between oatmeal cookies.*

---

*Serve cupcakes as dessert for your next dinner party. They are just as delicious as a slice of cake and make those who eat them feel like a child again. Decorate them with frosting and small candy. You could also use gel icing to monogram the cupcakes for a small dinner party. Practice your technique in advance and amaze your guests!*

# CHOCOLATE WALNUT FUDGE PIE

| | | | |
|---|---|---|---|
| 2 | squares unsweetened chocolate | ¼ | cup corn syrup |
| ¼ | cup (4 tablespoons) butter | 1 | teaspoon vanilla |
| ¾ | cup sugar | ¼ | teaspoon salt |
| ½ | cup brown sugar | 3 | eggs |
| ½ | cup milk | 1 | cup finely chopped walnuts |
| | | 1 | (9-inch) pie shell, unbaked |

- Preheat oven to 350 degrees.
- In a large saucepan over low heat, stir chocolate with butter until melted and combined.
- Remove from heat.
- Add sugar, brown sugar, milk, corn syrup, vanilla, salt, and eggs. Whisk until well blended.
- Fold in nuts.
- Pour into pie shell, and bake 45 to 55 minutes until filling is puffed. Allow to cool.
- Serve warm with ice cream.

*Yield: 8 servings*

*Use glass or plastic measuring cups for liquids. You should use the smallest cup available for the measurement. The larger measuring cups are not accurate for measuring small amounts of liquid. Pour the liquid into the cup and make sure that it comes to a rest before your read the measurement.*

# BLACK AND WHITE CHESS TARTS

*This versatile recipe makes individual vanilla tarts and chocolate tarts. What could be better?*

| | | | |
|---|---|---|---|
| ½ | cup (1 stick) butter | 6 | tablespoons buttermilk |
| 1½ | cups sugar | 10-11 | frozen tart shells |
| 3 | eggs | 2 | tablespoons cocoa |
| 1 | teaspoon vanilla | | |

- Preheat oven to 350 degrees.
- Melt butter in a large bowl in the microwave, and cool.
- Using an electric mixer on medium speed, beat melted butter and sugar. Add eggs 1 at a time. Add vanilla and buttermilk. Beat until smooth.
- Fill 5 tart shells ⅔ of the way full with batter.
- Place filled tart shells on a baking sheet with a rim.
- Add cocoa to the remaining batter stirring to combine. Fill remaining tart shells ⅔ full with chocolate batter.
- Place chocolate tarts on baking sheet.
- Bake for 30 minutes.
- Lower heat to 300 degrees, and bake an additional 10 minutes, until tarts are brown and set. Do not overbake.

*Yield: 10 to 11 tarts*

---

*You can easily make your own candied flowers. Hold the flower by the stem with a pair of tweezers. Then, using a child's paintbrush, brush the petals with beaten egg whites at room temperature. Sprinkle the flowers with superfine sugar and allow to dry on a baking sheet lined with wax paper. Store these in an airtight container. They should keep up to one year.*

# NEW BABY PEANUT BUTTER PIE

*This peanut butter fudge pie is delivered to many a new mother in Jackson! It may explain our large families!!*

| | |
|---|---|
| 1½ cups heavy whipping cream, divided | 1 chocolate sandwich cookie pie shell |
| 3 tablespoons butter | 4 ounces cream cheese, softened |
| 1 (6-ounce) package semi-sweet chocolate chips | ⅓ cup creamy peanut butter |
| | ½ cup confectioners' sugar |

- Simmer ¾ cup heavy whipping cream and butter in a medium saucepan over low heat until butter is melted, whisking until combined.
- Remove the pan from heat and add chocolate; whisking until chocolate is melted and mixture is smooth.
- Pour fudge mixture into pie shell.
- Cover and chill for 1 to 2 hours.
- In a small bowl, using an electric mixer on medium speed, beat cream cheese until smooth. Add peanut butter and confectioners' sugar beating until smooth.
- In a separate bowl, whip the remaining ¾ cup heavy cream until soft peaks form.
- Gently fold whipped cream into peanut butter mixture.
- Remove fudge pie from refrigerator, spread peanut butter mixture evenly over fudge layer.
- Cover and chill overnight.
- Garnish with chopped peanuts, chocolate curls or drizzle melted chocolate drizzled over pie.

*Yield: 8 servings*

---

*How to make chocolate shavings. Melt chocolate squares or morsels in a loaf pan lined with plastic wrap. Refrigerate until hard. Once hard, remove from pan and leave at room temperature for 1 to 2 hours. Take a sharp knife (or vegetable peeler) and place it on the end of the chocolate block away from you. Press down gently and pull the knife over the chocolate toward you.*

# ALMOND APRICOT TARTLETS

*These pretty tarts make a wonderful luncheon dessert!*

**Tartlets**

| | | | |
|---|---|---|---|
| 16 | unbaked tart shells, at room temperature | 1 | teaspoon almond extract |
| ¾ | cup almond paste | ¼ | teaspoon vanilla extract |
| 6 | tablespoons unsalted butter, softened at room temperature | 1 | tablespoon finely grated orange zest |
| 1 | cup confectioners' sugar | ⅓ | cup apricot preserves (chunky style) |
| 2 | eggs | 48 | sliced almonds |
| 1 | egg yolk | | Confectioners' sugar for garnish |

- Preheat oven to 350 degrees.
- In a mixer or a food processor, beat almond paste and butter until smooth and creamy, with no chunks of almond paste.
- Add next 6 ingredients (sugar through orange zest) and mix until smooth and well blended.
- Spoon filling ¾ full into tart shells.
- Spoon 1 teaspoon apricot preserves into center of each tart.
- Place 3 almond slices on top in a flower design.
- Place tarts on cookie sheet and bake until crust is golden, not too brown, 20 to 25 minutes.
- Remove from oven and allow to cool for 10 minutes.
- Remove from aluminum pie pans before serving and lightly dust with confectioners' sugar.
- Serve at room temperature.

*Yield: 16 servings*

---

*To make vanilla sugar, break a vanilla bean in 2 to 3 pieces and bury in 2 cups sugar in a tightly sealed container. Let stand for 1 week. Use the flavored sugar in coffee, to flavor whipped cream, over fruit, or in baking recipes. The sugar will keep up to six months.*

# APPLE CREAM PIE

*Everyone will ask for seconds when you serve this variation of the traditional apple pie.*

**Pie**

- 2 tablespoons flour
- 1/8 teaspoon salt
- 3/4 cup sugar
- 1 egg
- 1 cup sour cream
- 1 teaspoon vanilla
- 2 cups peeled, diced apples
- 1 (9-inch) pie shell, unbaked

- Preheat oven to 400 degrees.
- Sift together flour, salt, and sugar.
- Add egg, sour cream, and vanilla, beating until batter is smooth and thin.
- Stir in apples.
- Pour mixture into pie shell.
- Bake for 15 minutes, then reduce heat to 350 degrees and bake 30 minutes more.

**Topping**

- 1/3 cup sugar
- 1/3 cup flour
- 1 teaspoon cinnamon
- 1/4 cup butter, cut into small pieces

- Mix topping ingredients together.
- Remove from oven and sprinkle topping evenly over pie.
- Return to oven, increasing heat to 400 degrees, and bake 10 minutes, until brown.

*Yield: 6 to 8 servings*

# TENNESSEE PEACH PIE

*A summertime favorite!*

| | | | |
|---|---|---|---|
| 1 | (9-inch) deep dish pie shell | ¾ | cup sugar |
| 3 | large ripe peaches, peeled, pitted and sliced | 1 | egg |
| ⅓ | cup butter, softened | 1 | teaspoon vanilla |
| ⅓ | cup self-rising flour | ⅛ | teaspoon almond extract or 1 tablespoon amaretto |

- Preheat oven to 400 degrees.
- Prick the bottom of shell with a fork and partially bake pie shell for 4 minutes.
- Place the sliced peaches in the pie shell. Make sure that the peaches are below the rim of the crust.
- Mix the butter and remaining ingredients in a medium-sized bowl. Pour butter and flour mixture evenly over the peaches.
- Place the pie on a cookie sheet.
- Bake for 15 minutes. Reduce oven temperature to 300 degrees for 45 minutes. Cover the crust if it browns too quickly.
- Serve with ice cream or fresh whipped cream.

*Yield: 6 to 8 servings*

---

*When buying peaches, look for gold or yellow skin. To ripen peaches, store loosely covered in a paper bag. Check daily. They are ripe when they yield to slight pressure.*

# FARMERS MARKET BLACKBERRY COBBLER

*This cobbler is so quick and easy you can make it anytime!*

| | | | |
|---|---|---|---|
| 2 | pints fresh blackberries or 4 cups frozen, thawed and drained | 1 | teaspoon baking powder |
| 1 | tablespoon lemon juice | 1 | egg, beaten |
| 1 | cup flour | 6 | tablespoons butter, melted |
| 1 | cup sugar | 1 | tablespoon dark brown sugar |
| | | ¼ | teaspoon ground cinnamon |

- Preheat oven to 350 degrees.
- Wash blackberries well, drain.
- Place blackberries in an 8x8-inch baking dish and sprinkle with lemon juice.
- Mix flour, sugar, baking powder, and egg in a medium-sized bowl with a fork. It will be dry and crumbly.
- Sprinkle dry mixture evenly over blackberries, and drizzle with melted butter.
- Sprinkle brown sugar, followed by cinnamon evenly over flour mixture.
- Bake for 35 to 40 minutes, or until golden brown and bubbly. (Sauce thickens as it cools.)
- Serve warm with ice cream.

*Yield: 6 to 8 servings*

*Variation: This recipe works well with blueberries, too!*

---

*To soften lumpy brown sugar, place in a dish with a slice of apple and microwave for 15 seconds or until soft. Or add a slice of bread to bag and sugar will soften in a few hours. To keep your brown sugar from hardening, place a ball of aluminum foil in the bag.*

# GINGERED PEACH RASPBERRY CRISP

*This technique produces a perfectly cooked crisp every time!*

### Topping

| | | | |
|---|---|---|---|
| 1 | cup all-purpose flour | ½ | cup (1-stick) butter, slightly softened |
| ½ | cup packed brown sugar | | |
| ¼ | cup granulated sugar | ½ | cup sliced almonds |
| | Pinch of salt | ¼ | cup old fashioned oats |

- Combine flour, brown sugar, granulated sugar, salt, butter, almonds and oats in a small bowl.
- Using your fingers, blend mixture together until well combined and crumbly. Cover and chill until ready to use.

### Filling

- 1 tablespoon fresh lemon juice
- 2 teaspoons cornstarch
- 4 cups sliced peaches or 2 (16-ounce) packages frozen peaches
- 2 cups fresh raspberries or 1 (12-ounce) package frozen raspberries, thawed and drained
- ¼ cup granulated sugar
- 2 teaspoons fresh grated ginger

- Preheat oven to 375 degrees.
- In a small bowl combine lemon juice and cornstarch.
- In a large bowl, combine peaches, raspberries, granulated sugar, and ginger. Add cornstarch mixture and stir to coat fruit.
- Pour fruit mixture into an 8x8-inch baking dish.
- Sprinkle ½ of the topping over fruit. Return remainder of topping to refrigerator.
- Place dish on a baking sheet, and bake for 20 minutes. Remove from the oven and crumble remaining topping over the crisp. Return to oven and bake an additional 20 minutes or until lightly browned and bubbly.

*Yield: 6 servings*

*Note: If the butter becomes too soft, this mixture will not "crumble". Cover and chill. When the butter cools, the mixture will crumble easily.*

---

**Descriptions of different types of pans:**

**springform** *round deep pan with tall removable sides*

**jelly-roll pan** *15x10x1-inch used to make sponge cake and jelly rolls often called a baking sheet or cookie sheet.*

**tube pan** *tall sided round cake pan with a tube in the center, usually used for angel food cakes*

# BROWNIE TRIFLE

*This easy dessert makes beautiful presentation.
Use it for your next supper club or bring a dish!*

| | | | |
|---|---|---|---|
| 1 | (19.8-ounce) fudge brownie mix (plus ingredients called for on package) | 8 | (1.4-ounce) toffee flavored candy bars, crushed |
| 1 | (3.5-ounce) instant chocolate mousse mix (plus ingredients called for on package) | 1 | (12-ounce) container frozen whipped topping, thawed |
| | | | Chocolate curls for garnish |

- Prepare brownie mix and bake according to package directions in a 13x9-inch baking pan.
- Let cool and crumble.
- Prepare chocolate mousse according to package directions, omit chilling.
- Place half of the crumbled brownies in the bottom of a deep straight-sided clear bowl.
- Top with ½ each of mousse, candy bars, and whipped topping.
- Repeat layers with remaining ingredients, ending with the whipped topping.
- Cover and chill for 8 hours.
- Garnish with chocolate curls.

*Yield: 14 servings*

*Variation: After preparing brownie, prick top of warm brownies at 1-inch intervals using a fork; drizzle with ½ cup Kahlúa (or 4 tablespoons strong brewed coffee plus 1 tablespoon sugar). Cool, crumble, and prepare as directed above.*

---

*Make your own chocolate covered strawberries! Melt the desired amount of chocolate in the top of a very dry double boiler. (You can melt it in the microwave if you watch carefully to make sure that it does not burn.) Have your strawberries washed and dried. When the chocolate is melted, dip the strawberries in the chocolate, turning to coat. Lay on wax paper and allow chocolate to harden. Store in the refrigerator. These are a wonderful hostess gift or a beautiful garnish. You could also serve them as dessert.*

# CHOCOLATE CLOUD ROLL

*Your guests will be impressed with this delicious and decadent dessert!*

### Cake

| | | | |
|---|---|---|---|
| 6 | ounces bittersweet chocolate, broken into small pieces | ¼ | teaspoon salt |
| 3 | tablespoons water | 2-3 | tablespoons Dutch-processed cocoa powder, divided |
| 6 | large eggs at room temperature, separated | | Confectioners' sugar for garnish |
| ⅔ | cup sugar, divided | | |

- Preheat oven to 350 degrees.

- Grease a 15x10x1-inch jelly-roll pan. Line the pan with a large piece of waxed paper (19-inches), letting paper hang over the ends by 2-inches.

- In a small saucepan over low heat, melt chocolate with water, stirring constantly. Once melted, cool to lukewarm.

- In a large bowl, beat egg yolks, ⅓ cup sugar and salt in a large bowl with an electric mixer until thick and pale, about 5 to 8 minutes.

- Fold in chocolate and stir until blended.

- In a clean, dry bowl with clean beaters, beat egg whites until soft peaks form. Gradually add remaining ⅓ cup sugar, and beat until egg whites hold stiff peaks. Fold ⅓ of egg whites into chocolate mixture to lighten, then fold in remaining whites gently but thoroughly.

- Spread batter evenly into the prepared pan. Bake in center of oven until puffed and dry on top, about 15 to 18 minutes.

- Remove pan from oven to cool. Cover top of cake with 2 layers of damp paper towels, and let stand 5 minutes. Remove paper towels, and let cool completely. Using a sharp knife, loosen edges.

- Sift 1 tablespoon cocoa powder over cake layer. Overlap 2 layers of waxed paper lengthwise over cake. Place a baking sheet or a large tray over paper, and invert cake onto it. Gently peel off waxed paper lining. (Don't worry if cake breaks, it will hold together when rolled.)

---

*For fluffy whipped cream, freeze bowl, cream and beaters for 10 minutes before beginning to whip the cream. Whip just until stiff peaks form. If you whip cream too long it will become butter!*

## Chocolate Cloud Roll continued

**Filling**

| | | | |
|---|---|---|---|
| 1 | cup heavy whipping cream | 2 | tablespoons orange liqueur (optional) |
| 3 | tablespoons sifted confectioners' sugar | 1 | teaspoon finely grated orange zest |

- To make filling, beat cream with confectioners' sugar and orange liqueur on medium speed of electric mixer just until stiff peaks form. Do not overbeat. Fold in orange zest.
- To assemble cake, spread filling evenly over cake. Put a long serving platter next to the long side of the cake pan and using the waxed paper as an aid, roll up the cake jelly roll style, beginning with the long side.
- Carefully transfer rolled cake to the platter with the seam side down, using the waxed paper to slide cake.
- Dust the cake generously with cocoa and confectioners' sugar.
- Cover loosely and chill well.
- This may be prepared the day before.
- Garnish with raspberries or strawberries.

*Yield: 8 to 10 servings*

---

*Southern barbeque is the closest thing we have in the U.S. to Europe's wines and cheeses; drive a hundred miles and the barbeque changes.*

John Shelton Reed

# ORANGE CURD TARTLETS

*You can easily adapt this recipe to make lemon or lime curd!*

- 3-4 oranges at room temperature (enough to yield ⅔ cup juice)
- 1⅔ cups sugar
- ½ cup (1 stick) unsalted butter at room temperature
- 4 extra large eggs at room temperature
- ⅛ teaspoon salt
- 2 (15-count) packages of mini phyllo shells, baked as directed on package

- Remove zest from oranges with a zester or vegetable peeler. Be careful to avoid the white pith.
- Squeeze oranges to make ⅔ cup juice, set aside.
- Place zest in a food processor fitted with a steel blade.
- Add sugar, and process for 2 minutes until zest is finely minced.
- In a separate bowl, cream butter and sugar. Add orange zest.
- Beat in eggs, one at a time.
- Add juice and salt, mixing until well combined.
- Pour mixture into a medium saucepan and cook over low heat, whisking continuously for about 10 minutes until mixture is thick and smooth. Curd is ready when it coats the back of a spoon and leaves a clean line when you run your finger through the curd.
- Pour into a container; cover with plastic wrap directly on top of the curd.
- To prepare tarts, spoon curd into baked shells; garnish as desired.

*Note: Curd can be stored in the refrigerator for 2 weeks.*

*Variation: Substitute lemon or lime juice and zest for orange juice and zest. The curd is also delicious served with angel food cake or pound cake.*

---

*Make "blueberry flowers" as a creative garnish for the Orange Curd Tartlets. Place one blueberry on the edge of the tartlet. Add one mint leaf on either side of the blueberry so that it resembles a flower.*

# CREOLE BREAD PUDDING WITH BOURBON SAUCE

*Bananas and pineapples give this dessert a unique flavor!*

**Pudding**

| | |
|---|---|
| 1 | large loaf stale French bread |
| 2 | (12-ounce) cans evaporated milk |
| 2¼ | cups water |
| 2 | teaspoons almond extract |
| 4 | beaten eggs |
| 2 | cups sugar |
| 1 | teaspoon vanilla |
| 1 | teaspoon cinnamon |
| 1 | cup golden raisins |
| 1-2 | ripe bananas, sliced |
| 1 | (8-ounce) can crushed pineapple |
| ⅔ | stick melted butter |
| | Quick Bourbon Sauce |

- Preheat oven to 350 degrees.
- Tear bread apart and place in a 13x9-inch baking dish. Do not over fill.
- Pour evaporated milk and water evenly over the bread.
- In a small bowl, mix almond extract, eggs, sugar, vanilla and cinnamon. Pour over bread mixture in baking dish.
- Add raisins, bananas, pineapple, and butter to bread mixture. Toss well to coat bread and distribute fruit evenly.
- Bake for 45 to 55 minutes or until golden brown and firm, but not dry.
- Serve with Quick Bourbon Sauce.

**Quick Bourbon Sauce**

| | |
|---|---|
| ½ | cup (1 stick) butter |
| 1 | cup milk |
| 1 | cup sugar |
| 2 | tablespoons cornstarch |
| ⅓ | cup bourbon |

- Combine butter, milk, and sugar in a medium-sized, heavy saucepan over medium heat.
- Cook until butter melts and sugar is dissolved, stirring constantly.
- Combine cornstarch and water in a small bowl and mix well. Add cornstarch mixture to butter mixture, stirring constantly.
- Add bourbon, and bring mixture to a boil. Cook for 1 minute; and remove from heat.

*Yield: 12 to 14 servings*

---

*Make individual bread puddings by dividing the batter among individual (oiled) ramekins. Place on a baking sheet together and bake for 15 to 20 minutes. To serve, insert knife around edge of ramekin, invert ramekin onto a cutting board. Use a spatula to transfer to a plate. Garnish the plate with dollops of whipped cream (either fresh or use frozen with a pastry tip) and put fresh berries on top of whipped cream.*

# BREAD PUDDING WITH TENNESSEE WHISKEY SAUCE

*A Southern favorite!*

*Tennessee whiskey and bourbon are two different alcoholic beverages. Tennessee whiskey is slowly filtered through large vats of sugar maple charcoal which gives it a distinctively sweet flavor.*

**Pudding**

| | | | |
|---|---|---|---|
| 1 | loaf stale French bread, torn to bits | 1 | teaspoon grated orange zest |
| 4 | cups heavy milk | ¼ | teaspoon nutmeg |
| 1 | cup whipping cream | 1 | teaspoon vanilla |
| 5 | eggs | 1½ | teaspoons cinnamon, divided |
| 2 | cups sugar | ¼ | cup water |
| ¼ | cup melted butter | 2 | tablespoons butter |
| | | | Tennessee Whiskey Sauce |

- Preheat oven to 400 degrees.
- Place bread on bottom of greased 13x9-inch baking pan. Do not overfill.
- In a medium-sized bowl, combine milk and cream; pour evenly over bread. Mix together to coat.
- In a large bowl, combine eggs, 1½ cups sugar, butter, zest, nutmeg, vanilla, and ½ teaspoon cinnamon. Pour evenly over the bread.
- In a small saucepan, heat sugar, water, remaining 1 teaspoon cinnamon and 2 tablespoons butter. Stir until sugar dissolves. Pour sugar mixture over bread.
- Place on a cookie sheet and bake for 35 to 40 minutes. Cover with foil if it seems to be browning too quickly.
- Serve with Tennessee Whiskey Sauce.

**Tennessee Whiskey Sauce**

| | | | |
|---|---|---|---|
| ½ | cup (1 stick) butter | 3 | tablespoons light corn syrup |
| 1 | cup dark brown sugar | ⅔ | cup Tennessee whiskey |
| | Juice from 1 orange | 1 | teaspoon vanilla |
| ⅓ | cup confectioners' sugar | | |

- Combine first 6 ingredients (butter through whiskey) in a medium saucepan over medium heat.
- Bring to a boil, stirring occasionally; reduce heat to simmer and cook for about 30 to 45 minutes, until it is thick and syrupy. It will continue thickening as it cools.
- Stir in 1 teaspoon vanilla.
- Serve sauce with pudding and whipped cream.

*Yield: 12 servings*

*Note: The bread pudding may be made ahead, frozen; thawed in refrigerator and baked.*

# BAKED APPLES IN PUFF PASTRY WITH RUM SAUCE

*A warm rum sauce bathes these beautiful apple pastries!*

**Baked Apples in Puff Pastry**

| | |
|---|---|
| 6 | baking apples such as Granny Smith |
| 4 | tablespoons cold butter |
| 12 | teaspoons brown sugar |
| | Cinnamon |
| 2 | puff pastry sheets |
| | Rum Sauce |

- Preheat oven to 400 degrees.
- Peel apples. Core to make a hole in the center making sure to remove all seeds, but do not core all the way through.
- Fill the hole in each apple with 1 to 2 teaspoons firm butter and 2 teaspoons brown sugar.
- Sprinkle the top of each apple with cinnamon.
- Roll out pastry sheet to 11x11-inches. Cut into 4 squares, each 5½x5½-inches.
- Place 1 apple in the center of 1 square. Stretch the corner of the dough over the top of the apple; fold the opposite corner over the top. Moisten the under edge to seal.
- Continue with the other 2 corners and seal in the same fashion, completely covering apple.
- Poke a hole in the top of the pastry to allow steam to escape.
- Repeat with the other apples.
- Cover and chill until ready to bake.
- Place apples on a baking sheet and bake for 45 minutes until pastry is puffed and lightly brown.

**Rum Sauce**

| | | | |
|---|---|---|---|
| 2 | cups sugar | ⅓ | cup dark rum |
| 1 | cup water | | Juice of 1 lemon |

- Heat sugar and water in a medium saucepan over medium high heat; stirring until sugar is dissolved.
- Cook until thick and syrupy. Remove from heat.
- Add rum and lemon juice, stirring to combine.
- Pour about 2 tablespoon sauce over apples and serve warm.

*Yield: 6 apples*

*Note: The apples may be served warm without the sauce. They are delicious with ice cream or whipped cream.*

# CRÈME BRÛLÉE

*Try the many variations for this fabulous dessert!*

| | | | |
|---|---|---|---|
| 2 | cups heavy whipping cream | 1 | tablespoon vanilla |
| 5 | egg yolks | | Brown sugar |
| ⅓ | cup sugar | | |

- Preheat oven to 325 degrees.
- Combine heavy cream, egg yolks, sugar, and vanilla with a whisk until sugar dissolves.
- Pour cream mixture evenly among 5 to 6 (6-ounce) ramekins.
- Place ramekins in a 13x9x2-inch baking pan (or roasting pan with high sides) and fill pan with warm water to ½-inch depth.
- Bake for 50 to 55 minutes or until mixture is almost set (slight movement in the center is okay).
- Cool in a water bath in the pan on a wire rack at room temperature.
- Remove ramekins from the pan.
- Cover and chill for at least 8 hours, or up to 24 hours.
- Sprinkle the top of each ramekin with 2 to 3 teaspoons brown sugar and spread evenly.
- Place under broiler, just until sugar melts, 3 to 5 minutes.
- Let stand 5 minutes to allow sugar to harden. Serve immediately.

*Yield: 5 to 6 servings*

*Variations:* Berry Crème Brûlée: Place enough berries of your choice to cover the bottom of each dish. Top with custard and proceed as above. Almond Crème Brûlée: Reduce vanilla to 1 teaspoon; add 2 tablespoons almond liqueur, 1 additional egg yolk, and ¼ cup chopped, toasted almonds. Orange Crème Brûlée: Reduce vanilla to 1 teaspoon; add 2 tablespoons orange zest, 2 tablespoons orange liqueur, and 1 additional egg yolk. Black Bottom Crème Brûlée: Place a thin brownie in the bottom of each dish and top with custard.

---

*When preparing a custard, pudding or white sauce press plastic wrap directly onto the surface after cooking to prevent formation of film.*

# WARM CHOCOLATE SOUFFLÉS

*Serve this fabulous do-ahead dessert for your next special meal!*

| | | | |
|---|---|---|---|
| 1 | cup (2 sticks) unsalted butter | ¾ | cup sugar |
| 10 | ounces bittersweet or semi-sweet chocolate, chopped | 4 | large egg yolks |
| | | ⅔ | cup all-purpose flour |
| 6 | large egg whites | 2 | teaspoons vanilla extract |

- Preheat oven to 400 degrees.
- Butter 8 custard cups or (6-ounce) soufflé dishes.
- Melt chocolate and butter in heavy saucepan over medium-low heat until softened and smooth.
- Place chocolate mixture in a large bowl to cool.
- Beat egg whites with an electric mixer until soft peaks are formed. Gradually add sugar and beat until stiff, but not dry.
- Whisk yolks, flour, and vanilla into chocolate; gently fold in ⅓ egg whites and then the remaining egg whites.
- Divide batter evenly among dishes. Batter can be covered and chilled at this point for up to 24 hours.
- Bake until edges are set but wet batter is still attached when a tester is inserted in the center (about 20 minutes if refrigerated or for 15 minutes if at room temperature). Do not overbake. The edges will look set and the center will look soft and pudding-like.

*Yield: 8 servings*

*Note: You can dress up this luscious dessert with a dusting of confectioners' sugar, top with freshly whipped cream or open the top and pour a dessert sauce on top. We love the Tennessee Whiskey Sauce on page 244 or the Hot Fudge Sauce on page 261.*

---

*I was 32 when I started cooking; up until then I just ate.*

Julia Child (1912- )

# TOASTED ALMOND SEMI-FREDDO WITH WARM CHOCOLATE SAUCE

*An Italian ice cream dessert, it is amore!*

| | | | |
|---|---|---|---|
| 1 | cup sliced almonds, toasted and cooled | ¾ | cup egg whites (approximately 6 large egg whites) |
| 1 | cup sugar, divided | ½ | teaspoon almond extract |
| 2 | cups heavy cream | | Fresh sliced strawberries, for garnish |

- Grease bottom and sides of a 10-inch springform pan.
- Line bottom with waxed paper, cut to fit.
- In a food processor, pulse almonds and ¾ cup sugar only a few times, until almonds are slightly ground. (Over-processing will produce a paste.)
- Whip heavy cream with an electric mixer on medium speed until soft peaks form. Cover and refrigerate whipped cream until later.
- Whip egg whites in clean, dry bowl until soft peaks form. Add almond extract and remaining ¼ cup sugar and continue whipping until glossy and stiff, about 30 to 45 more seconds.
- Fold eggs into refrigerated whipped cream; then fold in nut and sugar mixture until well incorporated.
- Spoon into the prepared pan and smooth the top.
- Cover with plastic wrap and freeze from 4 hours up to 3 days.
- To serve, unmold, remove waxed paper and invert onto serving plate.
- Spoon Warm Chocolate Sauce over top of individual slices.
- Top with strawberries (if desired).

*Yield: 12 servings*

---

*Grease measuring cup with cooking spray before measuring honey, molasses or syrup. The sticky stuff will glide right off and will ensure an accurate measure.*

## Toasted Almond Semi-Freddo continued

**Warm Chocolate Sauce**

- 2 ounces unsweetened chocolate
- 8 ounces semi-sweet chocolate
- ½ cup light corn syrup
- ½ cup hot water

- In the top half of a double boiler, combine chocolates over simmering water.
- Stir until completely melted.
- Whisk in syrup and hot water until smooth.
- Serve warm over ice cream or cake.

*Yield: 2 cups*

Note: If consuming raw egg is a concern, ask your grocer about eggs pasteurized in the shell.

# BRANDY CHOCOLATE MOUSSE

- 7 ounces semi-sweet chocolate
- 6 tablespoons unsalted butter
- 5 eggs, separated
- ¼ cup brandy
- 1 cup heavy cream
- ¾ cup sugar, divided

- Melt chocolate and butter in the top of a double boiler.
- When butter is melted, remove from heat, and add egg yolks, one at a time, stirring after each addition until thoroughly mixed.
- Add brandy; let the mixture rest until it reaches room temperature.
- Whip cream with ½ cup sugar with an electric mixer on medium speed until stiff peaks form, cover and chill.
- In a separate bowl, whip egg whites with remaining ¼ cup sugar with an electric mixer on medium speed until stiff.
- Fold whipped cream and egg whites into chocolate mixture until well incorporated.
- Place mousse in a trifle bowl or individual serving bowls. Chill.
- Serve topped with whipped cream and shaved chocolate for garnish.

*Yield: 8 to 10 servings*

---

*When whipping eggs, use cold eggs when separating yolks from the whites (they separate more easily). Clean your bowl and beaters thoroughly before beating the egg whites, excess grease prevents egg whites from reaching their highest volume. Whip the eggs at room temperature in a stainless or copper bowl. If the recipe calls for the addition of cream of tarter, add it when the whites are loose and foamy.*

# FOUR-POUND BROWNIES

*One husband claims he gains four pounds every time his wife makes these addictive brownies!*

| | | | |
|---|---|---|---|
| 1 | (14-ounce) package of light caramels | ¾ | cup margarine, melted |
| ⅔ | cup evaporated milk, divided | 1 | cup chopped pecans |
| 1 | box devil's food cake mix | 1 | cup chocolate chips |

- Preheat oven to 350 degrees. Grease and flour a 13x9x2-inch baking pan.
- Melt caramels in heavy saucepan with ⅓ cup evaporated milk over low heat. Once caramels have melted, remove from heat, and set aside.
- In a large bowl, combine cake mix, margarine, ⅓ cup evaporated milk, and nuts.
- Stir until dough holds together.
- Press half of dough into the prepared pan, reserve the rest for topping.
- Bake for 6 minutes.
- Sprinkle chocolate chips over baked crust.
- Drizzle caramel mixture over chocolate chips.
- Crumble remaining dough mixture over top. It does not have to cover completely.
- Return to oven and bake for 15 to 18 minutes.
- Cool slightly; cover and refrigerate for 30 minutes.
- To ease slicing, cut bars after they are chilled. (Best if stored in refrigerator.)

*Yield: 36 bars*

---

*A wonderful use of cocoa! When baking a chocolate cake, use cocoa instead of flour to coat your pan to prevent sticking. This will prevent the chocolate cake from having a dusting of white on the top or bottom when you remove it from the pan.*

# MOCHA FUDGE BROWNIES

*This delicious recipe makes a large number of brownies.
It is perfect for a luncheon, shower or bring-a-dish!*

| | | | |
|---|---|---|---|
| 4 | sticks unsalted butter | 2 | tablespoons pure vanilla extract |
| 3½ | cups semi-sweet chocolate chips, divided | 1¼ | cups all-purpose flour, divided |
| 6 | ounces bittersweet chocolate | 1 | tablespoon baking powder |
| 7 | large eggs | 1 | teaspoon salt |
| 3½ | tablespoons instant coffee granules | 1½ | cups coarsely chopped pecans (may use 2 cups) |
| 2¼ | cups sugar | | |

- Preheat oven to 350 degrees.
- Butter and flour a 17x11x2-inch jelly-roll pan.
- In the top of a double boiler, melt butter, 2 cups chocolate chips, and bittersweet chocolate. Set aside and allow to cool slightly.
- In a large bowl, stir to combine eggs, coffee granules, sugar, and vanilla. Do not beat.
- Add the warm chocolate mixture slowly into the egg mixture, stirring to combine. Set aside, and allow to cool to room temperature.
- In a medium bowl, sift together 1 cup flour, baking powder, and salt.
- Add the flour mixture to the chocolate mixture.
- In a medium-sized bowl, toss pecans and remaining 1½ cups chocolate chips with remaining ¼ cup flour. Fold pecan mixture into chocolate mixture until well incorporated. Pour into the prepared pan.
- Bake for 20 minutes.
- Open oven, and bang the pan on the oven shelf to force out air between the batter and the pan.
- Continue baking for another 10 to 15 minutes or until toothpick inserted into the middle of brownies comes out clean.
- Let cool and refrigerate.
- Cut into small squares.
- Cover with plastic wrap and keep in the refrigerator up to 1 week.
- Garnish before serving with powdered sugar.

*Yield: 50 to 60 brownies*

---

*Baking soda does not keep indefinitely like baking powder. Therefore, you should buy baking soda in the smallest quantity available and date your can. Discard after three months.*

# RASPBERRY OATMEAL BARS

*Wonderful anytime, especially for an afternoon tea or luncheon dessert!*

| | |
|---|---|
| 1½ cups sweetened flaked coconut, divided | ½ teaspoon salt |
| 1¼ cups all-purpose flour | ¾ cup cold unsalted butter, cut into pieces |
| ¾ cup firmly packed light brown sugar | 1½ cups old-fashioned oats |
| ¼ cup granulated sugar | 1 cup seedless raspberry jam |

- Preheat oven to 375 degrees.
- Spread ¾ cup coconut evenly on a baking sheet; place on the middle rack of oven for 4 minutes. Stir. Continue cooking for 4 more minutes or until golden and toasted.
- Blend flour, sugars and salt in a food processor. Add butter and blend until dough forms.
- Place dough in a medium-sized bowl. Add oats and toasted coconut, and knead until well combined.
- Set aside ¾ cup of dough. Press remainder of dough into the bottom of a greased 13x9-inch metal baking pan.
- Spread jam over dough.
- Crumble reserved dough over jam, and top with remaining ¾ cup untoasted coconut.
- Bake for 20 to 25 minutes, or until golden.
- Cool completely.
- Remove from the pan in 1 piece by loosening sides and lifting with a spatula; transfer to a cutting board.
- Cut into bars.

*Yield: Approximately 24 bars*

*Variation: To make apricot bars, substitute apricot preserves for raspberry jam.*

---

*Good painting is like good cooking; it can be tasted but not explained.*

Maurice de Vlaninck
(1920 US columnist in Vogue)

# EASY COCONUT MACAROONS

*Bring these to your next holiday cookie exchange!*

- ⅔ cup (5.25 liquid ounce) sweetened condensed milk
- 1 egg white
- 1½ teaspoons vanilla
- ⅛ teaspoon salt
- 3½ cups (11.25-ounce) flaked or shredded sweetened coconut

- Preheat oven to 325 degrees. Line cookie sheet with parchment or waxed paper.
- In a medium-sized bowl, combine milk, egg white, vanilla, and salt.
- Stir in coconut until well blended.
- Drop scant measuring tablespoon full of dough in the 1½-inch mounds, spacing about 2-inches apart on cookie sheet.
- Bake 1 cookie sheet at a time in the upper third of the oven for 20 to 25 minutes, or until nicely brown.
- Transfer paper to wire racks, and let stand until the cookies are thoroughly cooled.
- Carefully peel the cookies from the paper.

*Yield: 20 cookies*

*Note: These cookies may be topped with a candied cherry during the holidays; or drizzled with melted chocolate.*

*You can substitute wax paper for baking if you do not have parchment paper.*

# GINGER COOKIES

*Deliciously chewy!*

| | | | |
|---|---|---|---|
| ¾ | cup butter | ¼ | teaspoon cloves |
| 1 | cup firmly packed brown sugar | ¼ | teaspoon nutmeg |
| ¼ | cup molasses | 1 | teaspoon ginger |
| 1 | egg | 1 | teaspoon cinnamon |
| 2 | cups flour | 2 | teaspoons baking soda |
| | | | Granulated sugar |

- In a large bowl, cream butter and brown sugar with an electric mixer on medium speed until smooth.
- Add molasses and egg, beating to combine.
- Sift flour, cloves, nutmeg, ginger, cinnamon, and baking soda together.
- Add flour mixture to butter mixture, beating until just combined. Cover and chill overnight. When you are ready to bake, preheat oven to 350 degrees.
- Roll dough into small balls, and roll in sugar.
- Place balls on a cool cookie sheet. Flatten balls slightly with the bottom of a glass and place on a baking sheet.
- Bake for 12 to 15 minutes.

*Yield: 3 dozen cookies*

*Variation: For a chunkier cookie, add ½ cup raisins.*

---

*When measuring brown sugar, use your measuring cup as a scoop and pack the brown sugar firmly into the cup with your hand outside of the bag.*

# TRIPLE THREAT CHOCOLATE CHIP COOKIES

| | | | |
|---|---|---|---|
| ¾ | cup butter flavored shortening | 1½ | cups self-rising flour |
| 1¼ | cups firmly packed brown sugar | 1 | cup chopped pecans |
| | | ½ | cup semi-sweet chocolate chunks |
| 2 | tablespoons milk | ½ | cup white chocolate chips |
| 1 | tablespoon vanilla | ½ | cup milk chocolate chips |
| 1 | egg | | |

- Preheat oven to 350 degrees.
- Combine shortening, brown sugar, milk, and vanilla in a large mixing bowl, beating at medium speed with an electric mixer until well blended.
- Beat in the egg.
- Gradually add flour to the mixture, continuing to beat at low speed, until blended.
- Stir in pecans and chocolates.
- Drop dough by heaping teaspoons on an ungreased cookie sheet.
- Bake for 8 to 9 minutes, cookies will appear moist. Do not overbake.
- Cool 2 minutes on cookie sheet before removing to a rack.

*Yield: 3 dozen cookies*

*When making drop cookies, always drop the dough onto cool cookie sheets to prevent spreading. You can cool them quickly by rinsing with cold water and drying thoroughly before using again.*

# LAST MINUTE COOKIES

*These are great to make when your child tells you at 8:00 p.m. that you need to take cookies to school in the morning!*

| | | | |
|---|---|---|---|
| 1 | box yellow cake mix | ½ | cup milk |
| 2 | eggs | 1 | (6-ounce) package chocolate chips |

- Preheat oven to 350 degrees.
- Mix all ingredients in a medium-sized bowl.
- Form dough into small balls and place on a cookie sheet.
- Bake for 12 to 15 minutes, or until edges turn brown. Do not overbake.

*Yield: 3 dozen cookies*

*Variation: The variations for this easy cookie are many. Try chocolate, white cake mix with peanut butter or butterscotch chips.*

# ALMOND CREAM CHEESE COOKIES

*You may not be able to eat just one of these light, yummy cookies!*

| | | | |
|---|---|---|---|
| 1 | cup sugar | ½ | teaspoon vanilla |
| 1 | cup (2 sticks) butter | ½ | teaspoon almond extract |
| 1 | (3-ounce) package cream cheese, softened at room temperature | 1 | cup sliced almonds |
| | | 2 | cups plus 3 tablespoons self-rising flour |

- Cream sugar and butter in a large mixing bowl with an electric mixer on medium speed. Beat until smooth.
- Add cream cheese, beat until smooth.
- Add vanilla, almond extract, almonds, and flour; beating until just combined.
- Shape into logs.
- Wrap in waxed paper, then wrap in foil.
- Chill for at least 2 hours.
- When you are ready to bake, preheat the oven to 350 degrees. Unwrap dough and cut into ¼-inch slices.
- Bake for 10 to 15 minutes, until edges are brown.

*Yield: 3 dozen cookies*

*Note: Can be frozen for up to 2 months in rolled form, then sliced while frozen and baked as needed.*

---

*Baked cookies or dough may be frozen for 6 months. Work the dough into the shape of a log. Wrap it first in plastic wrap then place in a zip-top freezer bag. Label the outside of the dough with the type of cookie and the date. Thaw the dough overnight in the refrigerator before baking.*

# LEMON MELT-AWAY COOKIES

**Cookies**

- ¾ cup (1½ sticks) softened butter or margarine
- ½ cup confectioners' sugar
- 1 tablespoon lemon juice
- 1 teaspoon grated lemon zest
- ½ cup cornstarch
- 1¼ cups flour
- Lemon Meltaway Frosting

- In a large bowl, cream butter and sugar with an electric mixer on medium speed until smooth.
- Add lemon juice, lemon zest, cornstarch, and flour; blend until well mixed.
- Divide dough in half; and shape each half into an 8x1-inch roll. Wrap each roll into plastic wrap, and refrigerate until firm, 1 to 2 hours, or overnight.
- When ready to bake, preheat oven to 350 degrees.
- Remove plastic wrap and cut each roll into ¼-inch slices with a sharp knife.
- Place 2-inches apart on greased cookie sheets.
- Bake 8 to 12 minutes, until set, but not brown.
- Cool completely on racks.
- Spread Lemon Meltaway Frosting on cooled cookies.

**Lemon Meltaway Frosting**

- ¾ cup confectioners' sugar
- ¼ cup softened butter or margarine
- 1 teaspoon grated lemon zest
- 2 teaspoons lemon juice

- In a small bowl with an electric mixer on medium speed, beat all frosting ingredients until well blended.

*Yield: 4 dozen cookies*

---

*On rainy days when you have run out of ideas, you can create your own play dough. The children will really enjoy being able to play with something that they helped to create in the kitchen. Mix one cup salt and one cup flour. Add one tablespoon vegetable oil to dry ingredients. If you like colored dough, add food coloring to one-quarter cup of water. Add water to the dry ingredients until it has reached the desired consistency.*

# GRAHAM CRACKER SANDWICHES

> Cooking is at once child's play and adult joy. And cooking done with care is an act of love.
>
> Craig Claiborne (1920- )

| 1   | (1-pound) box graham crackers | ½ | cup milk |
| --- | --- | --- | --- |
| 1   | cup sugar | 1 | cup sweetened flaked coconut |
| 1   | egg | 1 | cup chopped pecans |
| 1   | cup (2 sticks) butter, softened | 1 | cup graham cracker crumbs |
|     |   |   | Vanilla Frosting |

- Lay out ½ of graham crackers to completely cover a 17x11x1-inch cookie sheet.
- Beat sugar and eggs in a large bowl with an electric mixer.
- Add butter and milk, beating to combine.
- Place in medium-sized saucepan. Bring to a boil and remove from heat.
- Add coconut, pecans and graham cracker crumbs. Spread mixture over graham crackers.
- After spreading, place graham crackers over top to form sandwich.
- Spread frosting over Graham Cracker Sandwiches and refrigerate.
- When cool, cut into squares and strips.

**Vanilla Frosting**

| 6 | tablespoons butter, melted | ¼ | cup milk |
| --- | --- | --- | --- |
| 2 | cups confectioners' sugar | 1 | teaspoon vanilla |

- To prepare frosting, combine butter, sugar, milk and vanilla in a small bowl. Beat with an electric mixer until well combined.

*Yield: 40 cookies*

# PECAN WAFERS

| | | | |
|---|---|---|---|
| ½ | pound butter, softened | ½ | teaspoon powdered cloves |
| 1 | cup sugar | ⅛ | teaspoon salt |
| 1 | egg, separated | 2 | cups flour, sifted |
| 2 | teaspoons cinnamon | 1 | cup chopped pecans, divided |

- Preheat oven to 325 degrees. Grease a 17x11-inch cookie sheet.
- Cream butter and sugar in a medium-sized bowl with an electric mixer until smooth. Add egg yolk, cinnamon, cloves, and salt, beating until combined. Add flour and beat just until flour disappears. Fold in ¾ cup pecans.
- Spread dough onto the cookie sheet. Smooth with a wet table knife.
- In a small bowl, whisk 1 egg white until frothy and brush on top of dough.
- Sprinkle dough with remaining ¼ cup chopped pecans.
- Bake for 35 to 40 minutes.
- Cut immediately into 2-inch squares.

*Yield: 36 to 48*

*Use metal or plastic measuring cups with a flat top for solid or dry ingredients.*

# GRAPE SHERBET

| | | | |
|---|---|---|---|
| 16 | ounces grape juice | 3 | cups sugar |
| 1 | (8-ounce) can crushed pineapple | 16 | ounces heavy whipping cream |
| | Juice of 4 lemons | 3½ | quarts milk, more or less |

- Mix first 4 ingredients together; chill.
- Once cold, add heavy cream, and pour into a 1-gallon ice cream freezer.
- Add enough milk to reach fill line in freezer.
- Follow manufacturers directions and freeze to desired consistency.

*Yield: 1 gallon*

# ESPRESSO ICE CREAM SUNDAES

*A refreshing and easy summer dessert can be made from canned pears. Freeze one can of pears, puree and serve as a sorbet. Try this with other canned fruit that you may have on hand.*

### Espresso Chocolate Sauce

| | | | |
|---|---|---|---|
| 4 | tablespoons (½ stick) unsalted butter | 1 ½ | teaspoons instant coffee granules |
| 1 | cup sugar | ½ | can evaporated milk |
| 2 | ounces unsweetened chocolate squares | 1 ½ | teaspoons vanilla |

- Combine butter, sugar, chocolate, coffee, milk and vanilla into a 1-quart saucepan over low heat.
- Cook until chocolate melts; whisk and cook over medium-low heat 10 more minutes.
- Remove from heat, allow chocolate sauce to cool to room temperature.

### Sundaes

| | | | |
|---|---|---|---|
| 1 | bag pecan shortbread cookies, coarsely broken | 1 | bag chocolate-covered toffee bits |
| 1 | half gallon coffee ice cream with chocolate chunks, slightly softened | | |

- When ready to make Sundaes, layer ¼ cup broken cookie crumbs, ½ cup ice cream, ⅓ cup chocolate sauce in a large sundae dish. Sprinkle with toffee bits.
- If desired, freeze before serving. You may garnish before serving with whole cherries, whipped cream or a chocolate covered coffee bean, if desired.

*Yield: 8 sundaes*

*Note: You may serve these in mugs also for smaller portions.*

# HOT FUDGE SAUCE

*Delicious served over your favorite ice cream!*

| | | | |
|---|---|---|---|
| ½ | cup butter | ¼ | teaspoon salt |
| 4 | ounces unsweetened chocolate | 1¾ | cups evaporated milk |
| 3 | cups sugar | 1 | teaspoon vanilla |

- Melt butter and chocolate over low heat in a heavy saucepan whisking to combine.
- Remove from heat and stir in sugar, adding about ¼ cup at a time.
- Stir in salt, return to heat, and add milk.
- Cook 7 minutes, stirring constantly.
- Remove from heat and stir in vanilla.
- Serve immediately or store covered in the refrigerator and warm prior to serving.

*Yield: approximately 5 ¼ cups*

---

*When you melt chocolate alone, make sure that your container is dry. Any amount of liquid will make the chocolate solidify.*

# BALSAMIC GLAZED STRAWBERRIES OVER ICE CREAM

*This surprising flavor combination will make you want summer to last forever!*

| | | | |
|---|---|---|---|
| 6 | large ripe strawberries, hulled | 2 | tablespoons packed brown sugar |
| 2 | tablespoons balsamic vinegar | | Premium vanilla ice cream |

- Cut strawberries into wedges
- In a small heavy saucepan, heat vinegar and brown sugar over medium heat, stirring until sugar dissolves. Simmer for 1 more minute.
- Remove the pan from heat; add strawberries and toss to coat.
- Scoop ice cream into 2 bowls, top with warm strawberries. Serve immediately.

*Yield: 2 servings*

*Note: The ingredients can easily be increased to serve as many as needed.*

# PINOT GRANITA

*This icy dessert is pretty served in a wineglass.*

| | | | |
|---|---|---|---|
| 3 | cups water | 1½ | cups Pinot Noir wine |
| 1 | cup sugar | | Mixed fresh berries |

- Bring water to a boil in a non-aluminum saucepan and add sugar.
- Boil 1 minute or until sugar dissolves.
- Remove sugar mixture from heat and cool. Stir in wine.
- Pour into a 9x9x2-inch baking pan.
- Cover loosely with plastic wrap, place in the freezer.
- Freeze until solid, stirring occasionally.
- To serve, let soften in the refrigerator about 10 minutes and scoop out with an ice cream scoop.
- Serve in wine glasses and garnish with berries, if desired.

*Yield: 10 servings*

*Note: You may use a fork to scrape the frozen granita if you want to serve it straight from the freezer. This will give an icier texture to the dessert.*

---

*A fun activity for a Halloween or spring time children's party (or an activity for the children at a family party) is an old fashion taffy pull. Combine 2 cups molasses, 1 cup sugar, 3 tablespoons butter, and ¼ teaspoon baking soda. Boil ingredients until it reaches hard ball stage. Pour candy into a wet shallow pan. Allow to cool. When cool, pull the candy until it reaches the color you wish. Cut into sticks and enjoy.*

# ALMOND TOFFEE

*Make a batch to give to friends during the holidays!*

| | | | |
|---|---|---|---|
| 1 | cup sliced almonds, divided | 1 | (12-ounce) package milk chocolate chips |
| 1 | cup (2 sticks) butter | | |
| 1 | cup packed brown sugar | | |

- Sprinkle ½ cup almonds onto a cookie sheet lined with foil.
- Melt butter in a saucepan over medium heat. Add sugar, stirring until sugar is dissolved. Boil 5 minutes, stirring constantly.
- Add remaining ½ cup almonds to butter mixture, stir to combine.
- Remove from heat and pour butter mixture evenly over top of almonds on cookie sheet.
- Sprinkle chocolate chips on top of butter mixture. Allow to melt and spread evenly with a knife.
- Allow to cool. Invert toffee onto a solid surface, peel off foil and break into pieces.
- Store in an airtight container.

*Yield: 4 gift sized portions*

### We owe a special debt of gratitude to the many people who donated their talents to create *No Place Like Home*.

Those who contributed, prepared and tasted recipes, opened their homes for tastings and meetings, and supported this project since its inception.

Kirklands, Inc., for their generous support in helping to underwrite the printing.

Harbert Alexander, Sr., who provided the historical information about Jackson. Mr. Alexander is a true asset to this community. We appreciate all that he has done to record the history of our great city.

Lendon Hamilton Noe who gave so freely of herself and her artistic talents. The beauty of this book is a gift from her to all of us.

Delores Ballard for creating the introduction that personifies *No Place Like Home*.

Davis-Kidd Booksellers for the use of their meeting facilities and their support throughout this project.

The 2000 provisional class who pursued the idea of creating a cookbook.

And finally, our families, for their support and *many* sacrifices made during this project that sometimes seemed unending! We sincerely appreciate their patience and encouragement during the creation of *No Place Like Home*.

---

The Jackson Service League extends a heartfelt thank you to everyone who tested, developed, typed and edited recipes, brainstormed, developed and marketed this book. Many opened their homes and kitchens for meetings, tastings and more meetings. The League would like to specifically thank the following group of people for generously contributing their recipes to make our book possible.

We regret that we were unable to include all of the individual recipes due to similarity or availability of space. We hope that we have not inadvertently overlooked anyone who contributed to the creation of *No Place Like Home*.

| | | | |
|---|---|---|---|
| Carol Adkins | Becky Baxter | Laura Camp | Teresa Cobb |
| Nora Alexander | Bonita Beeken | Patsy Camp | Donna Coffman |
| Cecilia Alagappan | Sybil Benson | Missy Campbell | Cathy Howard Coggin |
| Margaret Sheppard Apple | Bobbie Blackard | Mona Campbell | Kim Cook |
| | Paul Bowden | Kathy Cantrell | Ceil Cowles |
| Kim Arnold | Lina Bowyer | Lou Anne Carlock | Connie Cowles |
| Debbie Atkins | Suzanne Boyd | Jean Chandler | Betsy Cox |
| Elizabeth Atkins | Geri Breeden | John Chandler | Kim Cox |
| Marty Atkins | Nancy Brooke | Kathleen Chandler | Kris Cox |
| Mary Jane Atkins | Ginger Buckley | Bonnie Chary | Bess Crane |
| Lisa Baldeck | Betty Butler | Lynn Cobb | Betsy Crook |

*continued on next page*

Kay Culbreath
Betsy Dement
Carlin Vineyard Diffee
Martha Dolinak
Gertrude Driver
Jane Edenton
Diane Edwards
Mrs. Edwin Edwards
Jill Egros
Cynthia Ellis
Sally Everett
Martha Jane Exum
Mary Ruth Faulkner
Lisa Findler
Susan Fisher
Kathy Fite
Stephanie Freeman
Connie Garey
Susan Garlock
Anne Garrard
Ashley Geisewite
Lynda Gilbert
Rhonda Greer
Merilyn Hamilton
Mary Claire Hancock
Helene Harris
Karen Harris
Susan Harris
Yolanda Harris
Anne Sanford Hawks
Clare Hickey
Barbara Higgs
Sylvia Hills
Kristina Hindmanper
Greta Hitchcock
Connie Hockaday
Margaret Hodges
Carol Holloway
Denise Homberg
Daphne Howard
Tiffany Howard
Marilyn Jackson
Ginger Jaggers
Valerie Johnstone
Celia Jordan
Mary Kenney
Katie Kibbe
Michelle King
Cindy Kirk
Alice Kirkland
Stacy Klein
Amy Koerner
Ann Lawrence
Doris Lawrence
Kim Lemons
Patty Lewis
Mimi Lundy
Jenny Lytle
David Lytle, Sr.
Cindy Magee
Clare Markos
Cokey Martindale
Judy Mascolo
Ann McGuire
Peggy McGuire
Nancy McMahon
Catherine McKnight
Nita Mehr
Caroline Merwin
Carol Messina
Heather Miller
Laura Miller
Carol Ann Mitchell
Katherine Mitchell
Teresa Morgan
Betty Morris
Dianne Morrison
Pat Morrison
Ginger New
Debbie Newell
Mandy Norsworthy
Kelly O'Rourke
Becky Ozment
Mary Jane Pakis
Nancy Pearson
Pam Perchik
Melinda Pierce
Ginka Poole
Joanna Priester
Sarah Pucek
Sally Rainey
Tracey Rector
Emily Richards
Mitzi Richardson
Leslie Rickman
Peggy Robbins
Lisa Roberts
Tammy Roberts
Sally Rowland
Cynthia Saif-Santana
Currie Sanders
Paula Shaw
Betty Louis Sheppard
Katie Stevenson
Mildred Stevenson
Mary Louise Stonecipher
Denise Stuart
Jamie Sullivan
Robyn Tabor
Janet Tankersly
Piper Taylor
Cynthia Teague
Sandra Teague
Jan Teer
Louise Thompson
Joan Tomlin
Laura Tomlin
Cyndi Turner
Leslie Underwood
Carolyn Vaughan
Kim Villarreal
Honey Wage
Marda Wallace
Mona Ward
Kristy White
Alleta Whitmire
Lindsey Wilhite
Mandy Williams
Michelle Williams
Michele Williamson
Mary Kay Woods
Marion Yarbro
Patti Yellen
Veronica Young

# Index

## A

Almond Apricot Tartlets ............................. 234
Almond Cream Cheese Cookies ................. 256
Almond Cream Cheese Danish ................... 107
Almond Jasmine Rice ................................ 159
Almond Toffee ......................................... 264
Angel Hair Pasta Flan ............................... 156

**APPETIZERS** *(see also Dips and Spreads)*

    Artichoke Cheese Puffs ............................ 29
    Asparagus with Wasabi Dip ..................... 24
    Bombay Blues .......................................... 25
    Brie Tartlets with Grape Salsa .................. 23
    Cece's Samosas ....................................... 43
    Cheesy Bacon Delights ............................ 31
    Chinese Chicken Bites ............................. 27
    Cilantro Lime Grilled Shrimp .................... 46
    Devils and Angels on Horseback
      with Balsamic Syrup ............................. 42
    Festive Bite-Size Cheese Balls .................. 34
    Five Pepper Quesadilla ........................... 40
    Fresh Tomato Tart ................................... 32
    Garden Party Canapés ............................ 33
    Green Chili Pick-Me-Ups .......................... 39
    Grilled Portobellos with
      Hazelnut Topping ................................. 44
    Marinated Cheese Tortellini ..................... 37
    Pepper Pecan Cheese Wafers .................. 34
    Pepperoni Praise ..................................... 35
    Petite Crab Cakes with
      Fresh Tomato Tartar Sauce ................... 30

    Rosemary's Walnuts ................................ 41
    Savory Goat Cheese and
      Walnut Cheesecakes ............................ 26
    Shrimp Quesadillas ................................. 45
    Skewered Shrimp with
      Warm Plum Sauce ................................ 47
    Spinach, Artichoke and
      Gruyère Pinwheels ............................... 28
    Tomato Bruschetta .................................. 41

## APPLES

    Apple Cream Pie ................................... 235
    Baked Apples in Puff Pastry
      with Rum Sauce ................................. 245
    Good Morning Glory Muffins ................. 111
    Gorgonzola and Walnut Terrine ............... 36
    Maple Mustard Pork Tenderloin
      with Caramelized Apples .................... 161
    Mediterranean Couscous ....................... 160
    Pork Chops with Apples and Raisins ........ 163
    Spiced Fresh Apple Cake ....................... 225
    Turkey Burgers with Smoked Gouda
      and Granny Smith Apples ................... 185

## APRICOTS

    Almond Apricot Tartlets .......................... 234
    Apricot-Glazed Cornish Hens
      Stuffed with Wild Rice ........................ 186
    Devils and Angels on Horseback
      with Balsamic Syrup ............................. 42
    Fruit Salad with Mint Syrup ...................... 80
    No Guilt Apricot Lemon Cake ................ 227
    Winter Fruit Salad .................................... 65

## ARTICHOKES

Artichoke and Blue Cheese Salad .............. 66
Artichoke Cheese Puffs ............................ 29
Artichoke Frittata ..................................... 95
Artichoke Garlic Bread ........................... 115
Italian Spinach and Artichoke Hearts ....... 143
Lemon Garlic Sautéed
    Artichoke Hearts ................................ 127
Pasta Salad with Sherry Dressing .............. 61
Scalloped Tomatoes and Artichokes ......... 125
Spinach, Artichoke and
    Gruyère Pinwheels ............................... 28
The Overnight Salad ................................. 71

## ASPARAGUS

Asparagus and Prosciutto Bundles............ 127
Asparagus with Wasabi Dip ...................... 24
Balsamic Roasted Asparagus ................... 126
Sesame Marinated Asparagus ................. 126
Aunt Lizzie's Punch ................................. 119

## AVOCADOS

Guacamole with Roasted Corn .................. 52
Mediterranean Salsa ................................ 49
Shrimp Quesadillas .................................. 45

## B

Bacon-Wrapped Meatloaf ........................ 196
Baked Apples in Puff Pastry
    with Rum Sauce ................................. 245
Baked Salmon with Roasted Tomatoes ......... 206
Balsamic Glazed Strawberries
    over Ice Cream .................................. 262
Balsamic Roasted Asparagus ..................... 126

## BANANAS

Banana Bundt Cake ................................ 226
Banana Delight Layer Cake ..................... 222
Banana Nut Frosting ............................... 222
Banana Punch ........................................ 120
Creole Bread Pudding
    with Bourbon Sauce ........................... 243
Italian Blizzard ....................................... 123
Spiced Orange Banana Bread ................. 102
Basic Cheese Dip ..................................... 53
Basil Marinated Corn on the Cob .............. 134
Basting Sauce ......................................... 164

## BEANS AND PEAS

Black Bean Salsa ...................................... 72
Black-Eyed Peas with Caramelized
    Onion and Country Ham ..................... 135
Cece's Samosas ....................................... 43
Citrus Black Bean Salsa ............................ 50
Cowboy Caviar ........................................ 54
Everybody's Favorite Green Beans ........... 128
Fabulous Chili .......................................... 83
Shrimp and Black Bean Salad ................... 72
Summertime Cherry Tomato
    and Green Bean Pasta .......................... 59

## BEEF

Bacon-Wrapped Meatloaf ........................ 196
Chipotle Baked Brisket ............................ 188
English Roast Beef with
    Whiskey and Ale ................................ 189
Fabulous Chili .......................................... 83
Flank Steak with Summer Salsa ................ 190
Garlic and Brandy Glazed
    Fillet of Beef ...................................... 191
Italian Roast Beef ................................... 192
Italian Stuffed Fillets .............................. 191
Jose's Queso ............................................ 53

Marinated Beef Tenderloin
   with Horseradish Sauce ........................ 193
Mushroom-Stuffed Tenderloin ................... 194
Sicilian Spaghetti Sauce ........................... 211
Spicy Grilled Steak ................................... 192
Steak au Poivre ........................................ 195

## BELL PEPPERS

Cowboy Caviar ........................................ 54
Five Pepper Quesadilla ............................ 40
Garden Party Canapés ............................. 33
Petite Crab Cakes with
   Fresh Tomato Tartar Sauce .................... 30
Pork Tenderloin with Red,
   Yellow, and Green Peppers .................. 166
Summertime Cherry Tomato
   and Green Bean Pasta ......................... 59

## BEVERAGES

Aunt Lizzie's Punch .................................. 119
Banana Punch ......................................... 120
Café Au Cacao ....................................... 122
Coffee Punch ........................................... 119
Famous Iced Tea ..................................... 118
Frozen Watermelon Margarita ................. 121
Hot Christmas Cider ................................ 124
Italian Blizzard ........................................ 123
Mojito .................................................... 122
Queen's Punch ........................................ 120
Refreshing Almond Tea ............................ 118
Sangría Blanca ....................................... 124
Sea Breeze in a Pitcher ........................... 121
Spicy Spiked Slush .................................. 123
Black and White Chess Tarts ..................... 232
Black Bean Salsa ..................................... 72
Blackberry Cobbler, Farmers Market .......... 237
Black-Eyed Peas with Caramelized
   Onion and Country Ham ...................... 135

## BLUEBERRIES

Blueberry and Lemon Soufflé Pancakes ....... 93
Fruit Salad with Mint Syrup ....................... 80
Bombay Blues .......................................... 25
Bow Tie Pasta with Olives and Pine Nuts ....... 58
Brandy Chocolate Mousse ......................... 249
Bread Pudding with
   Tennessee Whiskey Sauce ..................... 244

## BREADS

Almond Cream Cheese Danish ................. 107
Artichoke Garlic Bread ............................ 115
Cherry-Lemon Scones .............................. 106
Cinnamon Roll Ups ................................. 108
Cinnamon Strawberry Bread .................... 104
Gingerbread Muffins ............................... 110
"Good for You" Orange
   Cranberry Bran Muffins ....................... 112
Good Morning Glory Muffins ................... 111
Guilt Free Popovers ................................. 117
Mandarin Orange Brunch Cake ............... 109
Miss Jeanne's Corn Light Bread ................ 116
Raspberry Pecan Bread ........................... 103
"Ready When You
   Need Them" Dinner Rolls ..................... 113
Spiced Orange Banana Bread ................. 102
Sweet Potato Biscuits ............................... 114
Zesty Zucchini Bread ............................... 105
Breakfast Strata ....................................... 98
Brie Tartlets with Grape Salsa .................... 23

## BROCCOLI

Lemon Pepper Broccolini ......................... 128
Zesty Garlic Roasted Broccoli
   with Pine Nuts .................................... 129
Brown Sugar/Cinnamon
   Cream Cheese Spread ......................... 101
Brownie Trifle .......................................... 239

## BRUNCH (see also Breads)

Artichoke Frittata .................................. 95
Blueberry and Lemon Soufflé Pancakes ....... 93
Breakfast Strata .................................. 98
French Toast Soufflé .............................. 91
Grits Gruyère ...................................... 94
Mandarin Orange Brunch Cake ............. 109
Mushroom, Tomato, and Bacon Puff .......... 99
Panettone French Toast ............................ 92
Santa's Breakfast Surprise ........................ 96
Sausage Mushroom Quiche
  with Parmesan .................................. 97
Tom's Favorite Fruit and Nut Granola ... 100
Brussels Sprouts in Wine .......................... 130
Burgundy Lasagna ................................. 212
Buttery Glaze ...................................... 226

## C

## CABBAGE

Crunchy Chicken Salad ............................ 62
Oriental Slaw ...................................... 69
Spicy Thai Chicken Salad
  with Ginger Peanut Dressing ................. 73
Caesar Ravioli Salad ............................... 57
Café Au Cacao .................................... 122
**Cakes** (see Desserts)
Caramelized Almonds ............................. 75
Caramelized Onions ............................... 89
Caramelized Onion and
  Porcini Risotto with Sage ..................... 153

## CARROTS

Crowd Pleasing Carrot Cake
  with Cream Cheese Frosting ................. 220
Garden Party Canapés ............................. 33
Ginger Orange Roasted Carrots ............. 131
Good Morning Glory Muffins .................. 111
Lemon Carrot Sticks ................................ 130
Summertime Orzo Salad .......................... 78
Cece's Samosas ....................................... 43
Celebration Sauce .................................. 162

## CEREALS AND GRAINS (see also Rice)

Couscous Chicken Salad
  with Orange Ginger Vinaigrette ............. 60
"Good for You" Orange
  Cranberry Bran Muffins ...................... 112
Mediterranean Couscous ........................ 160
Raspberry Oatmeal Bars ........................ 252
Tom's Favorite Fruit and Nut Granola ....... 100

## CHEESE

Artichoke and Blue Cheese Salad ............. 66
Artichoke Cheese Puffs ............................ 29
Artichoke Garlic Bread ............................ 115
Asparagus and Prosciutto Bundles ............. 127
Basic Cheese Dip ................................... 53
Bombay Blues ....................................... 25
Bow Tie Pasta with
  Olives and Pine Nuts .......................... 58
Brie Tartlets with Grape Salsa ................. 23
Burgundy Lasagna ................................ 212
Caesar Ravioli Salad ............................... 57
Cheesy Bacon Delights ............................ 31
Chive Talking Fondue ............................. 51
Devils and Angels on Horseback
  with Balsamic Syrup ........................... 42
Festive Bite-Size Cheese Balls .................. 34
Feta and Vidalia Onion Risotto ................ 154
Five Pepper Quesadilla ............................ 40
Fresh Tomato Tart .................................. 32
Gorgonzola and Walnut Terrine ................ 36
Grated Cheese Potatoes .......................... 137
Greek Chicken Breasts ........................... 181
Green Chile-Pimento Cheese .................... 88
Green Chili Pick-Me-Ups ......................... 39

Grits Gruyère ............................................. 94
In A Crunch Corn Dip............................... 52
Jose's Queso ............................................ 53
Marinated Cheese Tortellini ...................... 37
Mediterranean Salsa ................................ 49
Monterey Salsa with Corn and Olives ......... 51
Pepper Pecan Cheese Wafers .................... 34
Roasted Chicken with Goat Cheese
   and Pine Nuts over Fettuccine............... 168
Roasted Pears with
   Gorgonzola and Pecans ....................... 152
Sausage Mushroom Quiche
   with Parmesan ...................................... 97
Savory Goat Cheese and
   Walnut Cheesecakes ............................. 26
Shrimp and Crabmeat au Gratin ............. 197
Shrimp Quesadillas ................................. 45
Spicy Rice Casserole .............................. 155
Spinach, Artichoke and
   Gruyère Pinwheels ................................ 28
Spinach, Gorgonzola, and
   Walnuts over Fettuccine ...................... 217
Spinach Lasagna ................................... 215
Spinach Parmesan Chicken ..................... 174
Spinach Queso ........................................ 53
Summer Squash Casserole ...................... 144
Summertime Cherry Tomato
   and Green Bean Pasta .......................... 59
Tailgate Cheese Spread ............................ 37
The Overnight Salad ................................. 71
Three-Way Queso .................................... 53
Turkey Burgers with Smoked
   Gouda and Granny Smith Apples ......... 185
Cherry-Lemon Scones ............................. 106

## CHICKEN

Chicken Breasts Sauté
   with Tarragon Cream Sauce ................. 183
Chicken Curry ........................................ 175
Chicken Jambalaya ................................ 178
Chicken, Sausage and
   Tasso Sauce Piquant ........................... 173
Chicken Tortilla Soup............................... 81
Chinese Chicken Bites ............................. 27
Couscous Chicken Salad with
   Orange Ginger Vinaigrette .................... 60
Crockpot Chicken with
   Mushroom Sauce ................................ 182
Crunchy Chicken Salad ........................... 62
Family Favorite Barbecue Chicken ........... 181
Greek Chicken Breasts ........................... 181
Grilled Chicken with Creamy Grits
   and Mushroom Sauce ......................... 176
Grilled Lime Chicken with
   Tropical Fruit Salsa.............................. 172
Lemon Thyme Grilled Chicken ................ 184
Mexican Chowder ................................... 84
Mushroom Chicken Crêpes
   with Sherry Cream Sauce .................... 170
Mushroom Glazed Chicken Breast ........... 180
Old Hickory's Chicken Salad .................... 63
Pecan Buttermilk Chicken ....................... 177
Picnic Chicken with Cumin
   and a Pine Nut Crust ........................... 169
Roasted Chicken with Goat Cheese
   and Pine Nuts over Fettuccine............... 168
Soccer Night Chicken ............................ 179
Spicy Thai Chicken Salad with
   Ginger Peanut Dressing ........................ 73
Spinach Parmesan Chicken ..................... 174
Summer Strawberry Salad
   with Sweet Surprise Pecans ................... 76
White Chicken Chili
   with Pine Nuts ...................................... 86
Chipotle Baked Brisket............................ 188
Chive Talking Fondue ............................. 51

## CHOCOLATE (see also Desserts)

Almond Toffee ....................................... 264
Black and White Chess Tarts .................. 232
Brandy Chocolate Mousse ...................... 249

Brownie Trifle .................................................. 239
Chocolate Cloud Roll .............................. 240
Chocolate Truffle Cake
   with Raspberry Sauce ......................... 228
Chocolate Walnut Fudge Pie .................... 231
Espresso Chocolate Sauce ....................... 260
Four-Pound Brownies ............................... 250
Hot Fudge Sauce .................................... 261
Last Minute Cookies ............................... 255
Mocha Fudge Brownies ........................... 251
New Baby Peanut Butter Pie ..................... 233
Toasted Almond Semi-Freddo
   with Warm Chocolate Sauce ................ 248
Triple Threat Chocolate Chip Cookies........ 255
Tunnel of Love Cupcakes .......................... 230
Warm Chocolate Soufflés ......................... 247
Cilantro Lime Grilled Shrimp ......................... 46
Cinnamon Roll Ups ...................................... 108
Cinnamon Strawberry Bread ....................... 104
Citrus Basil Grilled Shrimp ........................... 201
Citrus Black Bean Salsa ................................ 50

## COCONUT

Easy Coconut Macaroons ........................ 253
Good Morning Glory Muffins ................... 111
Graham Cracker Sandwiches ................... 258
Mama Nell's Strawberry Nut Cake .......... 223
Raspberry Oatmeal Bars .......................... 252
Strawberry Frosting .................................. 223
Coffee Punch ............................................... 119
Confetti Corn ............................................... 132
**Cookies** *(see Desserts)*

## CORN

Basil Marinated Corn on the Cob ............. 134
Citrus Black Bean Salsa ............................. 50
Confetti Corn ............................................ 132
Cowboy Caviar ........................................... 54

Curried Corn Soup..................................... 82
Farmers Market Fiesta Corn .................... 133
Guacamole with Roasted Corn ................. 52
In A Crunch Corn Dip................................ 52
Mexican Chowder .................................... 84
Miss Jeanne's Corn Light Bread .............. 116
Monterey Salsa with Corn and Olives ........ 51
Penne with Corn, Bacon,
   Leeks and Tomatoes ............................ 213

## CORNISH HENS

Apricot-Glazed Cornish Hens
   Stuffed with Wild Rice ........................ 186
Couscous Chicken Salad
   with Orange Ginger Vinaigrette ................ 60
Cowboy Caviar ............................................. 54

## CRANBERRIES

Cranberry Citrus Salsa ............................. 56
"Good for You" Orange
   Cranberry Bran Muffins ....................... 112
Hot Christmas Cider ............................... 124
Mediterranean Couscous ....................... 160
Sea Breeze in a Pitcher ......................... 121
Spinach Salad with Cranberries ................ 74
Cream Cheese Frosting Supreme ........... 221
Cream Cheese Spreads ......................... 101
Creamy Grits ........................................... 177
Creamy Raspberry Dressing ..................... 70
Crème Brûlée .......................................... 246
Creole Bread Pudding
   with Bourbon Sauce ............................ 243

## CRÊPES

Fresh Spinach Crêpes
   with Mushroom Sauce ......................... 140
Mushroom Chicken Crêpes
   with Sherry Cream Sauce ..................... 170
Crockpot Chicken with
   Mushroom Sauce ................................. 182

Crowd Pleasing Carrot Cake
  with Cream Cheese Frosting ............... 220
Crunchy Chicken Salad ........................ 62

## CUCUMBERS

Cucumber Sandwiches ....................... 87
Garden Party Canapés ....................... 33
Mediterranean Tomato Salad ............... 64
Spicy Thai Chicken Salad with
  Ginger Peanut Dressing ................... 73
Curried Corn Soup .............................. 82

## D

## DESSERTS *(see also Chocolate)*

### Cake Frostings

Banana Nut Frosting ......................... 222
Buttery Glaze ................................... 226
Cream Cheese Frosting Supreme ........ 221
Easy Cream Cheese Frosting .............. 226
Grand Marnier Buttercream Frosting ... 230
Lemon Meltaway Frosting .................. 257
Raspberry Sauce .............................. 229
Strawberry Frosting .......................... 223
Vanilla Frosting ................................ 258

### Cakes

Banana Bundt Cake .......................... 226
Banana Delight Layer Cake ................ 222
Chocolate Truffle Cake
  with Raspberry Sauce ..................... 228
Crowd Pleasing Carrot Cake
  with Cream Cheese Frosting ............ 220
Golden Circle Pound Cake ................. 224
Mama Nell's
  Strawberry Nut Cake ..................... 223
Miss Bess' Famous
  New York Cheesecake .................... 219
No Guilt Apricot Lemon Cake ............. 227

Spiced Fresh Apple Cake ................... 225
Tunnel of Love Cupcakes ................... 230

### Cookies and Bars

Almond Cream Cheese Cookies .......... 256
Easy Coconut Macaroons .................. 253
Four-Pound Brownies ....................... 250
Ginger Cookies ................................ 254
Graham Cracker Sandwiches ............. 258
Last Minute Cookies ......................... 255
Lemon Melt-Away Cookies ................ 257
Mocha Fudge Brownies .................... 251
Pecan Wafers .................................. 259
Raspberry Oatmeal Bars ................... 252
Triple Threat Chocolate Chip Cookies ... 255

### Pies

Almond Apricot Tartlets .................... 234
Apple Cream Pie .............................. 235
Black and White Chess Tarts ............. 232
Chocolate Walnut Fudge Pie ............. 231
Farmers Market Blackberry Cobbler .... 237
Gingered Peach Raspberry Crisp ........ 238
New Baby Peanut Butter Pie ............. 233
Orange Curd Tartlets ....................... 242
Tennessee Peach Pie ........................ 236

### Puddings and Desserts

Almond Toffee ................................. 264
Baked Apples in Puff Pastry
  with Rum Sauce ............................ 245
Balsamic Glazed Strawberries
  over Ice Cream ............................. 262
Brandy Chocolate Mousse ................. 249
Bread Pudding with
  Tennessee Whiskey Sauce ............... 244
Brownie Trifle .................................. 239
Chocolate Cloud Roll ........................ 240
Crème Brûlée .................................. 246
Creole Bread Pudding
  with Bourbon Sauce ...................... 243
Espresso Ice Cream Sundaes ............. 260

Grape Sherbet ..................................... 259
Hot Fudge Sauce ................................. 261
Pinot Granita ...................................... 263
Toasted Almond Semi-Freddo
  with Warm Chocolate Sauce ............. 248
Warm Chocolate Soufflés ..................... 247
Devils and Angels on Horseback
  with Balsamic Syrup ............................... 42

## DIPS AND SPREADS

Basic Cheese Dip .................................. 53
Brown Sugar/Cinnamon
  Cream Cheese Spread ....................... 101
Chive Talking Fondue ............................. 51
Citrus Black Bean Salsa .......................... 50
Cowboy Caviar ..................................... 54
Cranberry Citrus Salsa ........................... 56
Easy Everyday Salsa .............................. 49
Ginger and Water Chestnut
  Dip for Crudités ................................ 55
Gorgonzola and Walnut Terrine ............... 36
Guacamole with Roasted Corn ................ 52
In A Crunch Corn Dip ........................... 52
Jackie's Salsa ....................................... 50
Jose's Queso ........................................ 53
Lemon Cream Cheese Spread ................ 101
Mediterranean Salsa .............................. 49
Monterey Salsa with Corn and Olives ........ 51
Nutty Fruit Dip ..................................... 55
Scallion Cream Cheese .......................... 90
Smoked Salmon Spread ......................... 48
Spinach Queso ..................................... 53
Strawberry Cream Cheese Spread ........... 101
Sun-Dried Tomato Pesto Torte .................. 38
Sun-Dried Tomato Spread ....................... 48
Tailgate Cheese Spread .......................... 37
Three-Way Queso ................................. 53
Vanilla Cream Cheese Spread ................ 101
Wasabi Dip ......................................... 24

## E

Easy Coconut Macaroons ...................... 253
Easy Cream Cheese Frosting .................. 226
Easy Everyday Salsa .............................. 49

## EGGS

Artichoke Frittata .................................. 95
Breakfast Strata .................................... 98
Mushroom, Tomato, and Bacon Puff .......... 99
Santa's Breakfast Surprise ....................... 96
Sausage Mushroom Quiche
  with Parmesan .................................. 97
English Roast Beef with
  Whiskey and Ale .............................. 189
Espresso Chocolate Sauce ..................... 260
Espresso Ice Cream Sundaes .................. 260
Everybody's Favorite Green Beans ............ 128

## F

Fabulous Chili ...................................... 83
Family Favorite Barbecue Chicken ........... 181
Famous Iced Tea ................................. 118
Farmers Market Blackberry Cobbler .......... 237
Farmers Market Fiesta Corn ................... 133
Festive Bite-Size Cheese Balls .................. 34
Feta and Vidalia Onion Risotto ............... 154

**FISH** *(see also Seafood)*

Baked Salmon with Roasted Tomatoes ...... 206
Mahi Mahi with Pineapple
  Papaya Salsa .................................. 203
Maple-Glazed Salmon .......................... 207
Salmon Wellington ............................... 205
Smoked Salmon Spread ......................... 48
Wasabi-Glazed Salmon
  over Wilted Fresh Spinach .................. 204

Five Pepper Quesadilla .................................. 40
Flank Steak with Summer Salsa ................... 190
Four-Pound Brownies .................................. 250
French Toast Soufflé ..................................... 91
Fresh Spinach Crêpes with
    Mushroom Sauce .................................. 140
Fresh Tomato Tart ......................................... 32
Fresh Tomato Tartar Sauce ............................ 31
Frozen Watermelon Margarita .................... 121

## FRUIT *(see also individual listings)*

    Fruit Salad with Mint Syrup ....................... 80
    Grilled Lime Chicken with
        Tropical Fruit Salsa ............................ 172
    Tom's Favorite Fruit and Nut Granola ...... 100
    Tropical Romaine Salad ............................ 79
    Winter Fruit Salad .................................... 65
Fruit Salad with Mint Syrup ........................... 80

## G

Garden Party Canapés .................................. 33
Garlic and Brandy Glazed Fillet of Beef ...... 191
Garlic, Lemon Sautéed Artichoke Hearts ...... 127
Ginger and Water Chestnut
    Dip for Crudités ..................................... 55
Ginger Cookies .......................................... 254
Ginger Orange Roasted Carrots ................. 131
Ginger Peanut Dressing ............................... 73
Gingerbread Muffins .................................. 110
Gingered Peach Raspberry Crisp ................ 238
Golden Circle Pound Cake ......................... 224
"Good for You" Orange
    Cranberry Bran Muffins ......................... 112
Good Morning Glory Muffins ..................... 111
Gorgonzola and Walnut Terrine ................... 36
Graham Cracker Sandwiches ..................... 258
Grand Marnier Buttercream Frosting .......... 230

## GRAPES

    Brie Tartlets with Grape Salsa .................... 23
    Old Hickory's Chicken Salad .................... 63
    Grape Sherbet ....................................... 259
Grated Cheese Potatoes ............................. 137
Greek Chicken Breasts ............................... 181
Greek Pasta ............................................... 216
Greek Pasta Salad ....................................... 57
Green Chile-Pimento Cheese ....................... 88
Green Chili Pick-Me-Ups ............................. 39

## GRILLING RECIPES

    Cilantro Lime Grilled Shrimp ..................... 46
    Citrus Basil Grilled Shrimp ...................... 201
    Flank Steak with Summer Salsa ............... 190
    Grilled Chicken with Creamy Grits
        and Mushroom Sauce ......................... 176
    Grilled Lime Chicken with
        Tropical Fruit Salsa ............................ 172
    Grilled Portobellos with
        Hazelnut Topping ................................. 44
    Grilled Spinach Stuffed Vidalia Onions .... 142
    Grilled Zucchini Boats ............................ 150
    Guacamole with Roasted Corn .................. 52
    Lemon Thyme Grilled Chicken ................ 184
    Marinated Pork Tenderloin
        with Celebration Sauce ....................... 162
    Spiced Pork Tenderloin with
        Jalapeño Honey Sauce ........................ 164
    Spicy Grilled Steak ................................. 192
    Spicy Thai Chicken Salad with
        Ginger Peanut Dressing ........................ 73
    Turkey Burgers with Smoked Gouda
        and Granny Smith Apples ................... 185

## GRITS

    Creamy Grits ......................................... 177
    Grilled Chicken with Creamy Grits
        and Mushroom Sauce ......................... 176

Grits Gruyère .......................................... 94
New Orleans Style Shrimp 'n Grits .......... 198
Santa's Breakfast Surprise ........................ 96
Guacamole with Roasted Corn .................... 52
Guilt Free Popovers ................................... 117

## H

Herb Roasted Potatoes with
    Balsamic Vinegar ................................. 139
Honey-Lime Vinaigrette ............................ 160
Horseradish Sauce .................................... 193
Hot Christmas Cider ................................ 124
Hot Fudge Sauce ...................................... 261

## I

In A Crunch Corn Dip ................................ 52
Italian Blizzard ......................................... 123
Italian Roast Beef .................................... 192
Italian Spinach and Artichoke Hearts .......... 143
Italian Stuffed Fillets ................................ 191

## J

Jackie's Salsa ............................................. 50
Jalapeño Honey Sauce ............................. 165
Jícama Slaw .............................................. 68
Jose's Queso ............................................. 53

## K

### KIWIS

Fruit Salad with Mint Syrup ....................... 80
Tropical Romaine Salad ............................. 79

## L

Lamb, Pecan Encrusted Rack of .................. 187
Last Minute Cookies ................................. 255
Layered Garden Bake ............................... 149

### LEMONS AND LIMES

Blueberry and Lemon Soufflé Pancakes ....... 93
Cherry-Lemon Scones .............................. 106
Chinese Chicken Bites ............................... 27
Cilantro Lime Grilled Shrimp ..................... 46
Citrus Basil Grilled Shrimp ....................... 201
Cranberry Citrus Salsa .............................. 56
Famous Iced Tea ..................................... 118
Ginger Peanut Dressing ............................. 73
Grilled Lime Chicken with
    Tropical Fruit Salsa ............................. 172
Jícama Slaw ............................................. 68
Lemon Carrot Sticks ................................ 130
Lemon Cream Cheese Spread ................... 101
Lemon Garlic Sautéed
    Artichoke Hearts ................................. 127
Lemon Melt-Away Cookies ...................... 257
Lemon Pepper Broccolini ......................... 128
Lemon Thyme Grilled Chicken ................. 184
Mediterranean Couscous ......................... 160
Mojito .................................................... 122
No Guilt Apricot Lemon Cake .................. 227
Orange Lime Dressing ............................... 79
Queen's Punch ....................................... 120
Refreshing Almond Tea ........................... 118
Sangría Blanca ........................................ 124
Spicy Baked Barbecue Shrimp .................. 202
Spicy Spiked Slush .................................. 123

## M

Mahi Mahi with Pineapple
  Papaya Salsa ......................................... 203
Mama Nell's Strawberry Nut Cake ............. 223
Mandarin Orange Brunch Cake ................. 109
Maple Mustard Pork Tenderloin
  with Caramelized Apples ..................... 161
Maple-Glazed Salmon ............................... 207
Marinated Beef Tenderloin
  with Horseradish Sauce ........................ 193
Marinated Cheese Tortellini ....................... 37
Marinated Pork Roast ................................ 165
Marinated Pork Tenderloin
  with Celebration Sauce ......................... 162
Marinated Vegetable Salad Dressing ........... 74
Mediterranean Couscous ........................... 160
Mediterranean Salsa .................................. 49
Mediterranean Shrimp with
  Angel Hair Pasta ................................... 210
Mediterranean Tomato Salad ..................... 64
Mexican Chowder ..................................... 84
Mint Syrup ................................................ 80
Miss Bess' Famous
  New York Cheesecake ........................... 219
Miss Jeanne's Corn Light Bread ................. 116
Mocha Fudge Brownies ............................. 251
Mojito ....................................................... 122
Monterey Salsa with Corn and Olives ........ 51

### MUSHROOMS

Artichoke Cheese Puffs ............................. 29
Breakfast Strata ........................................ 98
Caramelized Onion and
  Porcini Risotto with Sage ..................... 153
Crockpot Chicken with
  Mushroom Sauce ................................. 182
Fresh Spinach Crêpes with
  Mushroom Sauce ................................. 140
Grilled Chicken with Creamy Grits
  and Mushroom Sauce .......................... 176
Grilled Portobellos with
  Hazelnut Topping ................................. 44
Mushroom Chicken Crêpes
  with Sherry Cream Sauce ..................... 170
Mushroom Glazed Chicken Breast ........... 180
Mushroom Sauce .......................... 141, 176
Mushroom-Stuffed Tenderloin .................. 194
Mushroom, Tomato, and Bacon Puff .......... 99
Parmesan Polenta with
  Wild Mushrooms ................................. 158
Sausage Mushroom Quiche
  with Parmesan ..................................... 97
Spinach Queso ......................................... 53

## N

New Baby Peanut Butter Pie ....................... 233
New Orleans Style Shrimp 'n Grits ............. 198
No Guilt Apricot Lemon Cake .................... 227

### NUTS

Almond Apricot Tartlets ............................ 234
Almond Cream Cheese Cookies ............... 256
Almond Cream Cheese Danish ................. 107
Almond Jasmine Rice ............................... 159
Almond Toffee ......................................... 264
Banana Nut Frosting ................................ 222
Bombay Blues ........................................... 25
Bow Tie Pasta with
  Olives and Pine Nuts ............................ 58
Caramelized Almonds ............................... 75
Cheesy Bacon Delights ............................. 31
Chocolate Walnut Fudge Pie .................... 231
Crunchy Chicken Salad ............................ 62
Festive Bite-Size Cheese Balls ................... 34
Four-Pound Brownies .............................. 250

Ginger Peanut Dressing ............................ 73
Golden Circle Pound Cake ...................... 224
Gorgonzola and Walnut Terrine ................ 36
Graham Cracker Sandwiches .................. 258
Grilled Portobellos with
   Hazelnut Topping .................................. 44
Mama Nell's
   Strawberry Nut Cake ........................... 223
Mocha Fudge Brownies .......................... 251
Nutty Fruit Dip .......................................... 55
Old Hickory's Chicken Salad ..................... 63
Orange-Walnut Salad with
   Sweet and Sour Dressing ....................... 67
Oriental Slaw ............................................ 69
Pecan Buttermilk Chicken ........................ 177
Pecan Encrusted Rack of Lamb ................ 187
Pecan Wafers ......................................... 259
Pepper Pecan Cheese Wafers ................... 34
Picnic Chicken with Cumin
   and a Pine Nut Crust ........................... 169
Raspberry Pecan Bread .......................... 103
Roasted Chicken with Goat Cheese
   and Pine Nuts over Fettuccine .............. 168
Roasted Pears with
   Gorgonzola and Pecans ...................... 152
Rosemary's Walnuts ................................. 41
Savory Goat Cheese and
   Walnut Cheesecakes ............................. 26
Shrimp with Spinach and Pine Nuts ......... 200
Spiced Fresh Apple Cake ....................... 225
Spinach, Gorgonzola, and
   Walnuts over Fettuccine ....................... 217
Summer Strawberry Salad
   with Sweet Surprise Pecans .................... 76
Sweet Surprise Pecans .............................. 77
Toasted Almond Semi-Freddo
   with Warm Chocolate Sauce ................ 248
Tom's Favorite Fruit
   and Nut Granola ................................. 100
Tossed Salad with Caramelized Almonds and
   Spicy Vinaigrette Dressing ..................... 75
Triple Threat Chocolate
   Chip Cookies ...................................... 255
White Chicken Chili with Pine Nuts ............ 86
Zesty Garlic Roasted Broccoli
   with Pine Nuts .................................... 129

# O

Old Hickory's Chicken Salad ..................... 63

## OLIVES

Bow Tie Pasta with Olives
   and Pine Nuts ...................................... 58
Caesar Ravioli Salad ................................ 57
Greek Pasta Salad ................................... 57
Mediterranean Tomato Salad .................... 64
Monterey Salsa with Corn and Olives .......... 5
Pasta Salad with Sherry Dressing ............... 61
Summertime Cherry Tomato
   and Green Bean Pasta .......................... 59

## ONIONS

Black-Eyed Peas with Caramelized
   Onion and Country Ham ..................... 135
Caesar Ravioli Salad ................................ 57
Caramelized Onion and
   Porcini Risotto with Sage ..................... 153
Cece's Samosas ....................................... 43
Chicken Jambalaya ................................ 178
Citrus Black Bean Salsa ............................ 50
Confetti Corn ......................................... 132
Cowboy Caviar ........................................ 54
Easy Everyday Salsa ................................ 49
Farmers Market Fiesta Corn .................... 133
Feta and Vidalia Onion Risotto ................ 154
Grilled Spinach Stuffed Vidalia Onions .... 142
Guacamole with Roasted Corn ................. 52
Jackie's Salsa .......................................... 50

Layered Garden Bake ............................ 149
Marinated Vegetable Salad Dressing ......... 74
Mediterranean Salsa ............................... 49
Mediterranean Shrimp
    with Angel Hair Pasta ........................ 210
Orange-Walnut Salad with
    Sweet and Sour Dressing .................... 67
Pasta with Garlic Shrimp
    and Zucchini ................................... 208
Penne with Pumpkin Sauce ..................... 157
Prosciutto Vodka Sauce .......................... 214
Shrimp and Black Bean Salad ................... 72
Shrimp and Crabmeat au Gratin ............. 197
Shrimp Creole with Saffron Rice ............. 199
Summer Squash Casserole ..................... 144
Summertime Orzo Salad .......................... 78
Tomato Vidalia Stacks ........................... 148
Turkey and Caramelized Onion Wraps ...... 89
Zucchini, Tomato and Onion Bake ........... 151

## ORANGES

Almond Jasmine Rice .............................. 159
Aunt Lizzie's Punch ............................... 119
Citrus Black Bean Salsa ........................... 50
Cranberry Citrus Salsa ............................ 56
"Good for You" Orange
    Cranberry Bran Muffins .................... 112
Mandarin Orange Brunch Cake .............. 109
Orange Curd Tartlets ............................. 242
Orange Ginger Vinaigrette ....................... 60
Orange Lime Dressing ............................. 79
Orange-Walnut Salad with
    Sweet and Sour Dressing .................... 67
Panettone French Toast ........................... 92
Sangría Blanca ..................................... 124
Spiced Orange Banana Bread ................. 102
The Overnight Salad ............................... 71
Tossed Salad with Caramelized Almonds
    and Spicy Vinaigrette Dressing ............ 75
Oriental Slaw ........................................ 69

## P

Panettone French Toast ........................... 92
Parmesan Polenta with Wild Mushrooms ..... 158

## PASTA

Angel Hair Pasta Flan ........................... 156
Bow Tie Pasta with Olives and Pine Nuts .... 58
Burgundy Lasagna ................................ 212
Caesar Ravioli Salad ............................... 57
Greek Pasta ........................................ 216
Greek Pasta Salad .................................. 57
Marinated Cheese Tortellini ..................... 37
Mediterranean Shrimp
    with Angel Hair Pasta ........................ 210
Pasta Salad with Sherry Dressing ............... 61
Pasta with Ale ...................................... 213
Pasta with Garlic Shrimp
    and Zucchini ................................... 208
Penne with Corn, Bacon,
    Leeks and Tomatoes ......................... 213
Penne with Pumpkin Sauce ..................... 157
Roasted Chicken with Goat Cheese
    and Pine Nuts over Fettuccine ............ 168
Seafood Fettuccine ............................... 209
Sicilian Spaghetti Sauce ......................... 211
Spicy Thai Chicken Salad
    with Ginger Peanut Dressing ................ 73
Spinach, Gorgonzola, and
    Walnuts over Fettuccine .................... 217
Spinach Lasagna .................................. 215
Summertime Cherry Tomato
    and Green Bean Pasta ........................ 59
Summertime Orzo Salad .......................... 78

## PEACHES

Gingered Peach Raspberry Crisp ............. 238
Tennessee Peach Pie ............................. 236

## PEARS

Pear Salad with Creamy
  Raspberry Dressing ................................ 70
Roasted Pears with
  Gorgonzola and Pecans ...................... 152
Winter Fruit Salad ...................................... 65
Pecan Buttermilk Chicken ........................... 177
Pecan Encrusted Rack of Lamb .................. 187
Pecan Wafers ............................................ 259
Penne with Corn, Bacon,
  Leeks and Tomatoes ............................. 213
Penne with Pumpkin Sauce ......................... 157
Pepper Pecan Cheese Wafers ....................... 34
Pepperoni Praise .......................................... 35

## PEPPERS

Cece's Samosas ......................................... 43
Chicken, Sausage and
  Tasso Sauce Piquant ............................ 173
Chipotle Baked Brisket .............................. 188
Citrus Black Bean Salsa .............................. 50
Cranberry Citrus Salsa ................................ 56
Easy Everyday Salsa .................................. 49
Five Pepper Quesadilla ............................... 40
Green Chile-Pimento Cheese ....................... 88
Green Chili Pick-Me-Ups ............................ 39
Jackie's Salsa ............................................. 50
Jalapeño Honey Sauce .............................. 165
Spicy Rice Casserole ................................ 155
Petite Crab Cakes with
  Fresh Tomato Tartar Sauce ....................... 30
Picnic Chicken with Cumin
  and a Pine Nut Crust ............................ 169
**Pies** *(see Desserts)*

## PINEAPPLE

Aunt Lizzie's Punch .................................. 119
Banana Punch ......................................... 120
Creole Bread Pudding
  with Bourbon Sauce ............................. 243
Crowd Pleasing Carrot Cake
  with Cream Cheese Frosting ................. 220
Grape Sherbet ......................................... 259
Mahi Mahi with Pineapple
  Papaya Salsa ....................................... 203
Tropical Fruit Salsa .................................. 172
Pinot Granita ........................................... 263
Plum Sauce, Warm ..................................... 47
Polenta with Wild Mushrooms,
  Parmesan ............................................ 158

## PORK

Asparagus and Prosciutto Bundles ............. 127
Bacon-Wrapped Meatloaf ......................... 196
Black-Eyed Peas with Caramelized
  Onion and Country Ham ...................... 135
Breakfast Strata ......................................... 98
Burgundy Lasagna ................................... 212
Cheesy Bacon Delights ............................... 31
Chicken, Sausage and
  Tasso Sauce Piquant ............................ 173
Confetti Corn .......................................... 132
Everybody's Favorite Green Beans ............. 128
Italian Stuffed Fillets ................................ 191
Maple Mustard Pork Tenderloin
  with Caramelized Apples ...................... 161
Marinated Pork Roast .............................. 165
Marinated Pork Tenderloin
  with Celebration Sauce ........................ 162
Mushroom, Tomato, and Bacon Puff ............ 99
Mushroom-Stuffed Tenderloin ................... 194
Penne with Corn, Bacon,
  Leeks and Tomatoes ............................. 213
Pepperoni Praise ........................................ 35
Pork Chops with Apples
  and Raisins ......................................... 163
Pork Tenderloin with Red,
  Yellow, and Green Peppers ................... 166

Prosciutto Vodka Sauce ............................ 214
Santa's Breakfast Surprise ......................... 96
Sausage Mushroom Quiche
   with Parmesan ..................................... 97
Sicilian Spaghetti Sauce ......................... 211
Spiced Pork Tenderloin with
   Jalapeño Honey Sauce ...................... 164
Tennessee Whiskey Spareribs .................. 167

**POTATOES** *(see also Sweet Potatoes)*

Cece's Samosas ........................................ 43
Grated Cheese Potatoes ......................... 137
Herb Roasted Potatoes with
   Balsamic Vinegar ............................... 139
Two Potato Roast ................................... 138
Prosciutto Vodka Sauce ............................ 214

**Pudding** *(see Desserts)*

**PUMPKIN**

Penne with Pumpkin Sauce ..................... 157
Pumpkin Harvest Soup ............................. 85

## Q

Queen's Punch ........................................ 120
Quiche with Parmesan,
   Sausage Mushroom ............................. 97
Quick Bourbon Sauce ............................. 243

## R

**RAISINS**

Creole Bread Pudding
   with Bourbon Sauce ........................... 243
Good Morning Glory Muffins .................. 111
Mediterranean Couscous ........................ 160
Pork Chops with Apples and Raisins ........ 163
Tom's Favorite Fruit and Nut Granola ....... 100

**RASPBERRIES**

Chocolate Truffle Cake
   with Raspberry Sauce ......................... 228
Creamy Raspberry Dressing ..................... 70
Fruit Salad with Mint Syrup ....................... 80
Gingered Peach Raspberry Crisp ............. 238
Pear Salad with Creamy
   Raspberry Dressing ............................... 70
Raspberry Oatmeal Bars ......................... 252
Raspberry Pecan Bread .......................... 103
Raspberry Sauce .................................... 229
"Ready When You Need
   Them" Dinner Rolls .............................. 113
Red Wine Vinaigrette ........................ 58, 71
Refreshing Almond Tea .......................... 118

**RICE**

Almond Jasmine Rice .............................. 159
Apricot-Glazed Cornish Hens
   Stuffed with Wild Rice ........................ 186
Caramelized Onion and
   Porcini Risotto with Sage ..................... 153
Chicken Jambalaya ................................ 178
Feta and Vidalia Onion Risotto ............... 154
Shrimp Creole with Saffron Rice ............. 199
Spicy Rice Casserole .............................. 155
Roasted Chicken with Goat Cheese
   and Pine Nuts over Fettuccine ................ 168
Roasted Pears with
   Gorgonzola and Pecans ...................... 152
Rosemary's Walnuts ................................. 41
Rum Sauce ............................................. 245

# S

## SALAD DRESSINGS

Creamy Raspberry Dressing ...................... 70
Ginger Peanut Dressing ........................... 73
Honey-Lime Vinaigrette ........................... 160
Marinated Vegetable Salad Dressing ......... 74
Mint Syrup ............................................. 80
Orange Ginger Vinaigrette ....................... 60
Orange Lime Dressing ............................. 79
Red Wine Vinaigrette ....................... 58, 71
Sherry Dressing ..................................... 61
Spicy Vinaigrette Dressing ....................... 75
Strawberry Poppy Seed Dressing ............... 76
Sweet and Sour Dressing ......................... 67

## SALADS

Artichoke and Blue Cheese Salad .............. 66
Bow Tie Pasta with Olives and Pine Nuts .... 58
Caesar Ravioli Salad ............................... 57
Couscous Chicken Salad with
   Orange Ginger Vinaigrette ................... 60
Crunchy Chicken Salad ............................ 62
Fruit Salad with Mint Syrup ...................... 80
Greek Pasta Salad .................................. 57
Jícama Slaw .......................................... 68
Mediterranean Tomato Salad .................... 64
Old Hickory's Chicken Salad ..................... 63
Orange-Walnut Salad with
   Sweet and Sour Dressing ..................... 67
Oriental Slaw ......................................... 69
Pasta Salad with Sherry Dressing ............... 61
Pear Salad with Creamy
   Raspberry Dressing ............................ 70
Shrimp and Black Bean Salad ................... 72
Spicy Thai Chicken Salad with
   Ginger Peanut Dressing ...................... 73
Spinach Salad with Cranberries ................ 74
Summer Strawberry Salad
   with Sweet Surprise Pecans .................. 76
Summertime Cherry Tomato
   and Green Bean Pasta ........................ 59
Summertime Orzo Salad .......................... 78
The Overnight Salad ............................... 71
Tossed Salad with Caramelized Almonds
   and Spicy Vinaigrette Dressing ............. 75
Tropical Romaine Salad ........................... 79
Winter Fruit Salad ................................... 65
Salmon Wellington ..................................... 205

## SALSAS AND SAUCES

Apricot Glaze ........................................ 186
Basting Sauce ....................................... 164
Black Bean Salsa ..................................... 72
Celebration Sauce ................................. 162
Citrus Black Bean Salsa ........................... 50
Cranberry Citrus Salsa ............................. 56
Easy Everyday Salsa ................................ 49
Espresso Chocolate Sauce ...................... 260
Fresh Tomato Tartar Sauce ....................... 31
Horseradish Sauce ................................ 193
Hot Fudge Sauce .................................. 261
Jackie's Salsa ........................................ 50
Jalapeño Honey Sauce .......................... 165
Mediterranean Salsa ............................... 49
Monterey Salsa with
   Corn and Olives ................................. 51
Mushroom Sauce ........................... 141, 176
Pineapple Papaya Salsa ......................... 203
Prosciutto Vodka Sauce ......................... 214
Quick Bourbon Sauce ............................ 243
Raspberry Sauce ................................... 229
Rum Sauce ........................................... 245
Scallion Cream Cheese ............................ 90
Sherry Cream Sauce .............................. 171
Sicilian Spaghetti Sauce ......................... 211

Spicy Tomato Thyme Sauce ..................... 218
Summer Salsa ......................................... 190
Tennessee Whiskey Sauce ..................... 244
Tropical Fruit Salsa ................................ 172
Warm Chocolate Sauce .......................... 249
Warm Plum Sauce ................................. 47

## SANDWICHES

Chipotle Baked Brisket ............................ 188
Cucumber Sandwiches ........................... 87
Green Chile-Pimento Cheese .................... 88
Turkey and Caramelized
   Onion Wraps .................................... 89
Turkey Basil Bites .................................. 90
Turkey Burgers with Smoked Gouda
   and Granny Smith Apples .................... 185
Sangría Blanca ...................................... 124
Santa's Breakfast Surprise ........................ 96
**Sauces** *(see Salsas and Sauces)*
Sausage Mushroom Quiche
   with Parmesan ................................... 97
Savory Goat Cheese and
   Walnut Cheesecakes .......................... 26
Scalloped Tomatoes and Artichokes ............ 125
Sea Breeze in a Pitcher .......................... 121

## SEAFOOD *(see also Fish)*

### Crab
   Petite Crab Cakes with
      Fresh Tomato Tartar Sauce ................... 30
   Seafood Fettuccine ............................. 209
   Shrimp and Crabmeat au Gratin ........... 197

### Scallops
   Seafood Fettuccine ............................. 209

### Shrimp
   Cilantro Lime Grilled Shrimp ................. 46
   Citrus Basil Grilled Shrimp .................... 201
   Mediterranean Shrimp
      with Angel Hair Pasta ........................ 210

New Orleans Style Shrimp 'n Grits ......... 198
Pasta with Garlic Shrimp
   and Zucchini .................................... 208
Seafood Fettuccine ............................... 209
Shrimp and Black Bean Salad ................ 72
Shrimp and Crabmeat au Gratin ........... 197
Shrimp Creole with Saffron Rice ........... 199
Shrimp Quesadillas ............................... 45
Shrimp with Spinach and Pine Nuts ....... 200
Skewered Shrimp with
   Warm Plum Sauce ............................. 47
Spicy Baked Barbecue Shrimp .............. 202
Seafood Fettuccine ............................... 209
Sesame Marinated Asparagus ................. 126
Sherry Cream Sauce .............................. 171
Sherry Dressing .................................... 61
Shrimp and Black Bean Salad ................ 72
Shrimp and Crabmeat au Gratin ............ 197
Shrimp Creole with Saffron Rice ............ 199
Shrimp Quesadillas ............................... 45
Shrimp with Spinach and Pine Nuts ............ 200
Sicilian Spaghetti Sauce ........................ 211
Skewered Shrimp with Warm Plum Sauce ...... 47
Skillet Tomatoes .................................... 146
Smoked Salmon Spread ......................... 48
Soccer Night Chicken ............................ 179

## SOUPS AND STEWS

   Chicken Tortilla Soup ........................... 81
   Curried Corn Soup ............................. 82
   Fabulous Chili .................................... 83
   Mexican Chowder .............................. 84
   Pumpkin Harvest Soup ........................ 85
   White Chicken Chili
      with Pine Nuts ................................ 86
Spiced Fresh Apple Cake ...................... 225
Spiced Orange Banana Bread ................ 102

Spiced Pork Tenderloin
  with Jalapeño Honey Sauce ..................... 164
Spicy Baked Barbecue Shrimp ..................... 202
Spicy Grilled Steak ..................................... 192
Spicy Rice Casserole .................................. 155
Spicy Spiked Slush ..................................... 123
Spicy Thai Chicken Salad
  with Ginger Peanut Dressing ..................... 73
Spicy Tomato Thyme Sauce ........................ 218
Spicy Vinaigrette Dressing ........................... 75

## SPINACH

Artichoke Frittata ....................................... 95
Burgundy Lasagna ................................... 212
Fresh Spinach Crêpes
  with Mushroom Sauce ........................... 140
Grilled Spinach Stuffed Vidalia Onions .... 142
Italian Spinach and Artichoke Hearts ....... 143
Orange-Walnut Salad
  with Sweet and Sour Dressing ................ 67
Shrimp with Spinach and Pine Nuts ......... 200
Spinach, Artichoke and
  Gruyère Pinwheels ................................. 28
Spinach, Gorgonzola, and
  Walnuts over Fettuccine ........................ 217
Spinach Lasagna ..................................... 215
Spinach Parmesan Chicken ..................... 174
Spinach Queso .......................................... 53
Spinach Salad with Cranberries ................ 74
Tomatoes Rockefeller .............................. 147
Wasabi-Glazed Salmon
  over Wilted Fresh Spinach ................... 204
Wok Sesame Spinach ............................. 139

## SQUASH

Layered Garden Bake ............................. 149
Squash Ribbons al Pomodoro ................. 145
Summer Squash Casserole ..................... 144
Steak au Poivre ........................................ 195

## STRAWBERRIES

Balsamic Glazed Strawberries
  over Ice Cream ..................................... 262
Cinnamon Strawberry Bread ................... 104
Fruit Salad with Mint Syrup ....................... 80
Mama Nell's Strawberry Nut Cake .......... 223
Sangría Blanca ....................................... 124
Strawberry Cream Cheese Spread ........... 101
Strawberry Frosting ................................. 223
Strawberry Poppy Seed Dressing .............. 76
Summer Strawberry Salad
  with Sweet Surprise Pecans ................... 76
Tropical Romaine Salad ............................ 79
Summer Salsa ......................................... 190
Summer Squash Casserole ..................... 144
Summertime Cherry Tomato
  and Green Bean Pasta ........................... 59
Summertime Orzo Salad ........................... 78
Sun-Dried Tomato Pesto Torte ................... 38
Sun-Dried Tomato Spread ......................... 48
Sweet and Sour Dressing .......................... 67

## SWEET POTATOES

Sweet Potato Biscuits .............................. 114
Sweet Potato Soufflé ............................... 136
Two Potato Roast .................................... 138
Sweet Surprise Pecans .............................. 77

## T

Tailgate Cheese Spread ............................ 37
Tennessee Peach Pie .............................. 236
Tennessee Whiskey Sauce ...................... 244
Tennessee Whiskey Spareribs .................. 167
The Overnight Salad ................................. 71
Three-Way Queso ..................................... 53

Toasted Almond Semi-Freddo
  with Warm Chocolate Sauce .................... 248

## TOMATOES

  Baked Salmon with Roasted Tomatoes ...... 206
  Basic Cheese Dip ............................................. 53
  Bow Tie Pasta with Olives and Pine Nuts .... 58
  Cowboy Caviar ................................................ 54
  Easy Everyday Salsa ....................................... 49
  Fabulous Chili ................................................. 83
  Fresh Tomato Tart ........................................... 32
  Fresh Tomato Tartar Sauce ........................... 31
  Jackie's Salsa .................................................. 50
  Jose's Queso ................................................... 53
  Layered Garden Bake ................................. 149
  Mediterranean Salsa ...................................... 49
  Mediterranean Tomato Salad ...................... 64
  Mushroom, Tomato, and Bacon Puff ........... 99
  Penne with Corn, Bacon,
    Leeks and Tomatoes ............................. 213
  Scalloped Tomatoes and Artichokes ......... 125
  Sicilian Spaghetti Sauce ............................. 211
  Skillet Tomatoes ........................................... 146
  Spicy Tomato Thyme Sauce ....................... 218
  Spinach Queso ............................................... 53
  Summertime Cherry Tomato
    and Green Bean Pasta ........................... 59
  Sun-Dried Tomato Pesto Torte ..................... 38
  Sun-Dried Tomato Spread ............................ 48
  Tomato Bruschetta ......................................... 41
  Tomato Vidalia Stacks ................................ 148
  Tomatoes Rockefeller .................................. 147
  Zucchini, Tomato and Onion Bake ............ 151
Tom's Favorite Fruit and Nut Granola .......... 100
Tossed Salad with Caramelized Almonds
  and Spicy Vinaigrette Dressing .................. 75
Triple Threat Chocolate Chip Cookies ......... 255
Tropical Fruit Salsa .......................................... 172
Tropical Romaine Salad ................................... 79
Tunnel of Love Cupcakes ............................... 230

## TURKEY

  Fabulous Chili ................................................. 83
  Turkey and Caramelized
    Onion Wraps ........................................... 89
  Turkey Basil Bites ........................................... 90
  Turkey Burgers with Smoked Gouda
    and Granny Smith Apples ................... 185
Two Potato Roast ............................................ 138

## V

Vanilla Cream Cheese Spread ...................... 101
Vanilla Frosting ............................................... 258

## VEGETABLES (see also individual listings)

  Jícama Slaw .................................................... 68
  Marinated Vegetable Salad Dressing .......... 74

## W

Warm Chocolate Sauce ................................. 249
Warm Chocolate Soufflés ............................. 247
Warm Plum Sauce ............................................ 47
Wasabi Dip ....................................................... 24
Wasabi-Glazed Salmon over
  Wilted Fresh Spinach .............................. 204
White Chicken Chili with Pine Nuts ............... 86
Winter Fruit Salad ............................................ 65
Wok Sesame Spinach ................................... 139

## Z

Zesty Garlic Roasted Broccoli
   with Pine Nuts ........................................ 129

## ZUCCHINI

Artichoke Frittata ....................................... 95
Farmers Market Fiesta Corn .................... 133
Grilled Zucchini Boats ............................. 150
Pasta with Garlic Shrimp
   and Zucchini ....................................... 208
Squash Ribbons al Pomodoro .................. 145
Summertime Orzo Salad ........................... 78
Zesty Zucchini Bread .............................. 105
Zucchini, Tomato and Onion Bake ........... 151

### JACKSON SERVICE LEAGUE, INC.
441 East Chester Street
Jackson, TN 38301
(731) 427-2080
or contact us at: www.jacksonsl.com

Please send _____ copies of *No Place Like Home*     @ $24.95 each _____

                Please add $4.50 per book shipping and handling     _____

                Tennessee residents add 9.75% sales tax     _____

                Make checks payable to *Jackson Service League, Inc.*

Please charge to     ❏ VISA     ❏ MasterCard

Card Number _____ Expiration Date _____

Signature _____

                                                        TOTAL $ _____

--------------------------------------------------------------------------

### JACKSON SERVICE LEAGUE, INC.
441 East Chester Street
Jackson, TN 38301
(731) 427-2080
or contact us at: www.jacksonsl.com

Please send _____ copies of *No Place Like Home*     @ $24.95 each _____

                Please add $4.50 per book shipping and handling     _____

                Tennessee residents add 9.75% sales tax     _____

                Make checks payable to *Jackson Service League, Inc.*

Please charge to     ❏ VISA     ❏ MasterCard

Card Number _____ Expiration Date _____

Signature _____

                                                         TOTAL $ _____